M🜨RMON SCIENTIST

THE LIFE AND FAITH
OF HENRY EYRING

MRMON SCIENTIST

THE LIFE AND FAITH
OF HENRY EYRING

HENRY J. EYRING

DESERET
BOOK

Salt Lake City, Utah

Library of Congress Cataloging-in-Publication Data

Eyring, Henry J.
  Mormon scientist : the life and faith of Henry Eyring / Henry J. Eyring.
    p. cm.
  ISBN-13: 978-1-59038-854-9 (hardbound : alk. paper)
    1. Eyring, Henry, 1901—Biography. 2. Scientists—United States—Biography.
3. Religion and science. 4. Mormon Church—Doctrines. I. Title.
Q143.E97E97 2008
289.3092—dc22
[B]   2007043842

Printed in the United States of America
Worzalla Publishing Co., Stevens Point, WI

10   9   8   7   6   5   4   3

For Parker Fairbourne Bradford, Hero
1989–2007

Greater love hath no man than this, that a man
lay down his life for his friends.

—JOHN 15:13

To accept the idea that the human personality ends with
death is to accept life as a futile, meaningless gesture. God
would be less compassionate than many good men if life ended
at the grave. Broken, uncompleted lives are the best possible
reason for a hereafter in which the scales of
justice are balanced by a just God.

—HENRY EYRING

He that endureth in faith and doeth my will, the
same shall overcome, and shall receive an inheritance upon
the earth when the day of transfiguration shall come.

—DOCTRINE AND COVENANTS 63:20

CONTENTS

LIST OF ILLUSTRATIONS

Photo section following page 152

* Property of Special Collections, J. Willard Marriott Library, University of Utah; used by permission.

ACKNOWLEDGMENTS

Many friends of Henry Eyring have made important contributions to this book. They include first and foremost the talented archivists at the University of Utah's Marriott Library. The work of an archivist goes largely unsung. And the task itself is laborious and often tedious. Take the archive of Henry's papers, for instance. It comprises eighty-eight boxes and consumes forty linear feet of shelf space. Henry was, among other things, a record-keeping pack rat. His archive's contents run the gamut from the precious to the pedestrian. There are, on the one hand, priceless documents such as original letters and transcripts of speeches; they sparkle with insight and life. But many of the archive's eighty-eight boxes contain documents that only Henry's mother might find interesting: membership directories for scientific associations; advance arrangements for Henry's speaking engagements; the results of his eye and hearing tests; even old tax returns.

The role of the archivist is to preserve and organize such disparate materials without prejudice, knowing that only time and circumstance can tell what might matter. There is the risk, of course, that none of it will be given due attention, or that a biased researcher will bring only certain materials to light, heedless of the archivist's evenhandedness. The archives of Henry Eyring's papers, photographs, and audio and video recordings have been masterfully preserved and organized. Thanks are due to generations of faithful archivists, and to those who have funded their efforts. It is hoped that they will take personal satisfaction from the publication of this book.

As the archival materials became a manuscript, many of Henry Eyring's descendants contributed. In particular, Henry's three sons, Ted, Hal, and Harden, provided special content and encouragement. He would be prouder than ever of them. Grandma Winifred Eyring, Henry's second wife and mother of Eleanor, Patricia, Joan, and Bernice, has presided over the work through the power of her personal example.

Many nonfamily members read the manuscript and made detailed suggestions. They include Joshua Allen, Jordan Clements, Eric D'Evegnee, and Rhonda Seamons. In addition, students of Dr. Allen's professional editing class at BYU-Idaho reviewed the manuscript over two semesters. This book is much better for their thoughtful effort.

The representatives of Deseret Book, including Jay Parry, Lisa Mangum, Richard Erickson, and Laurie Cook have been both professional and kind. Cory Maxwell, in particular, deserves credit for helping to finish what his father, Elder Neal A. Maxwell, started. In the final years of his life, Elder Maxwell repeatedly sounded the call, "You've got to write your grandfather's story." With Cory's having seen the book through to publication, the Eyrings are indebted to the Maxwells from beginning to end.

One more person is due special mention. Two years before Henry Eyring's death, Steven Harvey Heath undertook a biography in pursuit of a master's degree in scientific history. His unpublished biography, "Henry Eyring, Mormon Scientist," has proven invaluable in two ways. First, it is a thorough study of Henry's life, full of original insights. It is written with the skill of a professional historian and the respect of an admirer and friend. Second, Steven Heath's biography is significant because of the rich material that it added to Henry's archive. Steven conducted many interviews and helped Henry gather and organize materials. He arrived, providentially, in Henry's life just in time to pull the many pieces of the story together.

EVENTS IN THE LIFE

OF HENRY EYRING[1]

1901	Born February 20 in Colonia Juarez, Chihuahua, Mexico
1912	Driven from Mexico by revolution
1914	Settles with family in Pima, Arizona
1919	Graduates from Gila Academy in Thatcher, Arizona
1923	B.S., Mining Engineering, University of Arizona
1924	M.S., Metallurgical Engineering, University of Arizona
1924–1925	Instructor of Chemistry, University of Arizona
1927	Ph.D., Chemistry, University of California
1928	Marries Mildred Bennion
1928–1929	Research Associate in Chemistry, University of Wisconsin
1930–1931	National Research Foundation Fellow, Kaiser Wilhelm Institute, Berlin, Germany
1931	Birth of Edward Marcus Eyring
1931–1938	Assistant and Associate Professor of Chemistry, Princeton University
1932–1942	President of the New Brunswick, New Jersey branch of The Church of Jesus Christ of Latter-day Saints
1933	Birth of Henry Bennion Eyring

1933   "Best Paper" award from the American Association for the
            Advancement of Science

1935   Publication of ART paper

1938–1946   [Full] Professor of Chemistry, Princeton University

1939   Birth of Harden Romney Eyring

1941   Publication of *The Theory of Rate Processes*

1942–1945   President of the Princeton, New Jersey, branch of the
            Church

1944   Publication of *Quantum Chemistry*

1944–1946   Director of Textile Research Institute at Princeton

1945–1946   President of the New Jersey District of the Church

1946–1966   Dean of the Graduate School and Professor of Chemistry,
            University of Utah

1946–1971   Member of the Deseret Sunday School General Board of
            the Church

1948   CBS *Church of the Air* address, "Science and Faith"

1962–1968   Member of the National Science Board (appointed by
            President John F. Kennedy)

1963   President of the American Chemical Society

1965   President of the American Association for the Advance-
            ment of Science

1966   Receives National Medal of Science

1966–1981   Distinguished Professor of Chemistry, University of Utah

1967   Publication of *The Faith of a Scientist*

1969   Death of Mildred Bennion Eyring

1971   Marries Winifred Brennan Clark

1973   Publication of five hundredth scientific paper

1975   Receives Joseph Priestley Medal

1980   Receives Wolf Foundation Prize in Chemistry

            University of Utah chemistry building named for Henry
            Eyring

1981   International conference celebrating fiftieth anniversary of
            the publication of Michael Polanyi and Henry Eyring's
            paper on reaction rate theory, Berlin, Germany

            Dies December 26 in Salt Lake City, Utah

INTRODUCTION

By Steven M. Kuznicki

This is a story about a man named Henry Eyring.
Why should you care?

I knew Henry Eyring as one of the most renowned scientists of the twentieth century. But familiarity breeds contempt, or at least complacency. In researching this introduction I found a new appreciation for Henry's work, how it affected science and, more importantly, how it affected the way that you and I see this world, even if you have never heard his name.

This is a story about how someone can change the world without being overtaken by his own vanity. Henry saw himself much as you probably see yourself. He considered himself a common man. And yet, as you will see, he measurably changed the world. Therein lies the real reason you should care about this book. The lesson of Henry Eyring's life is that simple people, people just like you and me, can change the world. You do it every day, even without recognizing it. And you have the potential to change the world much more if only you can understand and use the gifts you have been given.

I first set eyes on Henry Eyring from a distance of perhaps

fifty yards. Though I had never seen him before, I knew his face instantly. There was a certain surety and humility that is rare and, I think, speaks of inner strength and peace. When I first met Henry, in 1976, he was already at an age, seventy-five, when most retire. He had endured the preceding three decades of being a world-renowned scientist. I say "endured" because endless praise is boring and a bit embarrassing to a man who would just like to keep moving ahead and discovering. Yet there was no conceit on his face, only serenity. His bearing was without evidence of vanity. In fact, Henry's lack of concern for appearances was legendary: his son Edward, also a noted scientist, once told me that his father had the ability to make a new thousand-dollar suit look rumpled. I would say rather that he looked comfortable in his own skin.

How do you endure a professional lifetime of praise without succumbing to vanity and conceit? How do you accept your ability to change the world without feeling that you are better than the people you walk by on the street every day? I guess it all starts with where you come from and who you chose as role models. Henry spent his early years on the Arizona-Mexico border. If you have not been there, it is as close to hell as I have ever seen on this earth; I don't know how even an animal scratches a living from such a wasteland. Yet his father managed to support a family of nineteen from this place. Henry idolized his father. Those who knew him well believe that Henry's strength stemmed from a boyhood of close observation of his strong, constant father. He also took strength from his many siblings. They were a kind of tribe in their alien environment. Henry remained unusually close to his brothers and sisters throughout his life, in some ways even closer than he was to his own children.

Such an upbringing disposes one to feel humble and common. You cannot endure such circumstances without realizing that there are forces greater than yourself and that you live at their whim and mercy. And yet this family rose above their material hardship. This book describes their remarkable achievements. The desert tribe produced, among other accomplished children, a daughter (Henry's sister Rose) who obtained a Ph.D. at a time when women were not, as a group, formally educated; one of Henry's brothers became a university president. The tribe was no ignorant or apathetic group. Though part of this derived from the father's great strength, Henry got perhaps even more determination from his mother, Caroline. She taught her children that they could do or be whatever they wanted. The lesson took, especially in Henry's case.

Like you and I, Henry was often in his own world. He wasn't always careful to observe or understand other people, to the point of sometimes being oblivious to them. He once confessed that he hadn't noticed his mother's being pregnant until the very moment of a new sister's birth. He likewise admitted that it took him until the age of sixteen to realize that a man is not well advised to marry two sisters.

Henry's father was a polygamist, his family being a remnant of the Mormon colonization of the American Southwest. Henry considered himself as having two mothers. The two large families lived side by side in something of a duplex, with his father spending alternate weeks with each family. You might ask how this could contribute to the construction of a genius. Well, a certain intellectual flexibility can be healthy, and learning to look at the world (and justify) nontraditional patterns might help one think in new directions. Or then again it might just leave one out of step. Apparently, in Henry's case it was beneficial.

Henry's mother taught him very early on that he could do whatever he wanted to do in this life. The way he jumped around in his early career as a scientist, it might be thought that he had taken her too literally. He received degrees in three distinctly different sciences. In 1923, at the age of twenty-two, he received a baccalaureate degree in mining engineering from the University of Arizona. He stayed on another year in Arizona, earning a master's degree in metallurgy. In 1925 he started a doctoral program, but this time in physical chemistry at the University of California at Berkeley. After graduating in 1927, he took a job as an instructor at the University of Wisconsin. Within another year the grass looked greener overseas, and he took a research position in the lab of a famous scientist, Michael Polanyi, in Germany. By 1930, he was back at Berkeley.

Having been both an executive in a multibillion dollar chemical company and also a professor at a large university, I have seen many thousands of resumes over the last twenty years. If I had been presented Henry Eyring's resume in 1931, at the height of the American Depression, I would not have given it thirty seconds' consideration. I would have seen him as an aimless drifter who had no guiding purpose in his life. Thankfully, I was not the one assessing him. In fact he was not aimless, but insatiably curious.

In 1931, Henry presented a scientific paper in Indianapolis at a meeting of the American Chemical Society. It so impressed the chairman, Hugh Taylor of the chemistry department at Princeton University, that Henry was offered a position at Princeton on the spot. Fortunately, he took it. The fifteen years that Henry spent at Princeton from 1931 to 1946 were magical. Princeton had assembled some of the finest minds in the world, including household names like Fermi and Einstein. Young Professor Eyring interacted with this group, and his scientific productivity exploded. So did the clearness of his thinking.

So what was Henry's world-changing idea? We will get to that, but first know that, just like yours and mine, his life had many chapters. During his fifty-year career Professor Eyring published over six hundred scientific articles on various topics, as well as a dozen textbooks, many of which were standards in their field and are still extensively quoted even today. He educated countless students and infected many of them with his love for science or, better put, the search for knowledge. He also wrote several texts reconciling science and a belief in God. Though it is seldom spoken openly, much of the scientific community never forgave him for that.

Now for Henry's world-changing idea. At Princeton, among many other scholarly contributions, he put forth something called the Absolute Rate Theory (ART). Essentially, this theory holds that when atoms or molecules collide, they briefly combine to form something new and different. They transiently enter a fourth dimension. These high-energy combinations of particles are unstable, and they must quickly collapse back into the three dimensions that we know. They may do so in the form of the particles they came from, or they may collapse into new configurations.

If the energy barrier to reach this "fourth dimension" is very high, things stay as they are for prolonged periods. Simply stated, whether particles change depends on energy states. If there is not enough energy, there is no change, essentially forever. The same holds true, by the way, for most people's lives.

That may sound simple, but it was a radical idea when it was proposed. It seems intuitively obvious only because it is now so ingrained in scientific thinking. That is why I believe that this man affected your view of the world, even if you have never heard of him.

The power of Henry's "great idea" has been described this way by colleagues who nominated him for prizes:

> Absolute Rate Theory (ART) has been one of the most potent forces to ever appear in Chemistry. This

theory represented a unifying point of view whose principles have been applied to areas of science ranging from quantum mechanics to catalysis. Areas as complex as the separation of atomic isotopes to the behaviour of fiber strands have been impacted. Theoretical Organic Chemistry is all but universally couched in terms of ART. The viscosity and behaviour of large molecules such as polymers has been explained and controlled using ART reasoning. Shock waves in explosives have been modeled, predicted and new configurations designed using ART. Long-term rates of corrosion of metals can be modeled and predicted using ART. The behaviour of proteins including enzymes has been modeled and predicted using ART, leading to, among other advances, enhanced effectiveness of anaesthetics. Even the rate of cell mutations leading to cancer can be predicted.

Henry's decade and a half at Princeton resulted in well over two hundred scientific works, many of them based on refinements and extensions of ART. But what is even more amazing is that while he worked so effectively in the realm of theoretical science—even to match some of his more commonly known Princeton colleagues—he simultaneously ran the school's Textile Institute. He was also devoutly religious and, much like a modern-day Mormon missionary, would preach on Princeton's common green to anyone who would listen to scripture. Then abruptly, in 1946, when his Utah-born wife, Mildred, told him it was time to go home, he went.

Henry was revered in Utah. He joined the faculty of the University of Utah as dean of the graduate school and professor of chemistry and metallurgy. More importantly to the people of Utah, he powerfully articulated the reconciliation of his faith in

God (and in the Mormon Church) and science. Among the books he wrote on this topic, *The Faith of a Scientist* (1967) stands out and is well worth a curious reader's time. Though he was already firmly established as *the* Mormon scientist in the Mormon community in Utah and the greater American West, this unofficial position became even more entrenched in the minds of many when his brother-in-law Spencer W. Kimball became president of the Mormon Church, in 1973. The family tradition of service to the Church has continued, most notably with his son Henry B. serving as one of three members of the First Presidency.

Henry's life from 1946 to 1981, when he died, was tremendously full—building a school of science, infusing countless young people with excitement for discovery, writing an additional three hundred-plus scientific papers, and receiving a continual stream of awards and accolades.

But he was still Henry Eyring of the "desert tribe." The man I met in 1976 was as simple and humble as any man who works the earth for a living. In this he puzzled many people. I recall clearly having dinner in 1988 with a professor from Canada who said this to me: "You knew Eyring; the people around him view him almost as sacred. The one time I met him, years ago, we had lunch at a café overlooking the Berlin Wall. I asked him if it [the wall] bothered him, and he told me that his God assured him that it would not be there all that much longer." Having reported this exchange with Henry, my colleague looked at me for some kind of reassurance that I thought it was crazy. I just smiled at him. The wall was gone less than two years later.

An internet site says this of Henry Eyring: "His transition-state theory (ART) is one of the most important developments in twentieth-century chemistry, and his failure to win a Nobel Prize has been a matter of surprise to many physical chemists." Myself a physical chemist by training, I have often joined in speculation about this Nobel "surprise." For years I presumed that I knew the reason why Henry didn't win a Nobel Prize—religious bigotry. (I make that observation, by the way, as one who is not a member of the Mormon Church.) To the modern-day intellectual elite, no man who can consistently stand and testify to his absolute belief in things greater than he (and the rest of us) could possibly deserve such an award, no matter how great his scientific contributions.

However, in preparing this introduction, I have come to believe that religious bigotry is only half the answer to the Nobel question. The rest of the answer may speak even more poorly of our current intellectual elites. Henry Eyring was a simple man. That simplicity bothered many of his peers who *had* been overtaken by their own vanity. In nomination materials prepared on his behalf for many awards, including the Nobel Prize, comments by colleagues are of two types. Of course, there is much unreserved praise: "The contributions of Dr. Henry Eyring touch practically every field of chemical science and technology in a very fundamental manner." "He has the Midas touch. Everything in science turns to gold when brought to the attention of his fertile brain."

But in contrast, there is another type of praise. It is fainter and even backhanded: "His approach to every problem is fresh, original and very frequently unorthodox. He tends to discover the facts rather than to read what others have found." "He paints with a broad brush. It is interesting that it comes out so well." Comments such as these admit Henry's genius. Yet they betray subtle contempt for the simplicity that others admired. Oh well, those who resented Henry's simplicity are all gone and forgotten, while his work lives on in our lives.

That is why you should care about this man's life and this story. You should read this book because it is about someone like you and me. Henry Eyring saw himself as simple. Great ideas come from simple people. It is simple ideas that can actually change the world. Henry Eyring instinctively knew the truth when he saw it. You know the truth when you see it. The truth is always simple. The lesson of Henry Fyring's life is that simple people, people just like you and me, can change the world. We do it a little bit every day. And we have the potential to change the world much more, if we can better understand and use our unique gifts.

Steven M. Kuznicki
Ph.D., Physical Chemistry, University of Utah, 1980
Professor, The University of Alberta

OVERVIEW

This story of the life and thought of Henry Eyring is organized differently than a traditional biography. Rather than proceeding chronologically through his life, we'll look first at the things he accomplished (his Legacy), then at the family experiences that shaped him (Heritage), and then at the unusual way he thought (Paradoxes). We will close with a section called Testament, in which Henry bears witness to those things of greatest importance.

In terms of accomplishments, or legacy, Henry was famous for three things. One, of course, was his science. He was, as Dr. Steven Kuznicki indicated in the introduction, among the notable chemists of the twentieth century. Of equal or greater importance to those who shared his faith, though, was his zeal in arguing that science and religion are mutually reinforcing, rather than conflicting. At a time when scientific theories such as organic evolution seemed to threaten the religious faith of many, Henry calmly declared that there was nothing to worry about.

Finally, there were many who knew Henry mainly as the eccentric professor who ran much-publicized footraces and told self-deprecating jokes, as though he were the kind of fellow anyone could talk to. In fact, he was just such an avuncular fellow, and the lifetime of conversations he had with anyone willing to listen left a great legacy of goodwill.

The first three chapters of this book explore each of these things for which Henry was famous: Science, Faith, and Friendship. They offer the kind of insight into his life we might have enjoyed as one of his neighbors, occasionally giving him a ride to work and talking along the way.

Such exposure to Henry, though, tended to leave his neighbors a bit puzzled. He wasn't what they expected of a famous scientist and respected Church authority. That was the reaction of his second wife, Winifred, the first few times she met him. Winifred moved into Henry's neighborhood not long after the passing of his first wife, Mildred. Seeing Winifred in Sabbath meetings, Henry was immediately charmed by her vivacity and her commitment to The Church of Jesus Christ of Latter-day Saints, to which she was a new convert.

Henry's overtures, however, initially worried Winifred. She noticed that he dressed shabbily and didn't attend church every Sunday. Given the Church's financial welfare program for its members, it seemed plausible that he had impure motives for attending at all; Winifred wondered if he was going to church just for a handout.

It was with reluctance, then, that she accepted a date with Henry. He invited her to attend a Sunday evening "fireside" address at a local meetinghouse. A large crowd had already gathered when they arrived. Henry escorted Winifred toward the front of the chapel. To her surprise, he stopped and seated her by herself in a pew before taking a position himself on the rostrum. She didn't know what to make of this apparent insult until the program began. It was only when Henry was introduced to speak on the subject of science and religion that she realized that her date was no deadbeat.

Such apparent contradictions appear often in our study of Henry's accomplishments in the chapters Science, Faith, and Friendship. He was simultaneously serious and gregarious, faithful and irreverent, distinguished and frumpy.

To begin to solve the puzzle of Henry's character, we'll want to meet his forebears and visit his childhood homes in Mexico and Arizona. He was, even more than most of us, the product of his family heritage. And, more than most, he actually liked that fact. From his earliest childhood he wanted to be just like his father and mother and grandparents. His father, Ed, was his lifelong hero, and his mother, Caroline, a ministering angel in his eyes. Likewise, Henry's grandparents were well-respected leaders of the Mexican colony in which he was born. He grew up admiring them and their experiences of frontier hardship and heroism.

Perhaps the most tangible—and best known—example of family influence on Henry's way of thinking is the story of his father's college send-off speech. Henry must have told this story a thousand times; it was a staple of his science-and-religion speeches. He described the tone of the conversation as "typical of my father's easy-going, under-selling way."[1]

It was a Friday evening in September, 1919. I had been hauling hay all day in Pima, Arizona. It had been very hot, and we'd been drinking lots of water. On Monday I was going to start classes at the University of Arizona, where I was to study Mining Engineering. In the evening my father, as fathers often do, felt that he'd like to have a last talk with his son. He wanted to be sure I'd stay on the straight and narrow. He said, "Henry, won't you come and sit down? I want to talk to you."

Well, I'd rather do that than pitch hay any time. So, I went over and sat down with him.

"We're pretty good friends, aren't we?"

"Yes," I said, "I think we are."

"Henry, we've ridden on the range, and we've farmed together. I think we understand each other. Well, I want to say this to you: I'm convinced that the Lord used the Prophet Joseph Smith to restore His Church. For me that is a reality. I haven't any doubt about it. Now, there are a lot of other matters which are much less clear to me. But in this Church you don't have to believe anything that isn't true. You go over to the University of Arizona and learn everything you can, and whatever is true is part of the gospel. The Lord is actually running this universe. I'm convinced that he inspired the Prophet Joseph Smith. And I want to tell you something else: If you go to the University and are not profane, if you'll live in such a way that you'll feel comfortable in the company of good people, and if you go to church and do the other things that we've always done, I don't worry about your getting away from the Lord."[2]

Thanks to Henry's lifetime of retelling this story, Ed's simple, private conversation with his son has resonated in the ears and hearts of generations of Latter-day Saints, especially those seeking to reconcile secular learning with faith. The phrase, "This Church doesn't require you to believe anything that isn't true," is so well known among Mormons that it might have been spoken by a prophet. However, it wasn't a prophet or even renowned scientist Henry Eyring who coined the phrase, but rather Ed Eyring, cattle rancher.

That is why understanding Henry's refreshing way of thinking requires knowing his parents and grandparents. He was the product of his upbringing, and of the parents and grandparents who brought him up. Their experiences became his, he built on the insights and achievements of his lineal forebears just as he did the discoveries of the scientists who preceded him. The chapter titles under the Heritage section of this book—Love, Ambition, Belief, and Fear—are a bit melodramatic. However, in each chapter we'll meet individuals who epitomized those traits and passed them on to Henry. For instance, the star of the Ambition chapter is Henry's maternal grandfather, Miles Park Romney. "Miles P.," as friends called him, was the personification of capability and ambition. He passed these traits down to Henry, who considered himself a Romney as much as an Eyring. Henry was proud of the family saying, "If a Romney drowns in a river, look for the body upstream."

Having explored Henry's legacy and heritage, we'll be armed to tackle his unusual way of thinking. As noted by Steve Kuznicki, Henry puzzled almost everyone who knew him. He was obviously intelligent and confident, but he often played the buffoon. He was driven to discover but was perfectly happy with the idea that not everything is knowable in this life. He respected God's omnipotence but also considered Him a personal friend. And so on.

Paradoxes such as these are the subject of the third section of this book. Most of the people who knew and admired Henry wished that they could somehow be more like him. They seemed to sense that his genius lay not so much in his undoubtedly high IQ, but rather in his unique perspective on things. The Paradoxes section accepts that premise and tries to explain Henry's way of thinking. Specifically, it explores six apparent contradictions of attitude that Henry embodied:

- Confidence and Humility
- Discipline and Creativity
- Freedom and Obedience
- Reasoning, More Than Reasons
- Fundamentals, Not Conventions
- People, Not Public Opinion

These attitudinal paradoxes, illustrated by events and sayings from Henry's life, capture much of his special way of thinking. They lie at the root of his ability to make a seemingly complex world simple.

Before proceeding, a disclaimer about the authorship of this book is in order. The real author is Henry Eyring. All of the stories and even most of the words are his. Moreover, he wanted everyone to share in them equally.

That can be said with certainty because of Henry's response to the request from leaders of the Church regarding his book *The Faith of a Scientist.* In 1969, they proposed that this hardbound book be slimmed down, published in soft cover, and distributed at the price of printing to the youth of the Church. In his letter of reply, Henry agreed without reservation, but with one condition:

> I will be happy to have you use the material from the book *The Faith of a Scientist* in the way you outline. I of course want no compensation but will be glad to edit what goes out over my name.[3]

This book has been published in that same spirit of inclusiveness. The cover price has been reduced by the amount of the author's royalty that otherwise would have been paid, in the hope that more readers might enjoy getting to know Henry and his ideas.

A related hope is that you will become a coauthor of the wiki version of this book, which can be found at mormonscientist.org. The wiki includes readers' memories of Henry Eyring, as well as their ideas about subjects such as the connections between science and religion. It also has electronic versions of two popular but out-of-print books, *The Faith of a Scientist* and *Reflections of a Scientist* (edited by Harden Eyring, one of Henry's sons).

Already, many readers have contributed to the wiki. Your contributions will make the story better still.

PART 1

LEGACY

Portrait of Henry by Alvin Gittins, 1969. The original hangs in the lobby of the Henry Eyring Building at the University of Utah.

SCIENCE

Ironically, science wasn't Henry's first professional love. If it hadn't been for the Mexican Revolution, he likely would have finished life the way he started it—on horseback. His father, Edward, was an affluent rancher whose holdings included fourteen thousand acres and several hundred head of cattle. As the eldest son, Henry rode the range with his father from the time he could walk. He loved being on horseback as much as his "Papa" did. Had circumstances allowed, they would certainly have stayed in northern Mexico, and Henry naturally would have assumed management of the ranch.

However, in 1910 war brought an end to his idyllic boyhood. Armed revolutionaries ultimately drove the Eyrings and their fellow Mormon colonists out of Mexico with nothing more than they could carry in their hands. The family took refuge for a year in El Paso, Texas, hoping that the revolution would pass and allow them to recover their land and lifestyle. As the war raged on, that hope faded. Giving up on a return to Mexico, Henry's family moved on to a tiny Arizona town called Pima, where they bought uncleared land and began to eke out a living as farmers.

Fortunately, Henry was a gifted student. There had been a good school in Mexico, a Church academy established by the colonists. Henry's mother was one of the teachers, and she made sure that he got almost as much exposure to books in those days as he did to horses. In spite of a lost year of study in El Paso, Henry was able to skip several grades in Arizona and graduate at the top of his class at the Gila Academy, another Church school.

A FAILED MINER AND METALLURGIST—FALLING ROCKS AND FIERY FURNACES

In 1919, at age eighteen, Henry used a $500 county scholarship to enter the University of Arizona. Having excelled in high school at math and science, and being from a major mining state, he decided to study mining engineering. As in high school, he excelled, but he soon began to doubt his choice of majors. During the summer before graduating with his bachelor's degree, he got his first real taste of mining. Initially, the job looked good: it paid twice as much as farming. However, nothing in his university coursework prepared him for the experience of working underground. In an early assignment, he was sent with an assistant to repair a "square set," a group of timbers holding up the roof of the mine. He recounts the harrowing experience that followed:

> We climbed to inspect the square set, and my veteran helper declared that he had no intention of being trapped in this particular hell hole, and, if it was to be repaired, it was up to me. He would wait down below, and I could call when and if I needed help. I had the usual ax and crowbar with which I could gingerly pry out the loose rocks until I had cleared enough space to put in new timber before it all caved in on me. I went about it as carefully as I could, but it was not long before a rock

12

somewhat bigger than my head fell from the ceiling and hit my boot. I soon had a boot partly filled with blood, and I was taken out of the square set and brought out on top.

I was once on another shift where there were three separate fatal accidents. There were also two other boys from Pima working in the mine that summer, and one of these had his arm crushed and later amputated. This just didn't make sense on a percentage basis. Although I wasn't frightened in the sense that I felt I needed to run away, those kinds of odds seemed prohibitive to me. Even though as an engineer I wouldn't have to take excessive chances, I would have to send others down, assuming responsibility for their safety.[1]

In addition to fear for the safety of himself and others, there was another important reason that Henry gave up mining: it wasn't interesting to him.

Actually I enjoyed my mining training. I did very well grade-wise, but I was not then, nor am I now, in my heart dedicated to getting rich. I was much more interested in how things worked. Mining did not provide this interest.[2]

Though unwilling to pursue a career likely to either kill him or bore him to death, Henry was practical enough not to entirely abandon his undergraduate training. Rather, he launched into a related field, metallurgy. Back at the University of Arizona, he won a Bureau of Mines fellowship and researched the practical problem of separating different types of ore. The results of his master's thesis were published (with appropriate attribution) by a scientist at the Bureau of Mines. At the time, Henry had no idea that he could publish the research himself. Yet while he didn't get full credit for his work, it established in his mind—and in the minds of his professors—his gift for chemical research.

As with mining engineering, Henry found the metallurgy coursework stimulating. However, upon graduating and entering the workplace he ran up against the same problem as before—the job was dreary.

> After completing my master's degree, I spent the summer of 1924 working in the United Verde Smelter at Clarksdale, Arizona. Again, I had a favored position as a prospective metallurgist and was rapidly shifted among different phases of the smelting operation. After being there a few weeks I was assigned to take samples from the blast furnaces. The sulfur dioxide smoke was especially strong, and I was holding a handkerchief soaked in baking soda over my face when the smelter superintendent came by, slapped me on the shoulder, and said, "Eyring, I like the way you are working out here at the smelter. I plan to put you in charge of these blast furnaces in a few weeks." That is when he lost a metallurgist.[3]

A Classroom Job in Chemistry

Fortunately, there was another career option: the University of Arizona had a one-year teaching position, in chemistry. Being a poor boy of greater-than-average self-confidence, Henry nearly walked away from the job when the salary was negotiated down to $1,400 from the $1,600 he was initially promised. However, memories of blast-furnace smoke and falling rocks helped him swallow his pride, and he took the offer even at the lower rate.

This full-time classroom job wasn't Henry's first exposure to teaching—he'd worked his way through school as a student instructor. This time, however, he enjoyed the perk of attending classes of his choice during free hours. He took courses from the university's most distinguished chemists, as well as one in introductory German. This choice to study German reveals his ambition and foresight. He had already planned a career in chemical research, and he knew that the cutting-edge chemistry was being done in Germany.

Given his hard work and demonstrated intelligence, it was easy to get the necessary recommendations for doctoral study. One of his professors at Arizona was from the University of Chicago and another from the University of California at Berkeley. Both professors recommended him, and both schools offered Henry admission to their Ph.D. programs.

Even when comparing the merits of two schools proffering untold prestige and opportunity, Henry was typically practical. He described his choice in these matter-of-fact terms:

> Obviously a decision had to be made based on very little information, since I had never been east of El Paso, Texas. I could hardly be called, at that point, worldly. But I did know the difference between $700 and $750. Since Berkeley offered $750, and since G. N. Lewis was the star, I decided in favor of the University of California.[4]

Gilbert N. Lewis, dean of the College of Chemistry at Berkeley, was then among the best-known and well-regarded American chemists. His educational background was as blue-blooded as Henry's was red-necked. The son of a Boston lawyer, Lewis graduated from high school at fourteen and earned a Ph.D. at Harvard when he was just twenty-four. He taught at both Harvard and MIT before becoming dean at Berkeley. By the time Henry applied to study at Berkeley, Lewis was recognized as one of the pioneers of chemistry and had organized a lab from which were flowing ground-breaking ideas about the way atoms bond to one another to form molecules. Lewis loved scientific discovery. When asked once to define his field, physical chemistry, he replied, "Physical chemistry is everything that is interesting." Before long, Henry would share that view.

Thanks to the inquisitive Lewis, the emphasis at Berkeley was on research rather than classroom study. As Henry later said,

> At Berkeley graduate students mingled with outstanding scientists who entertained no doubt that intelligent research was the most important activity in the world. This contagion infested everyone. Individual success in research was accompanied by a shedding of any undue veneration for the embalmed science of the past. The research atmosphere provided at Berkeley has probably rarely been equaled.[5]

After completing the Ph.D. at Berkeley, Henry continued his research at the University of Wisconsin, where he was offered a job as a laboratory instructor in 1927. His start at Wisconsin, though, was rocky. Upon arriving, one of his first duties was to varnish the floor of his lab. Ever the hard worker, he spent an entire Saturday at the task. The following Monday, the department chairman stopped by. He complimented Henry's effort, but then asked, "When will you apply the second coat?" At that Henry's impatience got the better of him, and he launched into a stern critique of Wisconsin's chemistry department, which he had already concluded to be inferior to Berkeley's. Specifically, he thought that classes weren't being taught by the department's best people.

Henry's teaching contract at Wisconsin was terminated after just one year, and he would later joke that his early criticisms were the cause. In any event, Henry's brashness didn't prevent others at Wisconsin from recognizing his brilliance. He was picked up immediately as a full-time researcher by Professor Farrington Daniels, who like G. N. Lewis was a Harvard Ph.D. and renowned scientist. Through the summer of 1928, Henry assisted in the study of Daniels' field of interest, chemical kinetics, or the rate at which molecules react with one another.

The study of molecular reactions that Henry began at Wisconsin would become his life's work. Many decades later, Daniels commented on the significance of their collaboration. To Henry he wrote, "I consider that one of my most important achievements in science was my success in getting you interested in chemical kinetics."[6]

Henry's second year at Wisconsin was significant for other reasons. One was the opportunity to meet and court Mildred Bennion, a graduate student from Utah whom Henry married in the summer of 1928. Another was the exposure he received to visiting lecturers by future Nobel laureates, including Werner Heisenberg and John Van Vleck. Heisenberg is famous today for the "uncertainty principle" that bears his name; he was also a father of "quantum mechanics," the complex mathematical model of what goes on inside of atoms. Van Vleck, an American, had just returned from Europe, where quantum mechanics was being developed. Van Vleck painted exciting pictures of how the new theory about what happens inside of atoms might explain physical phenomena—such as chemical reactions—that had theretofore defied understanding.

BERLIN

Amid such talk of scientific revolution in Europe, Henry must have been ecstatic to receive a National Research Fellowship to study at the Kaiser Wilhelm Institute in Berlin. With typical self-deprecation, he later explained the award as the Wisconsin chemistry department chairman's successful attempt to finally be rid of him. In fact, it was his mentor Farrington Daniels who recommended Henry for the fellowship and championed his cause.

In Berlin, the intellectual ferment was everything that a young American scientist could hope for. Henry described the heady research environment this way:

> Berlin in 1929 had pretty much recovered from the defeat in 1918 and was really the center of chemistry in the world. You could go to a meeting and find as many as eight Nobel people to a physics symposium.[7]

In Berlin Henry connected with yet another important mentor, Michael Polanyi (pronounced Poh-lan-yee). Ironically, Polanyi was Henry's second choice of research partners at the Kaiser Wilhelm Institute. The first was a world expert in the exact area of research Henry had been pursuing at Wisconsin. However, this other man was scheduled to be in the United States when Henry arrived in Berlin. Given just twelve precious months at the institute, Henry didn't want to lose a moment. He opted for a second choice, Michael Polanyi. This initially disappointing twist of fate was in fact the turning point in Henry's scientific career.

Compared to the man Henry had wanted to work with, Polanyi was young and less well credentialed. In fact, Polanyi was a medical doctor with only a year of formal chemistry training. Nonetheless, he headed his own department at the institute and was a renowned scientist. And, more importantly, Polanyi was a bold, creative thinker who liked Henry from the beginning.

Polanyi put Henry to work building on recent discoveries made in the lab. As at Wisconsin, the issue was the rate at which chemical reactions occur. For laymen, a familiar example of a chemical reaction that occurs at different rates is the spoiling of meat. Left at room temperature, uncooked meat spoils quickly, as the protein molecules that comprise the meat break down through chemical reactions. With refrigeration, the chemical reactions that cause spoiling are slowed, because the colder molecules have less energy and therefore are more inclined to stay in the same state Such differences in reaction rate soon captivated Henry.

In the year before Henry arrived in Berlin, another of Polanyi's researchers had used quantum mechanics to predict the rates of a few simple reactions. Making these rate predictions even in simple cases was an impressive achievement, because the science of the time allowed prediction of *whether* a reaction would occur, but not how fast; in fact, dogma held that such predictions of reaction rate were impossible.

Henry dreamed of defeating this it-can't-be-done dogma. He hoped to use quantum mechanics to expand rate-predicting power to all chemical reactions. That, it turned out, would require not only ingenuity, but a seemingly reckless disregard for traditional scientific methods.

SIMPLIFYING ASSUMPTIONS

First, Henry found a creative way to simplify what was initially a four-dimensional problem. One atom or molecule headed for a collision with another can move in the three dimensions of space: up-and-down, forward-and-back, and side-to-side. However, its likelihood of reacting with another particle also depends on its energy, a fourth "dimension" to be measured. Having to account for four dimensions—as opposed to just the three that we can see with our eyes—not only made the math horribly difficult, but it also precluded building a visual model of what was going on. In other words, you couldn't "see" the reaction happening in your mind's eye. That troubled both Henry and Polanyi, who were visual thinkers; they liked to imagine particles colliding as though they were down at the atomic level, watching it all unfold.

Henry's breakthrough on this point was to simplify the problem by assuming that the particles were moving in only two dimensions—say, forward-and-back and side-to-side, but not up-and-down. With only two spatial dimensions and the energy level to plot mathematically, you could create a three-dimensional map of the path an atom or molecule would travel as it moved toward reaction. In the succeeding years, Henry would refine this model, comparing a chemical reaction to a mountain summit, with the height of the mountain representing the energy required for a reaction to occur. Sufficiently energetic molecules climb over the mountain to the other side, becoming something new in the process. Less energetic ones stay as they are, stuck on their side of the energy "mountain."

As would often be the case, Henry was blessed with unexpected help in developing this novel approach to modeling a chemical reaction. With the model coalescing in his mind, he went to talk it over with Polanyi. In Polanyi's office at the time was, by chance, another young scientist, Eugene Wigner, a brilliant mathematician who would go on to win a Nobel Prize in Physics and would also be Henry's colleague at Princeton. When Henry described the simplified, three-dimensional model, Wigner replied, "Ah . . . that's exciting!" Over the next several years, Wigner and Polanyi and others would help refine the mathematics of Henry's model of the molecule and the mountain.

There was, though, another challenge. Quantum mechanics, the tool that was providing Henry new insights into chemical reactions, has a catch built into it. Quantum mechanics describes what happens inside of atoms, with special emphasis on energy levels. "Quantum" means "how much," specifically, "how much energy." With this emphasis on the energy levels of particles, quantum mechanics gives a much better picture of the atom than older theories, such as the planetary model, which envisioned electrons orbiting the nucleus of an atom like planets orbiting the sun.

However, quantum mechanics doesn't predict the whereabouts of an electron, at least not with the precision with which an astronomer knows where to find a planet in its orbit. In fact, the very essence of quantum theory is that you can't be exactly sure of the speed and position of the electrons orbiting the nucleus of an atom at any given moment; you can know only to varying degrees of probability. This dilemma is what Werner Heisenberg, the famous scientist Henry first met in Wisconsin, called the uncertainty principle. The upshot of this uncertainty is that the mathematical equations deriving from quantum theory are impossible to solve precisely.

Henry, though, wasn't bothered by the lack of mathematical precision. Again he simplified things. He began by making approximations—or educated guesses—about some of the unknown values in the equations. Then he tested the results against the outcomes of real laboratory experiments. When the results didn't match, he changed his equation until the match was better. Henry wasn't simply playing fast and loose with the math. His mathematical prowess was the gift that made him invaluable to Polanyi. The difference between Henry and other math geniuses, though, was his willingness to guess at an answer when there was no other way.

Henry knew that his simplifications would be criticized. However, he stood by the fact that (1) his new model made intuitive sense, as you envisioned the molecule and the mountain, and (2) it worked. In fact, the new approach proved unexpectedly powerful in predicting and explaining a wide range of chemical reactions. With due pride, Henry said of his scientifically unorthodox new approach, "This way we got an exciting, if only approximate, result and with it gained entrance into a whole new world of chemistry, experiencing all of the enthusiasm such a vista inspired. Our method made it possible to extend our calculations to all kinds of reactions."[8] Looking back seventy-five years later, Michael Polanyi's son John, a Nobel Prize–winning chemist more renowned even than his father, agreed about the significance of that moment: "The outlines of the hills over which the molecules would have to travel then emerged from the mists in which they had been hidden."[9]

REWRITING THE TEXTBOOKS

Armed with this powerful new research tool, Henry returned in 1930 from Berlin to Berkeley. He found the United States in the grip of the Great Depression. Jobs even for up-and-coming young scientists were scarce. Fortunately for Henry, a member of the Berkeley chemistry faculty had visited Berlin while he was there working with Polanyi. The Berkeley professor saw what Henry was doing and wrote to G. N. Lewis to suggest that he be hired. Even with this special recommendation, Henry was lucky to get a job; it would be five more lean Depression years before Berkeley could afford to hire new full-time faculty. However, Lewis had a one-year position, available because a tenured member of the faculty was on leave. Henry took it.

His second stint at Berkeley was significant not just for the opportunity to reconnect with Lewis, whom he idolized, but for a discovery that would grab the attention of the chemistry world. Using the new model developed in Berlin, Henry predicted that hydrogen and fluorine should not react with one another at room temperature. On its face, this prediction seemed ridiculous, because these two elements were known not just to react but to explode when brought into contact. All of the textbooks stated as much.

Nonetheless, Henry had enough faith in his model to present his prediction at a national meeting of the American Chemical Society. Among the attendees was Hugh Taylor, a friend of G. N. Lewis and chairman of the chemistry department at Princeton. Taylor was aware of recent experiments showing that hydrogen and fluorine in fact don't react at room temperature, so long as the two substances are brought together under just the right conditions. Taylor knew that the textbooks were wrong, and he recognized that Henry had shown why.

Taylor immediately wanted Henry at Princeton. He invited him on the spot to give two lectures there. Initially, Henry declined to go, citing prior commitments at Berkeley:

> I told him that I didn't see how I could, that I was teaching the freshman lab in Berkeley. He said, "Well, I'll take care of that. And I'll give you your expenses and $200 to give two lectures." Well, with me, $200 at that time was something that you worked for, alright, so I accepted. When I got to Princeton they had the whole physics department in to hear me, including Wigner (his friend from Berlin) and Von Neumann (a world-famous mathematician). Apparently it was very satisfactory, because after the lecture Taylor invited me to come to Princeton.[10]

PRINCETON

Notwithstanding Hugh Taylor's personal enthusiasm to hire Henry, Princeton was no more immune to the effects of the Depression than Berkeley. Princeton's offer was for just one year as an instructor (not a professor), at the same salary, $3,500, that Henry was making at Berkeley. Initially, Taylor was encouraging about Henry's long-term employment prospects: "I'm almost certain you'll be chosen for the faculty if you come back," he said. Within a matter of months, though, he wrote to Henry in California, reporting that the economic situation had gotten very tight and that there was no guarantee of Henry's being kept on after the one year as an instructor. Taylor said, "If you feel that you'd like to go someplace else, of course I'll release you." Henry wrote back, "I don't have any other place to go, so of course I'll come."[11]

As usual, Henry worked hard at Princeton, and he performed well. Yet the worsening economy meant that at the end of that first year Henry and three others hired with him were told that they'd be let go. Fortunately, Henry had an ace in the hole that the others apparently lacked. He was collaborating with so many senior faculty that they petitioned to keep him on, claiming that losing him would mean losing too much research-in-process. Henry's hard work—and Heaven's providence—saved him yet again.

Though he survived the 1932 layoff, Henry didn't receive regular faculty status; his employment remained on a year-to-year basis. Knowing that his professional situation was tenuous, he threw his energy into two activities. One was using his reaction-rate model to build three-dimensional pictures, or "surfaces," of the metaphorical mountain for a host of reactions. The work was extremely tedious, because each point of the picture required a complex calculation that had to be made with a slide rule (there were no computers in those days). After the calculations were made, the results had to be compared against experimental outcomes; often, the mismatch between predicted and actual results required reworking the calculations, again by hand. But Henry didn't let the tedium stop him: "I just built surfaces like mad, of all kinds of reactions without too much concern over whether or not it was exact. You could at least get rough surfaces, and then you could compare them against experiments."[12]

The other thing he did was publish papers. His first paper

appeared in print less than six months after his arrival at Princeton. Other papers followed in quick succession, most based on his painstaking "surface-building" and the predictive insights it produced. These papers were of high quality and naturally brought Henry some notoriety. His friend, Hugh Taylor, though, found a way to super-charge that notoriety, drawing on Henry's unique way of looking at chemical reactions.

On New Year's Eve, 1932, in Atlantic City, Henry presented a paper at a meeting of the American Association for the Advancement of Science. The paper generated much enthusiasm, even though few of the assembled scientists, especially the nonchemists, understood its contents. Dr. Taylor took this special opportunity to nominate Henry's paper as the best of the year—not just in chemistry, but in all of the sciences. More than simply making a nomination, Taylor aggressively lobbied the selection committee. His lobbying was not only unusual in scientific circles, it came at some personal sacrifice, as he was suffering at the time with the flu. Upon hearing at the eleventh hour that the committee members were wavering, he rose from his sickbed to make a final appeal for Henry. The lobbying worked, and Henry won.

The prize itself was significant: it was only the ninth ever awarded to that time, and it came with $1,000. Taylor, though, substantially increased the award's value to Henry, and to Princeton, by promoting the story to the national news media. On a serendipitously slow news day, New Year's Day, 1933, detailed stories about Henry's prize ran in major newspapers from coast to coast; a headline even appeared on the running electronic sign in Times Square. The story in the *New York Times* was typical:

> The prize of $1,000 given annually by the American
> Association for the Advancement of Science for the best
> paper submitted at the Winter meeting was awarded here

today to Dr. Henry Eyring, 32-year-old research associate of the Frick Chemical Laboratory, Princeton University. He was honored for his pioneering work in applying the principles of quantum mechanics, the latest tool of modern physics for delving into the mysteries of the subatomic world, to the laws governing the chemical bonds between elements.

Dr. Eyring has figured out mathematically the definite reactions that take place in a number of puzzling chemical combinations which later were verified independently by other workers through actual chemical experimentation. In one instance Dr. Eyring's calculations showed the present chemical textbooks to be wrong, and his predictions to that effect have been found to be true by experiment.

The *Times* article went on for nine more paragraphs, with bold subheadings reading, "Powerful Tool for Chemists," and, "Work Only at Its Beginning." Henry's hometown papers took credit for their native son. The front page of the *San Francisco Chronicle* read, "U.C. Graduate Awarded $1,000 for Outstanding Paper." In Arizona, the local paper gushed, "Pima Is Proud of Eyring's Success."

ABSOLUTE RATE THEORY

Notwithstanding the unusual generosity of these news stories, Henry's greatest professional success and notoriety lay yet ahead. The conditions for research and discovery at Princeton were ideal. He worked in the state-of-the-art Frick Chemical Laboratory, completed just two years before while Henry was in Germany. Throughout his fifteen years at Princeton his teaching load was light and his salary never cut, even in the depths of the

Depression. Perhaps most importantly, he was aided by a small army of bright, hard-working graduate students. Without them to test his ideas and write up the results, few papers would have been published.

Henry's most significant paper came in 1935, two years after the Atlantic City triumph. Building on his own research and on work done by Polanyi and Wigner after he left Berlin, Henry put the capstone on his reaction-rate model. He theorized that, when a reacting atom or molecule stands at the top of the mountain between one chemical state and another, it is actually part of a "transition complex." This transition complex is a combination of all of the particles involved in the reaction; for a brief instant, they act as one. Henry showed that the rate of a reaction depends on the number and the energy level of the transition complexes at the top of the mountain. He captured this relationship mathematically in what came to be known as Absolute Rate Theory (ART or, to many, the "Eyring Equation").

Fate gave Henry special help in writing the ART paper. In the summer of 1934, he took his wife and two young sons to visit their many cousins in Utah. On the return trip he was scheduled to present the ART paper at an American Chemical Society meeting in Cleveland. However, on their drive west the Eyrings met with a near-fatal accident. Outside of South Bend, Indiana, a woman coming in the opposite direction panicked when a wasp flew into her car. Trying to chase the wasp out, she lost control of her vehicle and crashed head-on into the Eyring's Model-A Ford. Nearly everyone in their car was injured, but Henry took the worst of it. He shattered the windshield with his head, broke the steering wheel with his hand, and had his leg fractured in a dozen places.

The Eyrings spent two weeks recuperating in an Indiana hospital. For Henry, the forced idleness was a first: never in his life had he had so much time with nothing to do. As usual, though, he made the best of a bad situation. Knowing that he'd miss the submission deadline for the Cleveland meeting, he turned the ART argument over and over in his mind. As he said of the paper finally published, "My enforced leisure gave me more time to put in on this paper. A more finished document resulted, so that was as finished a paper as I have ever written."[13]

Henry was fortunate that he gave this paper, the most important of his career, unusual attention. Even with the extra effort, it came back from the *Journal of Chemical Physics* rejected. The reviewers' criticisms would echo through the ensuing decades. Henry's peers objected to his mathematical technique of inserting arbitrarily chosen numbers into his predictive equation. To them, it was scientifically unacceptable to use a theoretical equation and then modify it based on empirical observation until it worked; they called his success "a happy cancellation of errors." Some doubted the very existence of the transition complex. One called the key mathematical term in the Eyring Equation a "fictitious" quantity.[14]

The strong negative response to Henry's paper may have been the result of his violating one scientific convention too many. To begin with, many of his fellow chemists resented the encroachment on their turf of hard-to-understand mathematical concepts from physics. Insights from quantum mechanics such as Henry's shed useful new light on chemistry, but quantum mechanics itself was foreign to all but a few chemists.

That said, Henry wasn't alone in trying to blur the conventional lines between chemistry and physics; had that been his only offense, the criticism of his work wouldn't have been so fierce. He had the audacity, though, to violate another convention—namely, that a scientist could either be a theorist or an experimenter, but not both. In other words, it was acceptable to build a purely theoretical model and then see how well the model explains reality. It was also all right to observe reality and draw conclusions about what is going on. Henry, though, was having it both ways: he had created a theoretical model, and then, based on things he observed but couldn't explain, he went back and tweaked the model until it worked for making predictions. To convention-bound scientists, that made him look more lucky than smart.

Of course, Henry cared less about the explanation for every piece of his model than about using it to make new discoveries. He was confident that the unanswered questions would be solved in time, and he meanwhile wanted to apply the model to any subject it could usefully illuminate.

A Fortunate Overruling

In fact, it was one of his earliest applications of the model—made even before the 1935 paper was written—that may have saved the model itself from the dustbin. In 1932 the American chemist Harold Urey discovered something called "heavy water." The discovery of heavy water, which would lead ultimately to the harnessing of nuclear power, was so important that Urey won the Nobel Prize for it. Like many others, Henry was fascinated by Urey's discovery. He also thought that his reaction-rate model could explain the mechanism by which Urey had been able to isolate the heavy-water molecules. In fact, the model did provide the answer, and Henry had published a paper on the subject even before Urey received his Nobel (and well before Henry submitted the 1935 reaction paper).

As it happened, Harold Urey was also the editor of the *Journal of Chemical Physics,* the one to which Henry submitted his paper. Henry was well aware of that fact. He also knew that Urey was, like him, a graduate of G. N. Lewis's Berkeley lab. How much trouble he expected from the reviewers of his 1935 paper is hard to say. However, he chose, in Urey, the ideal appeal judge to overturn a negative decision by reviewers of his paper. Upon learning of their rejection, Henry's Princeton colleagues Hugh Taylor and Eugene Wigner went to work on Urey, arguing that though the model might not be perfect, it was powerful—as evidenced by the earlier heavy-water paper. In the end Urey reversed the journal's decision to deny, and the 1935 paper was published.

This publication victory didn't end the controversy over Henry's unconventional model. It wasn't until 1962, almost three decades later, that new laboratory techniques allowed corroboration of the existence of the transition complex, the key concept behind ART. Apparently, even laboratory proof wasn't enough to settle the debate. Henry's biographical memoir, commissioned by the National Academy of Sciences after his death in 1981, still declined to grant ART full acceptance: "The validity of the basic assumptions of this theory frequently have been questioned, and the discussion on this continues to this day. Nevertheless, it is generally conceded that the theory provides a highly useful framework for the interpretation of chemical reaction rates."[15]

Unconcerned with criticism and unwilling to wait for universal acceptance, Henry went to work applying his model to any and every mystery he thought it might explain. By 1940 his name appeared on seventy-five published papers, an output that a team of half-a-dozen researchers would have been proud to produce in that amount of time. It was a feat that would lead Harvard's John Van Vleck, coincidentally one of the visiting lecturers at Wisconsin who inspired Henry's interest in quantum mechanics, to say, "Eyring's not a professor, he's a college."[16]

Van Vleck's comment spoke not just to the volume of Henry's work, but also to its variety. In addition to problems of traditional chemistry, he pursued questions of physics, biology, engineering and numerous other scientific disciplines. His Absolute Rate Theory could explain phenomena in fields in which he had no formal training, allowing him to roam freely across traditional academic boundaries. His work also ran the gamut from the most theoretical to the most practical problems. He was as happy to study the tearing of cloth as to imagine what it would be like to meet a person from an alternate universe. He published papers on both of these subjects.

Unconventional Methods

Henry also continued to disregard the traditional distinction between theoretical and experimental science. When, on occasion, he wanted to test some new idea, he would go out and find the necessary equipment to perform experiments. But his main focus at Princeton was on using ART to explain the experimental results of other scientists. For that, his primary laboratory tools were a blackboard and a piece of chalk. A Nobel Prize-winning Japanese physicist wrote of being surprised at the lack of traditional experimental equipment when he visited Henry's Princeton lab:

I visited Professor Eyring at Princeton, N.J. in May, 1940. It was the first time to meet Dr. Eyring, although I had known him for a long time through his interesting papers in quantum theory. He was younger than I expected. After talking about his current researches, he showed me around his laboratory and introduced his students to me. I saw only slide rules and several calculators on tables, but could not find even a simple piece of experimental apparatus in his laboratory. It was my first experience to observe such a chemical laboratory.[17]

Like ART itself, nearly all of Henry's research ideas were unorthodox. By his own admission, 95 percent of the notions he brought to work in the morning would, after exploration by his assistants during the day, prove fruitless. However, he came to work with so many ideas that the other 5 percent amounted to an impressive research output: by the mid-1940s he had published a total of 125 papers at Princeton.

Perhaps the seminal achievement of this time was the publication of a book, *Quantum Chemistry*, that would make him known to generations of chemists. The book was begun at the request of publisher John Wiley and Sons in 1933. Henry wrote with the help of a doctoral student, but even with that support his involvement in new research kept the book from progressing. Five years after they started, in 1938, he encouraged the graduate student to proceed without him: "It seems more important that our quantum mechanics be published than that I be a co-author. I wish, therefore, you would go ahead and finish it. You can acknowledge my past and future contributions, whatever they may be, in the preface."[18] The student co-author graciously suggested that they push on together to publication, which finally occurred after more than a decade.

In the scientific journals, *Quantum Chemistry* received mixed reviews. One reviewer complained that the book was "reliable" but "not easy," that it tried to cover too much too quickly.[19] However, *Quantum Chemistry* met with tremendous commercial success. It sold thirty thousand copies in its first thirty-five years and is still in print today. Italian and Japanese translations soon appeared. Even the Soviet Union admired the book, expressing its approval by translating a pirated copy into Russian. Throughout the world, Henry became known to generations of chemists studying quantum mechanics as the man who literally "wrote the book."

Notwithstanding critical reservations about Henry's scientific approach, his vast publication output soon won the battle of popular opinion. Before long every serious scientist and student accepted the notion of a transition complex and envisioned reacting molecules atop mountains. Today, thanks to computer graphics technology, those mountains are displayed on screens in undergraduate chemistry labs. The transition complex concept is taught even in good high school chemistry courses.

UTAH

In 1946, amidst this torrent of productivity, Henry surprised his colleagues with the announcement that he was moving to Utah. Hugh Taylor offered everything he had—including his own endowed chair—to keep Henry at Princeton. However, Mildred wanted their three sons to grow up among family and wouldn't let Henry decline an offer from the University of Utah.

The move to Utah looked like career suicide. Utah didn't even have a Ph.D. program in chemistry—or, for that matter, in any other field. Henry was recruited to change that. As the first dean of the graduate school, he set about immediately to create a research university from scratch.

He did so with a grand total of two years' experience as an academic administrator. In 1944 the national Textile Research Institute had been relocated from Washington, D.C., to Princeton, and Hugh Taylor had prevailed upon Henry to lead it. Until that time, Henry had been exempt even from faculty committee assignments, leaving him available to teach and do research full time.

Whatever the deficiencies in his administrative experience, Henry quickly distinguished himself as a natural leader at Utah. The graduate school's numbers speak to his capability. During Henry's twenty-year tenure as dean, Utah produced 749 Ph.D.s, and enrollment in the graduate school reached 2,500. [20] In its first full decade as a Ph.D.-granting institution (the 1950s), Utah ranked fortieth in degrees conferred in the U.S.

Henry himself supervised the work of more than 120 Ph.D.s.[21] Better still, he drew to Utah other gifted faculty who shouldered their fair share of the mentoring load and, like him, added luster to the university's academic reputation. Among them were some of his former students from Princeton.

Remarkably, the administrative success didn't come at the expense of his personal research productivity. Considering that he also taught a full teaching load year-round at Utah, more than twice what he ever did at Princeton, no one would have faulted him had the research output diminished. Yet rather than falling from the stratospheric Princeton levels, his publication rate at Utah actually rose. In his thirty-five years there, he published roughly 485 papers, an average of more than one per month. The key, of course, was the synergy between mentoring Ph.D. candidates and publishing: the more effectively he taught his students, the more they published together.

When he left Princeton in 1946 Henry had every reason to believe he'd be geographically and scientifically isolated in Utah. However, thanks to the advent of jet travel, he was at no greater disadvantage living in Salt Lake City than in Princeton. He traveled outside of Utah an average of one day in four, each year giving two hundred to three hundred lectures and consulting to twenty or more companies.[22]

EVERY PRIZE BUT ONE

Having been admitted to the major national scientific associations while at Princeton, Henry gradually rose through their ranks. In 1963 he became president of the 93,000-member

American Chemical Society. Two years later, he held the same position in the 100,000-member American Association for the Advancement of Science.

Throughout his time at Utah personal awards flowed. Among those were fifteen honorary doctorate degrees, including one from Princeton. Henry won the highest awards given by the American Chemical Society, including its premier Priestley Medal. In 1966 he received the National Medal of Science from President Lyndon Johnson. The presidential citation specifically mentioned ART, calling it "one of the sharpest tools in the study of rates of chemical reactions."

The two awards of which Henry was most proud were both international. One was the Brezelius Medal, awarded by the Swedish Academy of Sciences, which also selects the Nobel Prize winners. This award, named for Sweden's greatest chemist, is given only infrequently: Henry was just the tenth recipient, and he accepted the medal from Sweden's King Gustaf. The other cherished honor was Israel's Wolf Prize in chemistry, given for "achievements in the interest of mankind and friendly relations among peoples." The Wolf Prize, which came with a $100,000 honorarium, is generally considered chemistry's second-highest award after the Nobel Prize.

Of course, Henry would have liked to have won the Nobel, too. It was the only significant scientific honor to elude him. He was formally nominated at least half a dozen times, beginning in 1950. A final attempt was made in 1981, the year he died (and thus became ineligible for the prize). Merely nominating someone for a Nobel is a serious undertaking, requiring extensive documentation and written recommendations. That his colleagues went to this great effort is a sign of their admiration for Henry. That he allowed them to do it so often is a sign that he felt he deserved the prize.

The subject of the Nobel came up in an interview with Henry conducted by his nephew, Edward Kimball.[23] As they talked, Henry mentioned that Einstein had won the Nobel Prize in Physics not for the well-known theory of relativity, but for his discovery of a phenomenon called "the photoelectric effect." Kimball asked whether that meant that the photoelectric effect was a more important contribution to science. Henry responded with a clarification about what it takes to win a Nobel Prize. He also expressed his willingness to go to Stockholm, if asked:

> *Eyring:* [The] discovery of the photoelectric was clean cut. It was true; it was a discovery you could write something simple about, and it was his. All of those things go into a Nobel Prize. They tend to give the prize to people who have done other important things, but they ordinarily identify it with some specific contribution.
>
> *Kimball:* The head of one of the departments at Wisconsin mentioned that he thought you ought to have had the Nobel Prize long ago.
>
> *Eyring:* I am available.

Joking aside, not winning the Nobel Prize was more than just disappointing. In years when Henry was rumored to be on the short list, radio and television reporters would gather at his house as the announcement deadline approached. When he didn't win, his friends and supporters knew.

Nonetheless, Henry didn't let the lack of a Nobel committee nod dampen his enthusiasm or sap his confidence. He had seen enough divine intervention in the making of his unlikely career to know that if God had wanted him to win the Nobel Prize, he would have.

A Multi-faceted Legacy

Nor did his Nobel-bridesmaid status diminish the appreciation of those colleagues who knew him well. Hugh Taylor may have been foremost among them. Honoring Henry as he left Princeton for Utah, Dr. Taylor paid this lavish tribute:

> It is almost superfluous to say that these fifteen years comprise the fifteen most significant years of the Department—a history which stretches back into the earliest years of chemistry departments in the colleges of this country. Princeton may well have been the university where, during these fifteen years, the most significant contribution to physical chemistry has been made. Certainly it has been the happiest, pleasantest, most stimulating environment in which to live and work. We count ourselves indeed fortunate that we were able to add to the team of experimental scientists one of the outstanding theoretical chemists of this age, perhaps any age.
>
> One might say that he possesses the Midas touch. Everything in scientific research turns to gold when brought to the attention of his fertile brain. But there are none of the evils that beset the original Midas. Why this is so is realized by any who come into contact with him. Vigorous exponent of scientific truth and also of unpopular—one might even say lost—causes, he convinced everyone of his own disinterested selfless devotion to what he judges to be truth. And he has spared no energy or exertion in those causes.[24]

His scientific achievements made Henry famous among his professional colleagues. Heaven also cared enough to help, as evidenced by the providential support he received, especially early in his career. However, Henry's science has been long superseded by new discoveries. He'd be little remembered now, more than twenty-five years after his death, were it not for two other contributions to the world.

His colleague Hugh Taylor alluded to these other two contributions in the farewell speech for Henry at Princeton:

> Looking back over fifteen years I cannot recall a single sharp word or angry phrase in all our dealings together, and we oftentimes observed the scene of argument from other benches. We have learned together how much there can be in common in opposite approaches to a single problem, and it has been on many occasions an enriching experience. I have defended Mormonism among a community of Jesuits and pride myself on the issue though, of course, I had the great advantage that came from earlier argument with Henry.[25]

Hugh Taylor appreciated Henry for two things that went beyond science. One was geniality, the absence, as Taylor said, of "a single sharp word or angry phrase in all of our dealings together." We'll see more of Henry's gift for getting along with others in chapter 3, Friendship.

The other thing that Taylor appreciated was the way that Henry defended his Mormon faith. That unflinching defense of Mormonism—and of religion generally—is the subject to which we now turn.

The Eyring family (Ted, Hal, and Henry standing; Mildred and Harden sitting) newly moved to Utah, in 1949

2

FAITH

The first half of the twentieth century, when Henry began his career, saw unprecedented technological progress. Great good flowed from a wave of scientific discovery. Yet there was also great destruction of life and threat to traditional beliefs. Science had to take some responsibility for that, as well. The seeming tension between the good and ill that science wrought put Henry in an important, potentially difficult position.

THE THREAT OF SCIENCE

The world had changed so quickly. In 1900 the Wright brothers were preparing for their historic first flight. Marie Curie and her colleagues were just beginning to understand radioactivity. By the mid-1950s, the most terrible war in history had ended with the explosion of two atomic bombs; hydrogen bombs a hundred times more powerful were being tested. Sputnik, a Soviet satellite, could be seen overhead in the U.S. every ninety minutes. The world shuddered at the thought of combined missile and nuclear technology, of death raining down from space.

The religious faithful also shuddered at certain scientific developments. At the turn of the twentieth century, for instance, the theory of evolution was yet incomplete. Charles Darwin had demonstrated natural selection, or survival of the fittest, but couldn't show the mechanism by which a parent produced a more or less fit offspring. With the theory incomplete and the scientific community divided over the missing elements, evolution in 1900 was a subject of concern only to scholars.

That began to change rapidly, though, when Gregor Mendel's work on genetic inheritance was rediscovered in 1901, the year of Henry's birth. Within a few decades, the combination of Darwin's evolution and Mendel's genetics had resulted in a theory of evolution that the scientific community accepted as all but fact. The social influence of evolution was graphically apparent in 1925's "Scopes Monkey Trial," when the news media ridiculed William Jennings Bryan's defense of divine creation. Though the Scopes trial was legally inconclusive, it demonstrated evolution's wide acceptance in the media and its potential power even in children's classrooms.

As with the military threats of the day, science seemed to be at the root of this attack on religion. Ironically, the very radiation science that made nuclear bombs possible also provided evidence for an earth age much greater than previously thought. By studying the decay of radioactive elements in rocks, scientists determined the earth to be more than four billion years old. To creationism's critics, an old earth was helpful in two ways: it not only debunked the biblical creation time line, but it also provided the theory of evolution with an essential ingredient—enough time for man to evolve from lower species.

Of course, religionists were worried about where science was taking the world. However, the concern was shared by some scientists as well. Einstein, for example, is famously quoted as saying, "God does not play dice with the universe." Einstein's real statement, written in a letter to fellow physicist Max Born, is more complex and revealing.

Einstein was writing to Born about quantum mechanics, the theory that aided Henry's creation of ART. A key tenet of the theory is the "uncertainty principle," which holds that the exact position and speed of an electron cannot be known, only guessed at probabilistically. Quantum mechanics' enthronement of uncertainty as a principle overthrew centuries of science dedicated to understanding the universe with mathematical precision. To some, it cast into doubt the order and rationality of the universe, an order and rationality that many scientists took as evidence of a divine architect. That is the context for Einstein's actual statement to Born, which amounts to a caution:

> Quantum mechanics is certainly imposing. But an inner voice tells me that it is not yet the real thing. The theory says a lot, but does not really bring us any closer to the secret of the Old One. I, at any rate, am convinced that He does not throw dice.[1]

If all scholars were as reverential and deliberate as Einstein, the religious faithful would have had little to fear from the discoveries of the early twentieth century. That wasn't the case, however. Even in the schools and seminaries of The Church of Jesus Christ of Latter-day Saints, some instructors began to teach secular theories as though they superseded Church doctrines. These instructors, many educated in prestigious secular universities, saw an either-or choice between religious orthodoxy and scholarly credibility, and they chose the latter. Trusting, young Latter-day Saint students were in many cases led to doubt their faith.

AN ECCLESIASTICAL RESPONSE

Leaders of the Church moved to counteract this trend. The centerpiece of their response was an address given to the Church's full-time educators in 1938 by J. Reuben Clark Jr., a counselor in the Church's First Presidency. President Clark was an attorney by training, a former U.S. State Department lawyer, Undersecretary of State, and Ambassador to Mexico.

Speaking for the Church, President Clark made a powerful case for honoring faith. He reaffirmed the two key tenets of LDS faith, first that Jesus Christ is the Son of God and Savior of the World, and second that Joseph Smith was divinely authorized to restore the Church. Building upon that foundation, he then addressed the subject of religious education. He described the natural faithfulness of young LDS students, and he challenged the Church's teachers to have courage in their instruction:

> I mean intellectual courage—the courage to affirm principles, beliefs, and faith that may not always be considered as harmonizing with such knowledge, scientific or otherwise, as the teacher or his educational colleagues may believe they possess.
>
> Not unknown are cases where men of presumed faith, holding responsible positions, have felt that, since by affirming their full faith they might call down upon themselves the ridicule of their unbelieving colleagues, they must either modify or explain away their faith, or destructively dilute it, or even pretend to cast it away. Such are hypocrites to their colleagues and their co-religionists.[2]

President Clark also addressed the advance of scientific knowledge:

I urge you not fall into that childish error, so common now, of believing that merely because man has gone so far in harnessing the forces of nature and turning them to his own use that therefore the truths of the Spirit have been changed or transformed. It is a vital and significant fact that man's conquest of the things of the Spirit has not marched side by side with his conquest of things material. Remember always and cherish the great truth of the Intercessory Prayer:

"And this is life eternal, that they might know thee the only true God, and Jesus Christ, whom thou hast sent."[3]

This is an ultimate truth; so are all spiritual truths. They are not changed by the discovery of a new element or a new ethereal wave, nor by clipping off a few seconds, minutes, or hours of a speed record.[4]

President Clark's speech stands as a constitutional statement of the Church's commitment to faith in education. Then, as now, it strengthened the resolve of many instructors to stand by their faith even in the face of intellectual criticism.

Some Church leaders, though, felt the need to go further. One, Elder Joseph Fielding Smith, sensed that intellectualism—both within and without the Church—would only increase, and that science might produce discoveries more threatening to faith even than evolution. For instance, given the pace of exploration of invisible phenomena such as the working of the atom, it was perfectly reasonable to assume that scientists might soon explore and explain away spiritual phenomena, or even the human spirit itself.

Elder Smith was a member of the Church's Quorum of the Twelve Apostles, subordinate to President Clark but recognized nonetheless as a prophet, seer, and revelator. His father had been

President of the Church, and his grandfather, Hyrum Smith, was the brother of the Church's founder, Joseph Smith. At the time President Clark gave his 1938 speech, Elder Smith had already served as an Apostle for twenty-eight years and was the Church's official historian. He was also a master of scripture and Church doctrine.

The Church had taken no official position on either evolution or the age of the earth.[5] Elder Smith, though, felt the necessity of claiming the strategic high ground relative not only to these challenges, but also to any others that science might present. He did this by advocating scriptural literalism. In other words, all scriptural accounts—including those of the creation—were to be read literally, regardless of contrary evidence or opinions. The advantage of this position was that it preempted threats not only from existing scientific theories such as evolution, but also from any future discoveries potentially inimical to faith. The scriptures would be taken as authoritative, come what may. The drawback of this position, of course, was that it required scientific findings contrary to scripture to be disregarded.

THE FAITHFUL SCIENTIST'S DILEMMA— THE CASE FOR A VERY OLD EARTH

Believing LDS scientists and students thus found themselves in a quandary. It was one thing to hold fast to spiritual beliefs that couldn't be proven scientifically, as President Clark had challenged. It was another thing to deny—as a condition of faith—science itself.

The age of the earth was a particular problem. Whereas evolution was just a theory (albeit a broadly accepted one), virtually all serious scientists accepted a four-billion-year-old earth as fact. The evidence was both old and new. For hundreds of years before radioactive dating, geologists had compared observed rates of sedimentation (the pace at which mud accumulates at the bottom of an ocean or lake) to the thickness of sedimentary rock layers exposed in places like the Grand Canyon. They calculated that the time necessary for all of the observable sedimentary rocks to form would be over one billion years.

Radioactive dating makes the case for an even older earth. When certain radioactive materials decay, they produce lighter elements, such as the gas helium. In rocks formed deep in the earth's crust, trapped helium can come from only one source—radioactive decay. Thus, a scientist who knows how fast radioactive decay occurs can measure the amount of helium in a rock and tell how long ago it was formed. Using such rock "clocks," the earth is shown to be between four and five billion years old. The evidence is strong enough that arguing for a younger earth—such as the one implied by a literal reading of the biblical creation account in Genesis—is nearly as bold as arguing for a flat earth.

CALLING ON HENRY

It was natural, then, for LDS scientists and educators to wonder what Henry Eyring had to say on the subject. Here was not only the Church's most preeminent scientist, but a chemist whose early specialty was metallurgy or, in other words, the chemistry of metals such as those in radioactive "clocks."

Henry was also a faithful Church member. Throughout his fifteen years in New Jersey he served in lay leadership positions. At the time of the 1946 move to Utah, he was president of the New Jersey District, a fact recognized in the Church's official newspaper under the headline, "Noted American Scientist Presides over Church Unit."[6]

Upon arriving in Utah, Henry received an appointment to the

general board of the Sunday School, a general Church office that, though subordinate to the Twelve Apostles and the First Presidency, gave him substantial stature and opportunity to address the membership at large. He wrote articles, for instance, for official Church magazines, and in 1948 he gave a nationwide address on CBS's *Church of the Air* program. The title of the CBS address was "Science and Faith."

In "Science and Faith,"[7] as in hundreds of similar speeches that Henry would give throughout his life, both scientists and religionists could find support for their respective positions. The strength and source of his personal religious conviction was obvious:

> The four gospels tell the story of the Son of God who came into the world, lived an exemplary life, died, and was resurrected. If accepted as accurate, this record puts the necessity of being religious beyond question. History, unlike laboratory experiments, cannot be tried over again, just because we are not quite sure what the happenings meant. In this sense, religion differs from such laboratory sciences as chemistry and physics. We must depend in part on inference. In the end however, if the inquiry is broad and careful enough, we need be no less sure of our final conclusions.
>
> The Lord himself outlined the procedure when he said: "If any man will do his will, he shall know of the doctrine, whether it be of God, or whether I speak of myself."[8]

Henry made many arguments for faith similar to those of President J. Reuben Clark. For instance, having described the progress of scientists in exploring the majesty of the physical world, he challenged skepticism and preached the benefits of belief:

> Now, curiously enough, there are good people who would have you believe that man who conceives all these wonderful things, and masters them in part, is no more than the dust of the earth to which his body returns. To me, this is unbelievable.
>
> I would like to suggest to the youth who may feel inclined to disparage religion as they pursue other studies, that they might bring enrichment to their lives by cultivating faith and an interest in things of the spirit as they follow their other pursuits. Such faith will never detract from their abilities in other fields, but it will broaden their thinking and give added depth to their character.

Henry also preached the need for religious tempering of science:

> In times of uncertainty, such as the present, the increasing effort to understand man's place in the grand scheme of things proceeds at an accelerated pace. That understanding is a problem not alone for the laboratory; many of its answers will be found in the realm of the spiritual. It is important that all men of good will use their energies, their talents and their learning in their chosen fields, mutually assisting one another toward the building of a better world—that world which men of faith of all ages have envisioned and toward which they have labored.
>
> The scientific method which has served so brilliantly in unraveling the mysteries of this world must be supplemented by something else if we are to enjoy to the fullest the blessings that have come of the knowledge gained. It

is the great mission and opportunity of religion to teach men "the way, the truth, the life," that they might utilize the discoveries of the laboratory to their blessing and not to their destruction. There is a need for added spirituality, of the kind that leads to brotherhood, to go hand in hand with the scientific progress of our time.

God grant that in seeking the mysteries of his handiwork, we may also learn his great religious truths, which we have been prone to disregard, that our efforts might become a blessing to us.

BACKING BOTH SCIENCE AND RELIGION

President Clark himself could have asked for no better defense of faith. However, Henry didn't advocate just religion; he was also strong in his support of science. Remarkably, he used scripture in advocating scientific reasoning every bit as much as he had in advocating faith:

I am happy to represent a people who throughout their history have encouraged learning and scholarship in all fields of honorable endeavor, a people who have among their scriptural teachings such lofty concepts as these: "The glory of God is intelligence, or, in other words, light and truth." "A man cannot be saved in ignorance." "Whatever principle of intelligence we attain unto in this life, it will rise with us in the resurrection."[9]

We learned from the Prophet Joseph Smith that man lived before he was born; that life is a school where man is sent to learn the things the Lord intends; and that he continues on into life after death. Death is not the end; it is but one more step in a great forward march made possible by the redemption wrought by the Savior. This is the spirit of true science—constant and eternal seeking.[10]

The truly remarkable thing about Henry's stance was that he disappointed anyone hoping to resolve the supposed conflict between science and religion in favor of one side or the other. To him, there was simply no conflict:

> I have been announced as a student of science. But I also like to think of myself as one who loves the Gospel of Jesus Christ. For me there has been no serious difficulty in reconciling the principles of true science with the principles of true religion, for both are concerned with the eternal verities of the universe.
>
> And yet there are many people, and particularly among our youth, who regard the field of science and the field of religion as two wholly different spheres, the one entirely separated from and unrelated to the other. In fact, there are those in both fields who have done themselves and the causes to which they give their interests a distinct disservice in teaching that the two are opposed and that they cannot be harmonized with the other.

In support of his argument for harmony, Henry referenced the faith of great scientists, notably Newton and Gauss. As he said, their scientific expertise "seemed only to strengthen their sense of a great spiritual realm beyond their ken."

He went further, suggesting a symbiosis between science and religion:

> I am now going to venture to say that science has rendered a service to religion. The scientific spirit is a spirit of inquiry, a spirit of reaching out for truth. In the final

analysis, this spirit is likewise of the essence of religion. The Savior said: "Ask, and it shall be given you; seek, and ye shall find; knock, and it shall be opened unto you."[11] The scientist has in effect reaffirmed this great fundamental laid down by the Master, and in doing so has given a new impetus to religion.

Just as science has proved a help to religion, so religion in its finest expression has given impetus to science. I should like to quote again from modern scripture: "That which is of God is of light; and he that receiveth light, and continueth in God, receiveth more light; and that light groweth brighter and brighter until the perfect day."[12]

RECONCILING THE APPARENT CONFLICT

Had Henry left his argument at this, he might have been written off as little more than a hopeful diplomat promoting tolerance of conflicting opinions, rather than reconciling them. Yet he did in fact offer a theory of ultimate reconciliation. The catch is that the theory demands both humility and patience.

In essence, Henry argued that God's wisdom is so great that man is incapable of understanding—let alone reconciling—the apparent conflicts between science and religion. In support of that argument, he expressed his own humility as a scientist:

Contemplating the awe-inspiring order in the universe, extending from the almost infinitely small to the infinitely large, one is overwhelmed with its grandeur and with the limitless wisdom which conceived, created, and governs it all. Our understanding, great as it sometimes seems, can be nothing but the wide-eyed wonder of the child when measured against the Creator's omniscience.[13]

Henry argued that this kind of childlike humility is required of the religious faithful, who must expect to be given the truth line upon line, rather than all at once:

> The restored gospel teaches that certain things are known by revelation and study, but much more remains to be learned. God in his wisdom will reveal more as the need arises. We are engaged in a never-ending program of eternal progression.[14]

In short, Henry argued that apparent conflicts between science and religion are the result of incomplete understanding, an inevitability given our modest intelligence relative to God's. In the case of the creation of man and the Earth, for instance, he recognized the incompleteness of both scientific and religious understanding of the complex processes involved. He was sure, though, that however man and the Earth were created, "God was at the helm." He trusted that God, as creator of both Heaven and Earth, saw no conflicts between science and religion:

> The gospel, then, is the search for truth, and there is only one truth—there is a God in Heaven, who, if He is God over the world and over the universe, certainly understands everything, and inside His mind there must be no contradiction.[15]

Henry also had faith that, as his intelligence grew to approach God's, he too would see how the findings of science and religion ultimately meshed. Rather than being frustrated by his limited understanding, Henry reveled in the chance to learn and grow. He made it clear that he would continue both to believe and to study:

I should like to say that true religion was never a narrow thing. True religion concerns man and the entire universe in which he lives. It concerns his relationships with himself and his fellowmen, with his environment, and with his Creator. It is therefore limitless, and as boundless as that eternity which it teaches lies ahead of every son of God. "Be ye therefore perfect, even as your Father which is in heaven is perfect."[16] What a challenge to every man lies in these words from the Master, to develop himself, to strive, to learn, to seek, to go forward that he might become as God.

To us has come the following which we regard as a divine injunction: "Teach ye diligently and my grace shall attend you, that you may be instructed more perfectly in theory, in principle, in doctrine, in the law of the gospel, in all things that pertain unto the kingdom of God, that are expedient for you to understand; of things both in heaven and in the earth, and under the earth; things which have been, things which are, things which must shortly come to pass; things which are at home, things which are abroad; the wars and the perplexities of the nations, and the judgments which are on the land; and a knowledge also of countries and of kingdoms."[17]

Here is the spirit of true religion, an honest seeking after knowledge of all things of heaven and earth.

A PROPHETIC TRADITION OF CONFIDENCE

In fact, novel as it may have sounded coming from a twentieth-century scientist, Henry's philosophy of seeking truth via both science and religion was nothing new in the Church. He often cited Joseph Smith's statements advocating the pursuit of knowledge, as noted earlier: "The glory of God is intelligence, or, in other words, light and truth." "A man cannot be saved in ignorance." "Whatever principle of intelligence we attain unto in this life, it will rise with us in the resurrection."[18]

Joseph Smith's successor, Brigham Young, elaborated on the charge to seek truth, arguing that it be sought everywhere and that there was nothing to fear from scientific discoveries. Given that President Young was not himself a learned man, and that he had a fledgling church to protect, his confidence is remarkable:

> Our religion will not clash with or contradict the facts of science in any particular. You may take geology, for instance, and it is a true science; not that I would say for a moment that all the conclusions and deductions of its professors are true, but its leading principles are; they are facts—they are eternal. How long the Earth has been organized is not for me to say, and I do not care anything about it. As for the Bible account of the creation we may say that the Lord gave it to Moses, or rather Moses obtained the history and traditions of his fathers, and from these picked out what he considered necessary, and that account has been handed down from age to age, and we have got it, no matter whether it is correct or not, and whether the Lord found the Earth empty and void, whether he made it out of nothing or out of the rude elements; or whether he made it in six days or in as many millions of years, is and will remain a matter of specula-tion in the minds of men unless he give revelation on the subject. If we understood the process of creation there would be no mystery about it, it would all be reason-able and plain, for there is no mystery except to the ignorant.[19]

Of course, Henry's testimony lacked the prophetic weight of Brigham Young's. However, Henry's witness had several advantages. One was his scientific training. Whereas President Young disavowed knowledge of—or even interest in—the process by which the Earth was formed, Henry was both interested and expert.

Henry's declarations of faith also carried special weight because he had seen the wave of scientific discovery that occurred after President Young's time, including the broad acceptance of evolution. That he was unperturbed in the face of so much change was a great source of confidence to those who heard his testimony. In fact, far from being worried about new scientific findings, Henry welcomed them. He saw them as helping to focus the faithful on the core of their religious beliefs. As he said:

> It is interesting to recall that, in ages past, religious men felt that their faith hinged on the notion that the earth was flat. However, when it was found to be round, they discovered that their basic religious ideas had survived without perceptible damage. In fact, the great underlying principles of faith were brought into bolder relief when the clutter of false notions was removed from about them.[20]

THE CHURCH'S UNOFFICIAL SPOKESMAN AND ADVISOR ON SCIENCE

Henry's comforting view of the compatibility of science and religion was warmly welcomed by his faithful LDS colleagues. It also drew the tacit support of the senior-most leaders of the Church. Though the Church made no official statement on either the age of the Earth or evolution, Henry was privately encouraged to address the subject of science and religion as the opportunity presented itself. In 1951, for instance, he received an invitation to speak at a "Religious Emphasis Week" at the Oklahoma Agricultural and Mechanical College. Henry forwarded the invitation to the office of the Church's First Presidency, asking their opinion of his participation. In response, he received approval to proceed:

> We think it would be very desirable for you to accept this invitation, if you feel you are able to do so, having in mind your other duties and responsibilities. We congratulate you upon the receipt of this invitation and believe that you can render a real service in spreading the truths and principles of the Restored Gospel by acknowledging the invitation and performing the work outlined.[21]

The letter was signed by Church President David O. McKay and both of his counselors, Presidents Stephen L Richards and J. Reuben Clark, author of the landmark 1938 speech.

Henry's work at the Oklahoma Agricultural and Mechanical College must have been well-received. The following year, Presidents McKay and Clark again wrote to Henry. They had been contacted by the University of Oklahoma, which asked for a Church representative at their annual "Religious Emphasis Week." Presidents McKay and Clark identified Henry as their go-to man:

> We recalled the excellent service which you did on another occasion when you visited the Oklahoma A. and M. College. We decided that we would ask you to be good enough to fill this new assignment, if it be possible for you to do so.[22]

Henry accepted not just these requests, but many others. In 1955, four years after the First Presidency's initial request to speak for the Church, he made this report to them:

Dear Brethren:

I just returned from a Conference on Religion at the University of Oklahoma, where I gave twenty-two lectures and seminars during Sunday through Thursday, February 12–17. I treated various aspects of science and religion. The visit was pleasant, though strenuous, and what was said seemed well received. I hope that some good was done. This is my fourth religious conference in Oklahoma, twice at Oklahoma A. & M. and twice at the University of Oklahoma. I thought that you would be interested in this brief report.[23]

In addition to speaking publicly, Henry acted as an informal science advisor to the senior leaders of the Church. At the same time that the First Presidency were dispatching him to seminars, they sought his opinion on scientific matters. He was quick to reply, for instance, to a March 26, 1952, request from the First Presidency for insight into the age of the Earth. His reply included a mix of science and religious philosophy. He began with the science:

Accurate dating of events by radioactive elements decaying in the rocks and in textile fibers and elsewhere makes possible an accuracy in chronology which was undreamed of a generation ago. In effect, clocks are set going whenever these materials are laid down. These clocks can often be read with great accuracy. Such data, with many kinds of cross-checks, leads to an antiquity for life on this earth of at least some six hundred million years and an age of the Earth of upwards of two billion years. These conclusions are well known and will surprise no one.[24]

After adding several paragraphs about specific techniques for measuring Earth's age, such as carbon-14 dating, Henry closed with this insightful statement of religious philosophy:

> My conception of the gospel is that the scriptures record the dealings of God with His Prophets and His People. By living in accordance with their teachings, we may expect to reach the Celestial Kingdom. To be understood, the Lord must reveal Himself in a language His Children can understand. Of necessity, many things not necessary for their immediate progress are omitted, to be revealed later, and to be discovered by man's own enterprise. There are some people who throw away the scriptures and restrict themselves to science and related fields. Others use the scriptures to the exclusion of other truth. Both are wrong. Latter-day Saints should seek after truth by all avenues with earnest humility. There is, of course, no conflict in the gospel since it embraces all truth. Undoubtedly, however, science is continually challenging us to think through again our conceptions of the gospel. This should work both ways, of course.
>
> Since I think we don't accept Archbishop's Usher's chronology[25] as final, it seems to me of interest to check it against other available time scales. Such an investigation won't affect fundamentals but it will help us as teachers.[26]

Henry also gave advice, when asked, about the Church's educational strategy. For instance, a senior Church leader forwarded to him a complaint from a rank-and-file member who felt that Brigham Young University was being spiritually compromised by requiring Ph.D. degrees of its faculty. Specifically, the complainant alleged that "men are incapable of serving more than one master at a time and this practice tends to enforce upon the teachers the obligation to serve those who issue these degrees rather than the Lord."[27] The Church leader wrote to Henry asking what he would consider "a proper reply to such an inquiry." Henry responded as follows:

> The Gospel embraces all truth. Brigham Young especially emphasized the propriety of seeking all truth. The assumption that because a man understands something about the operation of the Universe he will necessarily be less faithful is a gratuitous assumption contradicted by numberless examples. God, who understands all about the Universe, is apparently not troubled by this knowledge.
>
> Some people drift when they study, but some people drift when they don't study. If the Church espouses the cause of ignorance it will alienate more people than if it advises men to seek after the truth even at some risk.[28]

A Delicate Dialogue

Henry continued to receive requests from Church leaders for his scientific opinions, particularly after 1954. That was the year that Elder Joseph Fielding Smith published a book called *Man, His Origin and Destiny*. In the book Elder Smith reiterated the position that scripture should be read literally as it pertained to the Creation.

One of Henry's wife's cousins, Elder Adam S. Bennion, wrote asking what Henry thought of *Man, His Origin and Destiny*. Henry responded with comments about both the book's strengths and also its shortcomings. On the latter score, he particularly noted the book's inconsistency with scientific findings and with the beliefs of two deceased Church leaders, James Talmage and John Widtsoe, both accomplished scientists and both former members of the Quorum of the Twelve Apostles. Henry concluded, "Since the Gospel is only that which is true, this book cannot be regarded as more than the private opinion of one of our great men to be admired for the fine things in it."[29] Significantly, he ended the two-page letter with this invitation:

> I hope my opinions offered for what they are worth will not seem presumptuous. Please feel free to make such use of this letter and the enclosed material as you may choose.[30]

Henry likely knew that, given this license, the letter would circulate. It did. Before long Henry heard from Elder Smith. In fact, it wasn't the first time that Elder Smith had written him. Four years earlier, in 1950, Elder Smith penned a five-page letter to Henry, explaining his view of the creation of the Earth.[31]

The 1954 letter from Elder Smith was similarly lengthy, but the tone was more emphatic.[32] Elder Smith stated his pleasure at Henry's achievements and his confidence in the divine inspiration behind great scientific discoveries. However, he reiterated his contrary views and challenged Henry to respond. He also warned sternly against scientific arrogance, and he referenced and even quoted from Henry's letter to Elder Bennion. Though the tone of Elder Smith's letter wasn't confrontational in a personal way, it seemed to invite a formal debate.

Henry replied to Elder Smith without delay. His letter was brief and conciliatory, but gave no ground:

> Thanks for your letter of April 15, 1955. I am happy that you read my letter, which you refer to, as it expresses accurately my point of view.
>
> Given the differences in training of the members of the Church, I never cease to marvel at the degree of agreement found among believing Latter-day Saints. So far

from being disturbed to find that Brother Talmage, Brother Widtsoe and yourself didn't always see scientific matters alike, this situation seems natural and as it should be. It will be a sad day for the Church and its members when the degree of disagreement you brethren expressed is not allowed.

I am convinced that if the Lord required that His children understand His works before they could be saved that no one would be saved. It seems to me that to struggle for agreement on scientific matters in view of the disparity in background which the members of the Church have is to put emphasis on the wrong place. In my judgment there is room in the Church for people who think that the periods of creation were (a) 24 hours, (b) 1000 years, or (c) millions of years. I think it is fine to discuss these questions and for each individual to try to convert the other to what he thinks is right, but in matters where apparently equally reliable authorities disagree, I prefer to make haste slowly.

Since we agree on so many things, I trust we can amicably disagree on a few. I have never liked, for example, the idea that many of the horizontally lying layers with their fossils are wreckage from earlier worlds. In any case, the Lord created the world and my faith does not hinge on the detailed procedures.

Thanks again for your kindly, thoughtful letter.[33]

Not long after this exchange of letters, Elder Smith invited Henry to his office to discuss the age of the Earth. Years later, Henry offered two versions of what happened that day. Both were positive, but the first was more diplomatic and philosophical:

A lively discussion ensued. As so often happens, each person brought up the argument which supported his position and we parted each with much the same position he held when the discussion began. But what was much more important, the discussion proceeded on a completely friendly basis without recrimination and each matter was weighed on its merits. So far as I am aware the matter ended there. No one was asked to conform to some preconceived position. The Church is committed to the truth whatever its source and each man is expected to seek it out honestly and prayerfully. It is, of course, another matter to teach as a doctrine of the Church something which is manifestly contradictory and to urge it in and out of season. I have never felt the least constraints in investigating any matter strictly on its merits, and this close contact with Elder Smith bore out this happy conclusion.[34]

At a later time, Henry implied, somewhat mischievously, that the conversation may have been a little more heated, at least on his part:

We talked for about an hour. He explained his views to me. I said, "Brother Smith, I have read your books and know your point of view, and I understand that is how it looks to you. It just looks a little different to me." He said as we ended, "Well, Brother Eyring, I would like to have you come and let me talk with you sometime when you are not quite so excited."[35]

THE FAITH OF A SCIENTIST

In the midst of private interactions such as these, Henry continued to write and speak publicly about science and religion.

Always it was by invitation. In addition to "fireside" talks to local groups, there were articles in official Church magazines, *The Instructor* and *The Improvement Era*. In 1961 Henry was featured in a Church-sponsored film, "The Search for Truth." The target audience was young people, and the film not only included Henry's testimony of the compatibility of science and religion, but also dramatized scenes from his youth.

As early as 1954, when *Man, His Origin and Destiny* was published, Henry's friends pushed him to write his own book. His brother LeRoy, a chemist at Iowa State University, made the case this way:

> Henry, the Church must publish a book by a man of great stature showing that the theories of science are tentative, to be sure, but when the real truth is known all the present evidence must be accounted for. The Church must not divorce itself from honest scientific thought. Most of all a person must realize that if it is true that the Earth is 4 billion years old there is still every reason to believe in God. If you can think of anyone who can write such a book who can do it better than you and you can persuade them to do so you are exempted from the task, but otherwise you must do it yourself.[36]

In 1957, Henry's friend Dr. Francis Kirkham made a similar proposal. Dr. Kirkham wrote, referencing a speech that Henry had given to a small group of Church members a few nights before. Dr. Kirkham was among those in the audience that night. Apparently, after Henry's formal remarks there had been a question-and-answer period. In Dr. Kirkham's opinion, the highlight of the evening was Henry's answer to a question asked by a bishop. Dr. Kirkham recalled the bishop's question and also his reaction to Henry's answer:

> [The bishop] stated that he faced the problem of young men and women attending the University of Utah who felt the new knowledge in the field of science, which they now receive, apparently conflicted with their faith in God and the teachings of the gospel. At the close of the meeting [the bishop] said to me, "I would give $100.00 for the record of Brother Eyring's talk tonight."[37]

Believing that others felt the same as this bishop, Dr. Kirkham proposed to collect Henry's published speeches and articles on the subject of science and religion and have the Church distribute them in book form. The idea to publish such a book was ten years in coming to fruition. Moreover, the book, *The Faith of a Scientist,* was published privately, rather than by the Church. It was long, a collection of twenty-seven articles and two biographical sketches. Some of the articles on science were quite technical. Nonetheless, *The Faith of a Scientist* proved popular, selling more than eight thousand copies. Scientifically minded Church members especially liked the book. One of them sent the following letter to Henry:

> Dear Dr. Eyring:
> I am a young member of our Church from Germany. Last year during my studies at Brigham Young University I got your book "The Faith of a Scientist" into my hands. Although it didn't appeal to me very much at first I bought a copy and sent it to my stepfather in Germany. He is a mathematician and loves his field. But in spite of my letters testifying of the truthfulness of our gospel I somehow doubted that he was at all interested in something what I called eternal truth. Nevertheless I tried to "infiltrate" little gospel messages into my regular letters addressed to my parents. Within a short period he had

read your book and my mother described the enthusiasm he showed about your book—I was surprised and delighted! A little over one year later my aged stepfather was baptized on his own accord even to the astonishment of my mother, his wife. This happened last December and only a few weeks had passed when a sudden illness overcame him. He might still live long but not recover as far as the physicians are concerned.

Please, Dr. Eyring, write him a few lines (not concerning his illness but rather from scientist to scientist!). Your words from the book must have had some impact and surely were not the smallest fragment of the key to his conversion. I am certain that my stepfather will more than appreciate some personal words from a brother in the gospel who is a fellow scientist as well and whose judgment he apparently esteems.[38]

Henry received many such letters from appreciative strangers; he seems to have responded to all of them. In this case he honored the young German student's request for a letter to his ailing stepfather:

Dear Dr. Oetcke:

Your stepson has said that you found my book "The Faith of a Scientist" interesting. I am glad that you did since I think nothing is more important than the gospel. The gospel is the way God looks at things—the truth. I am sure our understanding of the gospel is always provisional and incomplete but it is a great comfort to feel sure in one's own mind that life continues after death, as it must be if the seeming injustices are to be made right.

I wish we could have the opportunity of getting better acquainted, as I'm sure I would enjoy talking to you about science, mathematics and the gospel. Please accept my kindest good wishes.

Sincerely your brother in the gospel,
Henry Fyring[39]

A Paperback Version of *Faith*

Pointing to the popularity of *The Faith of a Scientist,* Dr. Kirkham encouraged the Church to officially sponsor a paperback version for young people. This idea was approved, and in 1969 Henry received a letter from a member of the Twelve, Elder Mark E. Petersen:

> Several of us have read and re-read your wonderful book, and like it immensely. We are sure it would be a boon to the youth of the Church if it were widely distributed.
>
> As our committee conferred on the matter, we felt that we would have a much larger readership if we could have a smaller volume made up of only about half of the chapters contained in the present book.[40]

Proposing to sell the book at its cost of production, Elder Petersen continued: "We would plan to print about 10,000 copies as the initial press run."[41]

Henry gave his consent and contributed to the editing of materials from the old book. Just three months later, the slimmed-down, paperback version of *The Faith of a Scientist* was ready for distribution. Reporting this, Elder Petersen seemed to suggest that expectations of the book's usefulness had risen:

> We are beginning a Church-wide distribution of this book, and it is our hope now that every high school and

college student in the Church will read it and obtain the strength from it that it can give.[42]

After another three months, Elder Petersen wrote to report that the higher expectations had been justified:

> The orders are still coming in but we have already exceeded the distribution of 112,000. The book is being very well received throughout the Church and we are surely thankful.[43]

In the end, 146,000 copies of *The Faith of a Scientist* were sold. The number of books distributed is a measure of Henry's impact on a generation of Church members, young and old alike. Countless readers found in *The Faith of a Scientist* the courage to stand firm in their testimonies of the Church as they pursued secular learning.

AN EDITOR AND A DIPLOMAT

Henry's influence wasn't limited to his own writing. As a member of the General Board of the Sunday School, his responsibilities also included compiling manuals for Sunday instruction. He took pride in creating lessons that built faith while also encouraging study.

Henry also served as editor of a special series of articles for *The Instructor,* the official Sunday School magazine. *The Instructor* solicited a dozen scholars for articles demonstrating the compatibility between their academic fields and Church doctrines. The chairman of this project described Henry's critical role:

> As a method of working, it is our plan to have Henry Eyring read all articles and make recommendations to

authors for revisions where needed. He is willing to do this. In fact, he will call the authors together and discuss the point of view to be expressed. He will also explain that we will not be obligated to publish anything that may be objectionable. However, it is the expressed desire of *The Instructor* Committee that authors present their views forthrightly, not as Church doctrine, but as their beliefs as members of the Church and as serious students in their own right. Considerable discussion was had in the committee on the point that we do not wish to inflate these problems beyond their importance. Brother Eyring was specific in stating that he thought controversy, as such, was definitely not our aim. He said he would like to bring these problems down to size in relation to basic religious belief and practice. He would like each author to be faithful in the Church and represent a high achievement of devotion to the Gospel in his own life. This would negate any criticism that study or differences arising from study of these problems was related to disbelief or agnosticism. Incidentally, during the discussion Brother Howard Bennion said he simply did not arrive at the same conclusions as Brother Eyring on some of these questions, to which Henry responded that he had never disagreed with anyone whom he respected more than Howard. This is the attitude which we hope will prevail in the series.[44]

Thanks in large measure to Henry's philosophy of conciliation and his personal efforts, the articles in *The Instructor* had their intended effect of building confidence in both religion and science.

He continued to exert a unifying influence throughout his life. Even after he was released from his position on the Sunday School

Board, Henry's opinion was sought regarding articles to be published in the Church magazines. As always, he weighed in forthrightly but respectfully. In 1971, for instance, he was asked to comment on an article that attempted to explain controversial scientific findings in the light of Church doctrine. The author was a faithful man but lacked formal scientific training. The editors were dubious about his arguments, and they wondered if Henry felt the same. He did. He wrote,

> I'm sure that [the author] is a fine man, and I like his zeal for the gospel. I feel that he has overstated his case to the point that it will offend many faithful Latter-day Saints who feel that God created the world but doubt that any man can find out how without intense study, and then only in part.[45]

The respect he conveyed for this writer with whom he disagreed was typical of Henry. No matter how much he differed with someone's opinions—or how they inveighed against his—he treated all with equanimity. His ability to disagree respectfully and even amicably was a tremendous asset in the delicate work of bridging science and faith. Others might have been as qualified and confident, but few would have been so kind. The combination of unimpeachable scientific and religious credentials, along with charity toward all, made him an unparalleled defender of faith and learning.

Of course, if Henry was good even to those who considered him a foe, one can imagine how he was loved by those who sought to be his friend. Along with his science and his faith, friendship, the subject of our next chapter, was Henry's other great legacy.

Seventy-year-old Henry chases three graduate students on the track at the University of Utah football stadium.

FRIENDSHIP

A casual observer of Henry might wonder how a man of his social tendencies could ever be credited with a legacy of friendship. He certainly wasn't one to pal around. He didn't have golf or fishing buddies. In fact, he had no "buddies" of any kind, no one with whom he regularly spent time socially. When he was away from home, it was for either work or Church-related duties. He enjoyed the companionship of his scientific colleagues, students, and fellow Church members, making ample time for personal talk. However, the context for nearly all of Henry's social relationships was either work or Church.

FRIENDS FROM A DISTANCE

Yet countless people felt a connection to Henry. Many who had known him only briefly remembered him throughout their lives. One such person, Frank M. Darrow, wrote a letter on January 10, 1982 (unaware that Henry had died two weeks earlier). Mr. Darrow was a chemist who recalled the precise details of events from almost sixty years before:

Dear Dr. Eyring:

I wanted to tell you that I recently read your 53-page book, *The Faith of a Scientist*. My first contact with you, that I remember, was when we took board at Glenwood Inn at Berkeley, Calif. on or about 1925. I remember four or five of us were having a religious discussion out in the yard after supper one evening. One fellow said, "There must be something unnatural and holy about the Bible because it makes predictions which are just now coming to pass after all those years." And you said, "The longer you wait for something to happen, the greater is the probability that it will happen within that interval." His argument was not much to you.

I remember seeing you strike out for Sunday School in the mornings in Berkeley with a bible under your arm or in your hand. Your book shows that you have not wavered in faith since those days.

My sister started reading your book this morning. She says she will read it all the way through.

You have gone far in chemistry, also. I have heard you lecture at seven or eight meetings in the United States.

I suppose that you do not Dean[1] men any more, but I hope this letter will find you.

> Sincerely,
> Frank M. Darrow[2]

Even complete strangers who wrote to Henry often bared their souls; they wrote of his impact on their lives and shared intimate details as though Henry were a trusted friend. Such a letter came in 1978 from a man who lived in Salt Lake City, only a few miles from Henry's home.

Dear Brother Eyring:

Although I am a stranger to you, I need to write and thank you because of what you have done for me and to me. Over the years you have been a great influence and help in my life. Many things you have written I have read with great interest and respect. Your life as a Latter-day Saint has moved me greatly.

In some small respect my life and experience has been similar to yours—

I was the sixth child in a family of twelve, born on a farm. At a critical time in my life my father set me on fire when he said, "There are important things for you to do in life." I kind of believed him. That fall he took me in a wagon, loaded with provisions, to a school presided over by David O. McKay.[3] There I was deeply inspired and really blessed.

In Logan at college,[4] I fell deeply in love with a choice girl who loved me beyond words. My life was glorified by her. We were happily married in the temple and our honeymoon lasted for fifty-four years. Six lovely children were sent to us. The first one, a boy, died as a child. Our hearts were broken. The other children have been successful and are happy.

Over the years I have believed in my church and have been active in it. I have loved, admired and believed in Joseph Smith. If Paul could have a revelation from God, why could not the boy Joseph have a similar experience?[5] His great life and story can be explained only by the fact that he had revelations.

I have met with some success in my profession. I compose and make gardens. I plant trees and shrubs and flowers. Some things I have done have been seen at Temple

Square and the Church offices in Salt Lake City, at the world's fair in New York City, at the Washington Temple, and even on the Mt. of Olives in Jerusalem.

Please believe me, in all my activity your life has been a moving factor. You have set a quiet but powerful example for me. Time after time I have been moved by what you *do,* what you *believe,* what you *are.* Again, thank you very much. My good wishes are expressed in some words attributed to the Coahuila Indians—

"May the four winds of heaven blow gently upon you and upon those with whom you share your heart and home."[6]

As these letters suggest, Henry's legacy of friendship stood on par even with his science and his faith. The question, though, is how a man who never joined a club or hosted a neighborhood party could have so many friends.

MAKING PEOPLE LAUGH

Part of the answer was humor. Anyone who ever met him or heard him speak could testify that his genius for science was equaled by his genius for making people laugh. Nearly always, the source of his humor was himself or his science. First-time acquaintances were often taken aback to hear this renowned scientist serving as the butt of his own jokes.

In a typical joke on himself, Henry told of being in Arizona on a Sunday School assignment. He stayed with his brother LeRoy in Tempe while attending meetings in nearby Mesa. LeRoy loaned Henry his car, and Henry drove himself to Mesa. After one meeting, Henry stayed late to talk with a boyhood friend and then drove this friend home. Rather than backtrack to Mesa and then proceed to Tempe over familiar roads, the friend urged

Henry to take a more direct route. Henry recalls how his best laid plans went shockingly awry:

> I didn't like the idea of picking my way over an unfamiliar route at 10 P.M., but finally consented to try it. I was uncertain where my brother's street was, so I inquired and was directed to the street and number. I found the house without difficulty, but was disappointed to find the front lights were out. I thought that was a strange thing for a brother to do, but knocked for some time without waking anyone. I inquired of the neighbors if they had seen the folks leave. They had not, so I decided to go around to the back, where I found the door open and the lights on, so I went in. I was startled to notice the refrigerator had been moved, but I went quickly to my room, only to find it was completely refurnished.
>
> No burglar ever made a quicker exit, and no wandering adventurer ever departed more relieved at not being shot. I had stumbled into Scottsdale instead of Tempe, and as I found out from my brother, an enterprising contractor had built two identical house divisions only a few miles apart in Scottsdale and Tempe, and I had gone into the identical house on the identical street in the wrong town. After I had quit shaking, I thought what a pity it was that I had robbed the newspapers of the headline, "Utah Chemist, President of the American Chemical Society, L.D.S. Sunday School Worker, Shot Dead in Scottsdale Last Night by Jealous Husband."[7]

Henry's gift for self-deprecating humor allowed him to connect not only with those who weren't as educated as he was, but also with people who had no inherent interest in what he was talking about. To sense that, imagine being in the audience of his June 14, 1952, address at the BYU Leadership Week.

The vast majority of attendees are females, homemakers enjoying the summertime beauty of BYU's verdant campus. Chemists in the audience, if any, are outnumbered 100 to 1. As usual, Henry's topic is "Science and Religion." He begins with his standard spiel on the compatibility of the scientific inquiry and religious faith. Then, without warning, he takes a right turn:

Having finished that, I would like to go on to some other matters. *Where are we with respect to fuel?* That is a question we ought to get straightened out. We used to burn mesquite in the stove in Pima. It was kind of hard to cut, but it heated the house well (although it was not as good as central heating). I went to the University of Arizona, and the old fellow there in mechanical engineering, bless his heart, sounded to me like a dummy. He used to say it is nonsense to keep studying coal all the time; we ought to get the energy out of the atom. As I have often said, I thought the fellow was balmy,[8] but he was right. He was way ahead of his time.

Yesterday I was in Los Angeles at a meeting. We were discussing the problem of organic reactors. Let me tell you what an organic reactor is (I am sure you are dying to know). After all, what you do is simply take uranium and you clad it (just like those of you who have clothes on are clad—the same way with uranium or uranium oxide), you simply put some aluminum around it or some other metal—molybdenum sometimes. The uranium atoms go to pieces and send out neutrons, and if you do not kill off the neutron by bumping into an atom that absorbs it, it will hit another uranium eventually, make that break in two, and give you two for one. That is always good: that is known as interest. It is also a chain reaction, and it is also the way the human race increases. You get an improvement that way. But in any case, in the whole process you get fission and the problems are all technical.

Heat is just heat, no matter how you get it, and you get heat from these things going to pieces. There are a lot of problems to managing it. If you want to make a heat engine out of it, all you have to do is have the fission go on, that is, have the uranium go to pieces and go into products shooting out these neutrons and let each bump another one and get two for one. That is good, as I said. You get lots of heat. Now you have to take the heat from the place where it is liberated in the uranium and take it over to a boiler just like you would have to if you built a fire, and they take organic materials to do that. You will be delighted to know that benzene, or di-phenyl (two benzenes tied together), can stand the gaff.[9] It is kind of punishing in there because it is hot as sin. Also, the particles, when they go through the benzene, just tear a limb off. That is considered bad for the benzene. All of those things tend to make the benzene go into other molecules, but benzene and di-phenyl are more stable than anything else. (This chemistry will just kill you, I mean, how interesting it is.)

The reason that benzene is so stable is because it is aromatic. I bet you think aromatic means it smells good. Well, it does smell good, but it also means something else—that the electrons do not stay home. In an ordinary well-behaved aliphatic[10] molecule the electrons stay right close where they ought to and hold atoms together, but in the benzene molecule they get expansive and spread around on everybody. As a result, the molecule does not come to pieces. Isn't that simple? (It cost several million dollars to make sure that that is the best thing to use, and here you are getting it for nothing. Of course it is after the fact, so you can't sell it.)[11]

He could go on like that forever, with a good one-liner to ease the pain of every chemistry principle. It was a skill he perfected in hundreds of speeches to large, nontechnical audiences.

A Mentor to the Young

Henry not only didn't mind teaching chemistry neophytes, he intentionally sought them out. Semester after semester he taught first-year university students. Among these freshmen were not just chemistry majors, but often nonmajors—students from English and social work and physical education who had to take his class to satisfy a graduation requirement.

Henry taught these young students year-round all of his life, including the year he died at age eighty. To colleagues who wondered at his willingness to perform this duty, considered the least desirable of teaching responsibilities, he would explain the personal benefits. He claimed that teaching novices required him to master chemistry at its most fundamental level. "If you can't explain something to an eight-year old," he would say, "you don't really understand it yourself."

Teaching freshmen might have increased Henry's clarity of thought, but there was more than that in it for him and his students. He taught not just understandably, but in a way that touched his students' hearts, and they loved him for it. That can be seen in a sample of teacher evaluations written in 1975, when Henry was seventy-four. At the end of the course, the students responded privately to questions about the class and the instructor.

The questions included, "What is the best aspect of this instructor?"; "How could this instructor improve?"; "Does he seem interested in the students?"

The students uniformly awarded high marks for Henry's interest in them as individuals. In answer to the question, "What is the best aspect of this instructor?" a radiation technology major said,

> His willingness to spend the needed time with the students to help them understand the subject matter. He doesn't pontificate—he teaches.[12]

A business student gave a similar answer to the same question about Henry's best aspect:

> The fact that he makes himself available for students to come in and get help. Anytime you have questions on text material or problems, he'll help you.[13]

It strains the imagination to envision freshmen students from other departments wandering into the office of the university's most distinguished researcher, but the record shows that it happened often. There was certainly the space to entertain students who had questions: Henry's dean's office had a large blackboard and more than a dozen chairs, and observers reported that the chairs were occupied more often than not.

Henry's concern for his students seemed to lift them over their struggles with the course content. An English major, offering thanks for Henry's use of analogies and simple explanations, said:

> Even though I don't always understand the calculus involved, I can usually understand the principles being explained, and their importance.[14]

The same student recognized that taking a course from Henry Eyring meant more than just learning chemistry:

> This class has been an opportunity to gain insight into the functioning of a great mind. He constantly challenges our minds and his own.

In answer to the final question, "If you have to take another chemistry course, would you like to have the same instructor?" 92 percent of these chemistry nonmajors said, "Yes."

Henry's concern for young people, as manifest by his kindness to these teenage university students, seemed to have no lower bound. He also loved, and was loved by, children. In 1976, for example, Henry traveled to Montana to give several speeches. He was accompanied by his second wife, Winifred. In Bozeman Henry and Winifred stayed at the home of a family with young children. One of them, a boy, later wrote this note:

> Dear Brother and Sister Eyring,
>
> I enjoyed having you stay at our house, and thanks again for the five dollars you gave my brother and I, don't worry I'll use it wisely. How was your trip back? Oh, sorry I didn't stay till you left but I was about to cry a little bit. You were so nice when you were here it was almost like having our grandma and grandpa visit us. I don't think I'll ever figure out why you thought I was a good kid, I didn't act very nicely to prove it to you. Brother Eyring, don't worry I'm planning on getting an A in Science. Best wishes, I hope I see you again.[15]

At the bottom of the letter, in Henry's hand, is written the word "*Answered.*"

FRIENDSHIP

FRIENDS FROM WORK

Henry was especially appreciated by his professional colleagues. And he had a broad, egalitarian definition of what it meant to be his "colleague." For example, at the retirement of the employee who delivered the mail to his office for twenty years, Henry arranged to have the university confer on the mailman an honorary Ph.D.—a "Doctor of Letters."

He was also unusually generous and loyal to his student researchers. Graduate students' names always appeared before his on joint publications. In addition, they could depend on him to be a faithful defender of their best efforts. Once, a cantankerous professor threatened to deny graduation to one of Henry's students, raising subjective concerns about the student's thesis. Henry got a copy of the professor's thesis and confirmed his suspicion that the man was asking more of Henry's student than he had delivered himself in the same position. At the next meeting of the thesis review committee Henry asked the adverse professor, "Why don't we look at your thesis and decide what we think of it?" The fellow immediately got the point, and Henry's beleaguered student received his diploma without further incident.[16]

Henry showed similar concern for a Ph.D. student, John Morrey, who arrived early for his oral exam, a rite of passage only slightly less terrifying than the thesis defense. As Morrey recalled, Henry helped ease the tension:

> I came in a little early, and he was the only member of the committee there. He sensed, I'm sure, that I was pretty nervous. And so he said to me, "John, have you ever seen me jump on the table from a standing position?" There was a big oak table in his room. I said, "No." He jumped, but he didn't make it. He sprawled out over the table, catching his shins on the edge. It must have nearly killed

him. I'm sure it hurt terribly. He winced, backed off, and he said, "I didn't make it." He jumped again. And that time he did.[17]

Henry's close colleagues knew him well for such table-jumping, a trick he showed them until his sixties, when misses became more common and he had to retire for the sake of his shins.

FLEET-FOOTED PROFESSOR

It wasn't until he was nearly eighty, though, that Henry stopped running against his graduate students. The footrace tradition actually began in 1958, when his secretary, Belva Barlow, inadvertently insulted him. Hearing stories of Henry's running races in Princeton in his younger days, Ms. Barlow expressed doubt about his ability to do the same thing at his then-advanced age (fifty-seven). The next thing Belva knew, she had been challenged to a race. She initially ignored the challenge, but Henry stood firm. The race was set for the next day in front of the University of Utah's administration building.

Belva arrived for the race well-outfitted in running shoes and pedal pushers (calf-length pants). She felt confident of victory over her boss, who was shorter than average height and a bit portly. With the starter's call of "go," however, she realized that her confidence was sadly ill-founded: "He took off like a rocket and made me look like I was standing still."[18]

Full of his victory over bewildered Belva and eager for more fun, Henry sought fresh competition. Within days he had publicly challenged two administrative colleagues, University of Utah Academic Vice-president Homer Durham and Sterling McMurrin, Dean of Arts and Letters. Both men accepted. A crowd of five hundred gathered on race day, and there was much spectacle—

Dr. McMurrin appeared in his academic robes, with running shorts underneath. Years later, Henry recalled the race with typical good humor:

> It was really quite sad. It was a fifty yard race, and before we had gone ten feet Dr. McMurrin's legs had failed; he fell down in a heap. Dr. Durham was more successful. He stayed right to the end, and you can be sure I was putting on all I had. The way I tell it, I was just a bit ahead, but in any case he fell down just at the end of the race. I came out victorious because all of my colleagues fell down. Although there are great stories going around about how fast I run, that is the only time I ever beat everybody. But they did keep the time, and I think that was rather interesting. Actually, Professor Nielson, who was presiding at the time with a stop watch, apparently forgot to stop the watch when we got to the end, so he invented a time. This fifty yards, according to the newspaper report, was done in five seconds, which is a little bit better than the world record.[19]

After this competitive and comedic triumph, Henry made the footrace an annual event. His fellow administrators having learned to stay away, he would challenge the twenty or so graduate students who worked for him (who of course had little choice but to compete). There were prizes for the winners—$15 for first, $10 for second, and $5 and $4 for third and fourth, respectively. Sometimes there was also a 50-cent prize for last place. Henry never ran in the money, but at least until age sixty-eight he was claiming to beat about half of the field. After the race, he bought lunch for all.

The annual summer event drew considerable public attention, especially as Henry got older. The three local network affiliates regularly sent television crews; everyone in Utah knew Henry as the famous footracing scientist. National newspapers also covered the event, just as they had his 1935 award for the year's best research paper.

In 1971, CBS featured the race nationally on Charles Kuralt's "On the Road" program. The university sent its marching band and cheerleading squad to enhance the spectacle. Aged seventy by then, Henry finished closer to last than first. However, Mr. Kuralt seemed to understand. Summarizing the spirit of the annual event, he described Henry as "the race favorite: not the favorite to win, just the favorite."[20]

A GOOD-NATURED MORMON

Henry enjoyed friendly competition and banter with colleagues throughout his life. The jokes weren't limited to desk jumping and footracing. Among his friends not of the LDS faith, for example, Henry's religion provided a good target for humor. In a typical practical joke, two of his Princeton graduate students, George Halsey and Howard White, hid themselves in his office closet. When Henry came in, they called out in unison, "Henry, this is the Angel Moroni, prepare to meet your fate." They were immediately scolded, "George and Howard, get out of there."[21]

Non-Mormon colleagues especially liked ribbing Henry about his abstinence from alcohol, coffee, and tobacco. One of his many Korean graduate students recalls playing a horseshoes-like game with Henry at Princeton. A ring was drawn with chalk on the cement floor of the laboratory, and contestants stood back and tried to toss erasers into the ring. This student, who went on to become the acknowledged father of modern chemistry in Korea, recalled:

> Henry was the most skillful player among us: his throwing was stable and exact. We tried to beat him, but in vain.

At last we discovered the reason why Henry was so skillful. It was very simple: because he did not drink sake or coffee at all, he had good equilibrium and steady hands.[22]

Occasionally, Henry emerged with the upper-hand in banter about his religion. That can be seen in a 1973 letter from a professional acquaintance:

Dear Henry:

I have many times in family and personal discussions referred to the incident in the Gunter Hotel here in San Antonio when you were visiting us in which you expressed your faith that I ultimately would see the light of the ways of the Mormons. Possibly in part because that story and its overtones has been so often repeated in our family, I myself have not seen that light, but I am writing to tell you that I am (reluctantly) turning over my first born son in my place.

The writer went on to explain that his son had converted at age seventeen and then, several years later, volunteered to serve a mission. The boy's father continued,

We are quite familiar with the activities of the Mormon missionaries and know that he will be in good hands. Our family, with its close-knit family ties, with its interest and activity in family genealogy, its apparently rather severe moral and ethical standards and its willingness to inquire into the Mormon religion and to discuss comparative religions, has for many years been a tantalizing target for the young missionaries, male and female, and I suppose the good southern cooking has been a help also. At any rate on Thursday, the 23rd, he departs for Salt Lake City to start his missionary tour, reporting to the

Mission Home on the 25th. Then on the 30th as I understand it leaves for the Bloomington, Minnesota mission. I am sure that if his zeal for the Mormon church continues he will one day be prominent in it, and if you don't meanwhile wear yourself out foot racing with your graduate students you will cross paths with him. I know he will be looking forward to that event since he has been familiar with your name for so long. When this occurs you may attribute it in part to our conversation in the Gunter Hotel in San Antonio some 20 years ago.[23]

A CHERISHED—IF PUZZLING—FRIEND

Given the affection he elicited from so many people, it is surprising that even his closest friends didn't feel that they knew him well. It wasn't just that they couldn't comprehend his science; there was much more that they found puzzling about him. In particular he had an unusual way of looking at things that often seemed contradictory.

The one thing that his friends knew for sure, though, was how good it felt to be with him. That sentiment was eloquently expressed by friend and neighbor Sterling Sill, who wrote to thank Henry after a lecture. Sterling was an accomplished business and religious leader, and no intellectual slouch. Nonetheless, in his letter he poked fun at his limited understanding of Henry's work. He noted that Henry had been introduced before the lecture as having a long list of research interests; the list ended with the word, "etc." "That last one," Sterling wrote, "was the only of your interests that I understand."

Sterling continued:

As I listened to your lecture last Friday, I was impressed that if I had nothing else to do for fifty years, I could understand many of the things that are lying across the front of your mind. But even then I don't think I would enjoy my dinner or my walk to work more than I already do. But, if I ate my dinner with you or walked to work with you, I would enjoy them both more."[24]

There are no more opportunities for dinner or a walk to work with Henry, the kind that Sterling Sill longed for. However, there is a still a chance to discover why he had such a positive influence on the world and the people who encountered him. The answer lies largely in the unique way he thought about the world. That unique way of thinking began with his forebears and upbringing, the subjects to which we turn next.

PART 2

HERITAGE

Newlyweds Edward and Caroline Romney Eyring,
in Mexico, 1893

LOVE

Henry's friendliness—the kindness and concern that he showed for others—was a product of training. He was taught love in his youth. That can be seen in his view of his unusually difficult family situation. Rather than resenting his half-brothers and sisters, children of his mother's sister Emma, he embraced them as equals:

> My father's two wives were sisters. They had the same father and mother. As far as breed and genetics goes, they were the same. I always felt the same way about Aunt Emma's children as I did about Mother's. I never felt any distinction.[1]

In fact, Henry did more than just treat his half-siblings and "Aunt Emma" kindly. Though he fully sustained the Church's directive to cease the creation of new plural marriages, he took the lead in treating the two families as one. From the time they were driven out of Mexico, Henry worked and turned his wages over to his father, Ed, for the support of the family. That was true even after he left home. As a university student and later as a professor at Princeton he contributed each month to the mortgage on the Arizona farm. Occasionally, he would also send small sums—typically five dollars—to his mother. Whenever he did that, he also included five dollars for Emma. Henry later explained his reasons for this unusual behavior:

> I had been treated kindly always by my father. He was a nice guy. I would have broken my neck if necessary for my parents. I also admired and respected Aunt Emma. The only thing that my mother was ever bothered with me about was when I would come from college she would want me to go and see her sister, but she didn't think I needed to stay too long. She wanted everything to be proper, but if I had a good time at it, that was a little too bad. She was human, but awfully nice about it really. Mother was just disturbed to find I found my aunt as pleasant as I did. My aunt was always very pleasant to me because I was very pleasant to her. So she felt like I was the cement helping to hold the family together.[2]

PIONEER GIRL

Notwithstanding his mother's naturally mixed feelings about Henry's kindness to Emma, it was she, Caroline, who was his model of love. By all accounts of her children, Caroline was unusually selfless and kind. Henry in particular felt nearly unbounded admiration for his mother:

> From my earliest memories Mother suffused the whole world with warmth and happiness. She was a strong, buoyant wonderful person whom I took completely for granted. To her the world and everything in it

was beautiful and wonderful, and one couldn't help being swept along on a cloud of rosy optimism. At four I nearly died of typhoid, but I remember it principally as a time when the small magnolia tree in our yard was in bloom and when I was loved and spoiled even more outrageously than usual.[3]

It was impossible for my mother to be either idle or pessimistic. Her devotion to the Church was expressed in good works. She served vigorously in all the organizations and when she died at eighty was still a member of the stake[4] Sunday School Board. Each of her eight living children had the feeling that they were special to her. They all did well in school, and she never failed to praise them for it. It was a happy home. Her example of hard work and selflessness made us all anxious to "pull our own weight." The most severe chastisement I ever received from her was once or twice being correctly characterized as "an ungrateful little wretch." Idleness and tardiness were abominations to her. At one o'clock when it was time to be in the hayfield it was easier to go to work than continue reading some interesting book while she was racing around doing her work. An indelibly remembered remark from long ago is "Henry, of course I want you to be good, but I hope you will be good for something." A lifetime of effort is still too little repayment to an optimistic, selfless mother.[5]

Henry's mother, Caroline Romney Eyring, learned optimism and selflessness the hard way. She grew up in poverty incident to the frequent dislocation of her father's family, who were persecuted for practicing polygamy. No sooner had they established themselves in one frontier town than they were forced to flee to another. Of the privations of her youth—and the character thus engendered—Caroline recalled,

> Mother made our shoes out of denims with rawhide bottoms for soles, and we used to get along with these as our only shoes. Once when I was ashamed of my shoes and didn't want to go to Sunday School, my father said, "You go on; nobody will ever know you are there."
>
> Many times we had little but bread and gravy, and many times I have been hungry, largely due to our inability to get supplies in. Sometimes when I fixed the food for my brothers and there was too little to eat, I made them say they had plenty and were full.[6]

LOVE AT FIRST SIGHT

Notwithstanding the difficulties of her youth, Caroline was a happy mother. A major reason for that was her love of Henry's father, Ed, whom she met in Mexico when they were both young. Apparently, the young couple were smitten the moment they set eyes on one another. Caroline later recalled meeting Ed in a mountain meadow:

> Mother and I were out picking flowers when I first saw Ed coming. He told me later he said to himself, "There's the girl I am going to marry." We were having a party that night and he was a guest. We were playing forfeits[7] and he had to pay. We all sang, "Kneel to the wittiest, bow to the prettiest, and kiss the one you love best" so he kissed me that first night. The other girls said they did not like him very much, but I said I did. I made up my mind that he was the one I wanted.[8]

Later in his life, Ed corroborated Caroline's romantic version of the story with one of his own, told to Henry:

> As a young man I didn't believe as I believe now. Both Mother and I feel that we knew each other in the world before this. Of course there is no proof of this, but it is our belief. I have a firm belief that birth, marriage, and death are timed and governed by a kind of Providence more than we have any idea of.
>
> Grandfather Romney invited me to go with him up to his home one weekend. We went horseback. . . . Just before coming into a little valley near Cliff Ranch your mother and grandmother were there picking flowers. Your mother was a very pretty girl, sixteen years old. I felt like I never had felt before toward any girl—in other words, it was love at first sight.[9]

Love at first sight, however, didn't mean an easy courtship. In fact, though Ed was an early favorite of his future father-in-law, Miles Park Romney, an indiscretion nearly cost him everything. Caroline later recalled how Ed incurred the wrath of her sometimes ferocious father:

> When I was seventeen I promised to marry Ed Eyring and my father and mother were both very happy about it, as they thought so much of his parents. He had asked me to go to the dance with him on a certain night. He went to Casas Grande that day and was unfortunately seen smoking a cigar,[10] and my father heard about it. He thereupon forbade me ever speaking to him again. He said he would rather see me dead than to marry a man who would do this. I did not have anything to do with Ed for

two years except to see him at the dances. In the meantime three older men proposed to me.

During the two years I was not permitted to see Ed, I had four persistent suitors. I did not dare go with anyone without their asking Father first. Jim McClelland came once to see me without having seen Father and he got a terrible bawling out. Pleas Williams was most persistent. He would not give up. I told him I liked Ed Eyring and I did not like him. He persisted. Brother H. said he knew I was to be his wife. All in all, four men proposed to me and finally Father relented toward Ed because he was being hounded so much by the other suitors.[11]

SUPPORTING A MISSIONARY HUSBAND

With Grandfather Romney's blessing, Ed and Caroline finally wed in 1893. At first, life was pleasant, even blissful. Northern Mexico, to which their families had fled to avoid persecution in the United States, produced a good living. Their fathers were both well established financially, and through hard work and skillful horse-trading Ed soon had assets of his own.

However, after only a few years of marriage and with a two-year-old daughter, Camilla, Ed accepted a call from the Church to serve a mission to Germany. Such calls to young fathers were not uncommon, but Ed's proved to be especially trying for his young wife. Caroline described her painful three years without Ed this way:

> When Papa was on his mission, Camilla was two years old. Father went to Germany. I was so sick that I couldn't throw the bedding across the bed. Papa thought he had arranged so we would have plenty while he was gone. He had rented his two span of mules and wagons and the

young man was going to pay an amount weekly. He went off with them and has never been heard of yet. Papa had debts due to him and expected them to be paid to us, but they were never paid. I worked what I could at sewing, making overalls and sacks for Brother Davis, who lived near us. I rented my bed to two school teachers; and I slept on the floor with the baby, Camilla.[12]

Caroline's family—including the brothers she used to convince they were full—helped as they could. However, she bore the brunt of the financial burden alone. In addition, there were other hardships. A second child, Mary, was born six months after Ed left for Germany. Caroline's eleven-year-old sister, Ethel, was staying with her when labor began; Camilla was sick with whooping cough. Caroline sent Ethel to fetch the midwife, but the midwife refused to come for fear of the whooping cough. Caroline delivered the baby with only Ethel and two-year-old Camilla in attendance.

This was not the end, though, of the trials incident to Ed's German mission. As little Mary grew, Caroline recognized that her baby couldn't hear:

> I gradually came to know that Mary was deaf when pounding a pan or slamming doors near her failed to awaken her. I would not let anyone know of Mary's condition, but carried my sorrow secretly. I feared that Ed would return from his mission if he knew. Finally Camilla and Mary both took very sick with diarrhea,[13] and I feared they would die. I was sick in bed with nervous prostration.
>
> One day when we all three were sick, I being so nervous that I could not raise up without numbness or faintness, the Bishopric Brothers Harris and Taylor and

another were sent for and came and administered[14] to Mary and to Camilla. Mary was worse than Camilla. When they administered they said, "Don't cry, little girl, you're alright." I said, "Don't talk to her that way; she can't hear a word you say." Then when I realized they knew my secret, I begged them not to tell so it would not get to Ed.[15]

None of the bad news—neither the financial troubles nor Mary's deafness—became known to Ed before his return from Germany. As he later said, "My wife was very brave, never making a single complaint during my absence. She worked extremely hard while I was away and was able to earn and collect enough means to keep me on my mission."[16] When Ed returned, the news of Mary's deafness came as a blow, but he saw the glass as half-full: "I think I never felt so badly in all my life over anything. Nevertheless, I felt to praise the Lord that all was as well as it was."[17]

A KIND, QUIET PAPA

Not long after the end of Ed's German mission, in 1901, Henry was born. Ed continued to build his ranching interests; in time he would become one of the Mexican colonies' largest landowners. He was also a devoted father, beloved by his eldest son, Henry, who described Ed this way:

> I idolized my father. To me he always seemed gracious, courageous and wise. If he ever worried I never knew it. He was very successful financially in Mexico and managed with the help of his large family to solve our financial problems in Arizona. He grew up in the cattle business and was skillful with saddle horses and rope, but this was

only incidental. He would have been successful in any-thing that interested him.[18]

As did Caroline, Ed taught Henry love by example. In partic-ular, he had a special gift for treating his son as an equal. In later life, Henry liked to illustrate this with a story of horse trading with his father when he was just five years old:

> At about this time Father gave me two goats, which became a nuisance by climbing on top of a board fence and then jumping down into the neighbors' lot. His solu-tion to this problem was typical of the gracious way he dealt with people. He bought a pretty little sorrel horse and rode him into the lot where I was playing and asked me if I would like to trade the two goats for Chivo ("goat" in Spanish). Of course I would. Who wouldn't? I rode Chivo quite a bit, but Father decided to get me another horse that he thought was better suited to me, and again he offered to trade with me and again I gladly accepted. Even at that age I knew that when he traded with me he aimed to get the worst of the bargain.[19]

As Henry grew, Ed took him along to work. Ed wasn't demonstrative in his affection, and on occasion he could even be tough on Henry. However, the symbolic act of involving a ten-year-old boy in dangerous ranch duties conveyed both love and respect, a message that Henry picked up on:

> I rode with my father on the range from my earliest days, and he was always kind. Riding with him was inter-esting. He had his own thoughts. I was a talker and was always wanting to get some more information. If I asked him a question about twice he would come to and talk to

me, always politely. He never said you shouldn't bother him; he just had other thoughts on his mind.

I remember one occasion when we had ridden together up on the ranch. We saw a cow that had just had a calf. The next day he said, "I've got to go to high council.[20] I would like you to go up and find that cow and bring her and her calf down to the house." I said, "I don't think I can find her." He said, "You can find her. She won't be a hundred yards from where we saw her." I said, "I don't know; I don't think I can do it." It annoyed him a little bit. It is the only time he ever paddled me in my life. He said, "Come outside." So he gave me a splat or two and we came back in. All of my siblings smiled because they had seen me punished. It hadn't amounted to much, but it was a little hard on my pride. My father was very kindly; he was just out of patience. I said, "I can do it. I'll go and do it." He said, "I wouldn't let you." I didn't go. I think that was part of the punishment. He didn't know how to be mean to anybody or to any horse. He was just not that kind of man. [21]

As he worked side-by-side with his father, Henry could see that Ed's kindness wasn't limited to family members. The Mexican laborers on the Eyring ranch were paid five times what they could make working for local "patrons."[22] In fact, both Henry's father and his mother treated their employees as equals:

Father had men working for him. At branding time there would be quite a few men. One man worked all the time, Don Francisco Quintana. He and his family lived on our place and worked. Father always instructed him as to what needed to be done. Father would get in and work on the hauling of the hay, which I thought was interesting.

He would do anything that he thought was useful. Don Francisco liked him very much; they were very good friends. Father always was especially friendly to the Mexican people and spoke Spanish as well as they did. So there was no friction of any kind.

Mother was a worker, so she didn't have Mexicans do anything that she could do for herself. We didn't have Mexican cooks. We weren't running a showplace.[23]

A SECOND WIFE

Not long after returning from Germany, and before real prosperity had been achieved, Ed took a second wife. In 1903, he married Caroline's younger sister, Emma Romney. He was encouraged to do so by his father-in-law, who had declared Ed "an ideal husband."[24] The Church had instructed its members in the United States to cease the formation of polygamous marriages in 1890, thirteen years earlier. However, polygamy was not prosecuted in Mexico—that was the reason for both the Eyrings and the Romneys being there—and Church leaders in the Mormon colonies continued to selectively encourage polygamy until a final, worldwide prohibition was issued by the First Presidency in Salt Lake City in 1904.

Ed's taking a second wife redefined his life. Already the father of four children, he would ultimately become "Papa" to eighteen, nine by each wife. One of the last faithful Church members to contract a polygamous marriage, he would preside as patriarch over his two families into the late 1950s.

Ed's decision to marry her sister Emma was hard for Caroline. Emma was pretty, and she was younger than Caroline by ten years. The two Romney girls knew the burdens and blessings of polygamy firsthand. Their mother, Catherine, was the third wife of their father, Miles Park Romney; she was appreciated as the family's great peacemaker. Yet in spite of her mother's example, sharing Ed was a great sacrifice for Caroline. Henry, who personally chose to see only the upside of his large family, nonetheless recognized the hardship on his mother and her sister:

> They were always cooperative on everything. There was no division. I'm sure that they had the same reservation that any two people would have in having a husband in common. They were both very devout; they were much alike. I rarely saw anything or heard anything in the way of differences. I'm sure they were human, so in first approximation they were two women who were proud and wished that they had a husband by themselves. I think that is a fair statement. Maybe they were even sorry they were sisters since they couldn't dislike the other one as much and feel good about it. Outwardly it was completely like living in any home that is well organized.[25]

There were several keys to the unusual household's equanimity. One was Ed's commitment to strict equality. Another was his easygoing manner. Henry commented on both of these qualities:

> The idea of equality was central in Father's thinking. That bothered my mother a little bit because she thought as the first wife that she and he had accumulated quite a bit before the second marriage. Her sister was ten years younger. I suspect she wanted it to be equal but at least with a little more attention as the first wife. My father said, "The only way I know how to run this family is to treat all equally."[26]
>
> He was also a very genial person. If there was anybody that was complaining a little, he would try and get them

out of feeling bad. He was never bossy or anything of that kind. He was strong. There was no question about that, but he was very much respected. I had nothing but the kindest feelings toward him and to my Aunt Emma and my mother, of course. So I think I couldn't have lived in a home where there was more harmony than there was in that home.[27]

Henry knew that he saw his home life through rose-colored glasses; he could sense the inherent tension. However, in honor of both his mother and his father, he chose to overlook it. That he continued to treat all of his siblings—including the half-brothers and sisters—with the same unqualified love even after the death of his parents suggests that, in time, his refusal to see any tension made it truly disappear in his mind.

No Half-Brothers

Henry's egalitarianism was in fact part of a broader family ethos. Later in his life he gathered a group of his grandfather Miles Park Romney's descendants to record their memories and begin writing a biography of their great progenitor, "Miles P." Among the group was a cousin of Henry's, also a child of a polygamous family, who remarked:

I want to say something about our family. Someone asked, "Is Gaskell Romney your half brother?" And I said, "No, I don't have any half brothers. They all have two legs and two ears." Well, the thing was, that there were no half brothers or half sisters in our family.[28]

Perhaps in part because of Henry's example, his mother also came to embrace the principle of complete equality. As Henry later reported,

Mother was also very strict when they got older that the property be divided equally. They had accumulated about two hundred acres of irrigated farming land. Mother insisted before Father died the property be divided exactly equally. Nobody insisted more strongly than she that it be definitely divided, and all agreed. Aunt Emma's part and Mother's part were perfectly definite.[29]

The Eyring family was unusual, by any standard. It wasn't entirely harmonious. As Henry said, by the time he was sixteen he had realized that marrying two sisters was not a good idea.

However, the natural divisions between the two families never grew into divides, because the home was built on an unshakeable foundation of love. For Caroline and Ed, it began in a Mexican meadow, when they saw one another for the first time and knew that they would someday wed. Their love was tested through a series of escalating trials: from a father-in-law's temporary wrath to an overseas separation and ultimately to the addition of another wife. Along the way the family went from rags to riches to rags again. Eldest son Henry saw how the love never wavered. He learned charity for all, in good times and bad. That charity was at the root of his kindness to both friends and strangers, as well as his equable treatment even of would-be detractors to his work as a scientist and defender of faith.

BELOVED, CONFIDENT SON

Henry also reaped another benefit of his parents' love—unfaltering confidence. His parents' praise of him knew few limits. That can be seen in a letter Caroline wrote in 1929, when he was an instructor at Wisconsin:

I am so proud of you dear boy. I can hardly contain myself to be the mother of such a son. Papa says there is only one Henry in this whole wide world. I know he loves you just a little more than anyone else in this whole wide world, and I know father and son were never more devoted on this earth. I am so happy about it.[30]

The frightening thing is that Henry accepted this kind of praise as natural. Having no reason to doubt that he deserved it, he naturally grew confident. He admitted as much later in life:

Being born in 1901 in Colonia Juarez, Northern Mexico into a happy home, in good financial circumstances, fostered a feeling of optimism and security which has persisted. My mother, Caroline Romney, in particular always saw the bright side of everything, including her children's performance. This same support also came from a kindly father. The feeling of self-confidence this engendered has made it easy to go wherever my judgment dictated without undue concern for contrary opinions.[31]

The love of doting parents made Henry not just kind, but confident of himself. Throughout his life that confidence worked to his benefit. It did so hand-in-glove with another crucial trait, one he inherited from his Romney forebears—Ambition.

Miles Park and Catherine Cottam Romney, Henry's maternal grandparents

5

AMBITION

Henry was a born competitor. He often told the story of falling off his father's horse and into a stream from which the horse was drinking. According to his parents, his first words after having been pulled from the water were, "Put me back on the horse." He was three at the time.

Later in life, Henry's competitive streak took him where others wouldn't have dared venture. For example, at five feet eight inches tall, he started at center for his high school basketball team. He played every minute of every game his senior year, and his team won the area championship.

The next year, he was off to the University of Arizona. Literally just off the hay wagon, he nonetheless wasn't about to be intimidated by the older college boys. He relished telling the story of how he opposed their traditional efforts to welcome him and his fellow freshmen to campus:

> Hazing was in full swing. I found it distasteful that, as a freshman, I was expected to wear a green "beanie." The sophomores would throw freshmen not wearing their

beanies into the pool. However, it was against the rules to carry hazing into the dormitories. Since I thought I could outrun my tormentors, I left the dormitory without my beanie, believing they would have to quit the pursuit when I reached the door, or else they would be in trouble themselves. It was a miscalculation. I beat them to the dormitory and then to my room, where I slammed the door, but they kept coming. Since my door was locked, they tried to climb in through the transom,[1] but I blocked their entry by working on their hands with a broom handle. By this time, they were annoyed and threatened to break down my door if I did not come out. I was pretty sure I would be paying for the door if they broke it down, so I came out. There were plenty of sophomores, and I was soon face down in the air with someone holding on to each arm and leg, and another fellow enthusiastically swinging a large wooden paddle where it would do the most good. This did not engender love for authority in me, but it did engender respect for it when backed up by sufficient "lynch law."[2]

Henry's competitive streak was not without family precedent. In fact, it was a trait found in nearly all of his Romney cousins (who, thanks to plural marriage, numbered in the hundreds). Extraordinary ambition could be traced back to the family patriarch, Henry's grandfather Miles Park Romney.

FRONTIER ARISTOCRAT

Miles P. Romney was a natural leader, a kind of frontier aristocrat. Junius Romney, one of Miles P.'s sons, recalled his father's ability to exert influence almost effortlessly:

My earliest recollections of my father were that he was the dominating personality in the family and in the community. In my mind he was the leader of social, business, and religious affairs. I never remember his chastising me with physical punishment, but when I needed correcting he would talk to me in such an impressive manner that I would have much preferred a thrashing. I am sure he never milked a cow, cut a stick of wood, or cut a chicken's head off.[3]

Miles P.'s grandson Henry didn't know his grandfather for long, but he had similar impressions of his aristocratic progenitor:

I was born in 1901 and he died in 1904, so I wasn't very old, but I can remember that he came to our house. We had a long table, and I was apparently situated here at one place, and I remember that I had never done this before in my life. I was obliged to stand there, because he and my Grandmother marched in and my father and mother marched in behind them, and I was very much impressed with the grandeur of the occasion—at this parade going by.[4]

Miles Park Romney didn't begin life as an aristocrat. The son of an early convert to the Church, he was born in Nauvoo, Illinois, in 1843, one year before the martyrdom of Joseph Smith. Two years after that Miles P.'s family, along with twenty thousand other Saints, was expelled from their home. The Romneys stopped briefly in St. Louis before migrating west to Salt Lake City, where, like everyone else, they started from scratch.

Miles P. trained as a carpenter, and he married young, at eighteen. Less than a month later, he was called by Brigham Young to serve a mission to the British Isles. He was gone for three years.

The mission was challenging, characterized less by proselytizing success than by persecution. Polygamy was an especially hot topic. Debating daily with detractors of the Church, Miles P. became an effective orator and confident leader among his fellow missionaries. When the mission finally ended, he led a company of Scandinavian Saints across the ocean and the American plains to Salt Lake City.

A LIFETIME OF BUILDING

Almost immediately after Miles P. returned home, President Brigham Young had another call for him:

> "Brother Romney, would you like to go to heaven?" Whereupon the answer came, "Yea, Brother Brigham, I think I should like to go there." "Then," said President Young, "you must take charge of all the building operations in Southern Utah."[5]

The years that followed saw an unending string of sacrifices and achievements, as the Romney family tamed the elements of Utah's southern desert. During this time of struggle Miles P. married again, to Catherine Cottam, who would become Caroline's mother. Just two years after this marriage, Miles P. was called on another mission, this time to Wisconsin and the neighboring states. When he left, Catherine was expecting her second child; Hannah, Miles P.'s first wife, had six children.

Upon his return from the upper Midwest, Miles P. began a rise to prominence in St. George, Utah. He was almost entirely unschooled; he never entered a classroom past age twelve. However, he had the family gift for overcoming obstacles, including the lack of formal education. He was an avid reader and, at one point, a newspaper editor. Without assistance, he studied for and passed the legal bar. He gradually assumed leadership in business and civic institutions, and he was called to leadership in the local Church as well. He became a bishop, president of the local builder's union, county school superintendent, and a favorite actor in the community theater.

Unfortunately for the Romney family, though, the good times in St. George didn't last. In 1881 the First Presidency of the Church assigned Miles P. to strengthen the Mormon presence in the frontier town of St. Johns, Arizona, just over the border from New Mexico. To make the move, Miles P. had to dispose of his furniture and lumber business, as well as his real estate holdings in both St. George and Salt Lake City; he sold all of his property at substantial discounts to its true value.

In St. Johns the Romneys met stiff religious persecution. Most residents were fiercely anti-Mormon, and they resented Miles P. in particular for his industry and forthrightness. Though the Romneys weren't living high on the hog, they were envied for their property (160 acres bought with the proceeds of the sales in Utah) and for the newspaper that Miles P. ran. Worse, they became targets of persecution for their polygamy. Caroline, less than ten years old at the time, described the family's hardships:

> While in St. Johns, it was almost impossible to get men to carry the mail and much harder to get them to bring foodstuff. They generally traveled at night, as the Indians were less likely to attack them. Many times we were hungry, and the boys said we had soup made of the muddy Colorado River water and one bean to the quart. Many times our lands were jumped and our little shanties moved off and someone else's put on. The Mexicans and Jews had established the town and so were not very friendly to the Mormons. The cowboys were very unwise,

and many times they would ride through the streets firing in the air.

On the 24th of June, 1882, the cowboys and Mexicans had a fight by our home, some of them hiding behind the house. They sent for Ammon Tenney's father to come and make peace, but he was shot and killed, as well as one on the other side. To make things worse for us, Father was editor of the only newspaper in town and told all the facts, which didn't please everybody, so they were determined to imprison Father at any cost.[6]

ON THE UNDERGROUND

Along with these local political problems, the family was harassed by federal marshals. As Miles P.'s second wife, Catherine (Caroline's mother and Henry's grandmother) was forced to spend months in hiding to preserve her freedom. Young Caroline was just old enough to understand what was going on. She recalls overhearing her father's plan to move her mother and another wife, Annie, from a nearby safe haven in Snowflake, Arizona, all the way back to St. George:

> I, being the oldest child on the Underground, heard the folks talking that they were going to send Mother and Aunt Annie farther away over to Snowflake to get them away from the deputies. I knew that Mother was coming one particular night to see us kids before she left. When she came, she came up and kissed us as we lay in bed. I was awake, but I did not move, as I was not supposed to know that they were coming. The two women, dressed in men's clothing, kissed us all good-bye, and in the darkness they went out over the hills, avoiding the roads, and on to

Snowflake. They had to ride horseback, even though this was only three weeks before Mother delivered a baby.

How well I remember when my brother Thomas and I were finally to go to see our mother after weeks of separation. Brother Lewellyn Harris sat in the back of the wagon with his gun while father drove the horses, and we lay flat in the wagon box as we went through the little town of Concho. They expected the guards to fire, as every road was guarded. The night was so dark that they had to strike matches and feel along the ground to find the road.

For two years Mother and we children lived with her father in St. George.[7] President Wilford Woodruff[8] and wife were also living with them. He would stay in the house all day and often he would work in the temple at night. Mother would iron, sew, or work at anything to keep us children in school.

At the end of two years we went on the train to Mexico. When we reached Ascension[9] we all came down with scarlet fever, and several of us were so sick we were not expected to live. One, our brother Claude, took pneumonia and died.[10]

SANCTUARY—BUT NOT REST—IN MEXICO

After years on the run, the Romneys finally found peace in northern Mexico. As he had done many times before, Miles P. quickly established his family and fortune. By the time Henry was born, his maternal grandfather was the most prosperous, prominent man in the community.

In the meantime, Miles P. had passed on the Romney legacy of drive to his daughter and Henry's mother, Caroline. As the

115

self-described "oldest child on the Underground," she had learned to take nothing for granted. She was busy every waking moment, and she expected the same of her children. Henry's youngest sister, Rose, recalled how, though they loved their mother dearly, she wasn't easy to please:

> I remember Mother as a tremendously dynamic individual, the kind of person that makes the world go round. She wasn't, however, the most comfortable person to be around, because she felt that others, too, should be up and doing. There wasn't a lazy hair on her head, and she tolerated no laziness in others, particularly her children. One of her strongest words of condemnation was, "For goodness sake, Child, don't be a lazy lout!" I often thought it would be fun to be a "lout" just now and then.
>
> If something needed to be done, Mother wanted it done right now—no dillydallying. And she was very strong willed. As Dad sometimes said, it was a good thing that what she willed was usually right, for nothing could stop her once she decided a thing must be done. He often said facetiously that he suspected that even the Lord Himself would hesitate to cross her, but fortunately, He wouldn't need to.[11]

Caroline's particular concern for her children was that they gain education; from their childhood, she pushed them to study. Almost immediately upon arriving in Mexico, the Mormon colonists had established a school, the Juarez Academy, which they financed through a commitment of 8 percent of their annual income. Henry's grandmother Catherine Romney was the first teacher.

Caroline also taught for a time at the school, and even after giving up those formal teaching duties to raise her children, she maintained a strong commitment to their education. In 1905, when Henry was four, Ed and Caroline moved their home so as to be closer to the academy, even though it meant a seven-mile ride for Ed out to the ranch.

The children knew that they were expected not just to attend school but to master their studies. Henry recalled his mother's high expectations and subtle techniques of encouragement:

> Mother expected me to stand at the head of my class in school, and it never occurred to me to try for anything less. Very little was said about it directly except that every small success was duly noted and appreciated. Mother and Father seldom scolded, but they never passed up a chance to commend us.[12]

A PSYCHOLOGY OF PRAISE

Ed and Caroline were motivational masters. Praise was the leading tool. One of Henry's brothers, Joseph, noted the power of their parents' positive reinforcement, especially Caroline's encouragement:

> I'm confident that this "build-up" she gave us had much to do with the superior educational attainment of most of her children. We didn't dare fail Mother, for she had such high hopes and aspirations for us.[13]

Henry's sister Rose likewise described Caroline's subtle but powerful gift for motivating her children:

> Mother seemed to have an intuitive understanding of psychology, though she hadn't studied in any university. How well I remember the time in the third grade when I

came home with all E's (for excellent) except for a P (poor) in deportment. Mother used her usual approach—praised first and then showed how there was a little room for improvement. And how vividly I recall the time my brother Joe was having a bit of trouble with his oral reading. His teacher had a number of complaints against him, among them being that he mumbled his words dreadfully. Mother told Joe what a fine boy and a good student his teacher thought he was—but that he had one little fault: he didn't speak quite distinctly enough when he read aloud. This praise did wonders, and it wasn't long until Joe was the best reader in the class. Even to this day he is still a good, loud, even bombastic reader.[14]

In addition to praising the children's scholastic achievements, Caroline also created the conditions for their success, as another daughter wrote:

> Should we be asked to do something publicly, Mother would surround us with books and articles on the subject, release us from other responsibilities and have us go to a secluded spot in the house where we could work undisturbed.[15]

Caroline's many strategies for motivating her children to learn proved stunningly successful. Of her eight children, including Mary, whose deafness kept her out of college, six earned bachelor's degrees, four went on for master's degrees, and three earned Ph.D.s. The magnitude of this achievement seems less today, when one out of four adults has a college degree. When Caroline's children were in school, though, that number was one in twenty-five.[16] By this measure, her children had fifteen times more higher education than the general populace. Even before some of the younger children had graduated, a local newspaper noted that Ed's family held the record in the state of Arizona for their number of college degrees.[17]

A Compulsive Little Worker

Henry, of course, led out in these educational achievements. Even as a boy, he was known for his prodigious effort and prowess in the classroom. Once, as punishment for some minor misbehavior, an elementary school teacher made him stay after class to memorize a stanza of Gray's "Elegy." After an hour had passed, she asked him to recite. He quoted the first stanza of the poem, but then continued on, as though he would recite all thirty-two stanzas. "Stop," she finally exclaimed, "That will be enough."

Henry excelled in school, and he naturally took pride in his academic success. That pride shows in an archival record of his educational achievements that his mother penned. Caroline's record is of course complimentary; she included even the smallest achievements. It is interesting, though, to see edits that Henry appears to have made after the fact. One line, written in Caroline's beautiful, round hand, reads, "[Henry] was valedictorian of his eighth grade graduating class and class president of his High School class 1915 and 16." In the space after "1915 and 16" is added, in Henry's more angular style, "& 18–19."

Henry kept on competing throughout his life. He sought to distinguish himself even in everyday situations that almost no one else would have treated as competitive. In one particularly humorous case, he sought to impress a judge. As a Mexican citizen, Henry had to seek naturalization as a United States citizen. He did so while a professor at Princeton. Knowing that naturalization included a test of his knowledge of the Constitution and the U.S. government, he boned up on those subjects.

When the day of the test came, he arrived at the courthouse prepared to impress the presiding judge with his newfound legal expertise. But he never got the chance. Upon learning that Henry was a professor at Princeton, the judge launched into a story of meeting and quizzing Albert Einstein under similar circumstances. By the time he was through talking about Einstein, the judge had little interest in testing Henry's knowledge of U.S. politics. Rather than feeling glad to skip the test, Henry was annoyed not to have the chance to show his stuff.[18]

Of course, Henry's congenital ambition manifested itself most powerfully in his research publication record. Publicly, he shrugged off the attention that his huge raft of research papers drew. He joked repeatedly, for instance, in a media interview after the publication of his five hundredth paper, describing himself as a "compulsive little worker" with "the tenacity of a plowhorse and a lingering *disease verbosa*." He added,

> It's disgraceful! You'd think if a fellow had something to say he could compress it.[19]

For all the professed modesty, though, Henry's research record was no accident. Of course he found scientific research inherently interesting. But a merely curious man wouldn't have published anywhere near as much as he did. Working hard—and being recognized for it—was in his breeding and upbringing. "I've always worked hard," he admitted. "I never knew I didn't have to."[20]

Henry's congenital ambition was a Romney family gift. That's not to say, of course, that his Eyring forebears weren't accomplished. As Henry himself noted, "My Grandfather Eyring spoke seven languages and had a good education and was very much in favor of education."[21]

However, the Eyring side of Henry's family was more reserved than the Romneys. They tended to be thinkers more than talkers. They also had powerful stories of their conversion to Mormonism. From them, his Eyring forebears, Henry inherited a special gift of religious belief. We see that next.

Henry and Mary Bommeli Eyring, Henry's paternal grandparents

6

BELIEF

Henry's examples of religious belief were not exclusively family members. Nor, in fact, were they all members of The Church of Jesus Christ of Latter-day Saints. A student not only of science but also of great scientists, Henry often spoke of the faith of his scientific heroes. He particularly liked to cite Max Planck, the great German physicist:

> Planck himself says that "God existed before there were human beings on the earth, and that he holds the world, believers as well as disbelievers, in his omnipotent hands, since the beginning of eternity, and that he will continue to rule from his heights inaccessible to human imagination long after the earth and everything on it will have crumbled to dust."[1] One cannot help believing that it was this unwavering faith in an omnipotent ruler of the universe which gave Planck the courage to intercede with Hitler in behalf of Fritz Haber and the other suffering Jews. His son, Edwin Planck, was executed for his part in the unsuccessful attempt to get rid of Hitler. Planck as a

case history is pertinent and interesting because we find [that] in him a deep faith in God was accompanied by resolute honor and the highest scientific attainments. One could wish for no finer example for emulation.[2]

Henry also admired the belief of Louis Pasteur, the great French biologist, who like Planck suffered terrible family tragedy:

Pasteur had the simple faith that made him certain that he would live again with his family. These included his parents, his sisters, and the two little daughters who had preceded him in death, in addition to the devoted wife, married son and daughter and grandchildren whom he left behind.[3]

In his book *The Faith of a Scientist* Henry included this statement of Pasteur's:

There are two men in each of us: the scientist, he who starts with a clear field and desires to rise to the knowledge of Nature through observation, experimentation and reasoning, and the man of sentiment, the man of belief, the man who mourns his dead children, and who cannot, alas, prove that he will see them again, but who believes that he will, and lives in the hope—the man who will not die like a vibrio,[4] but who feels that the force that is within him cannot die.[5]

A TESTIMONY OF JOSEPH SMITH

As much as he valued the faith of Planck and Pasteur and other great scientists, Henry's religious beliefs went beyond theirs. Specifically, Henry's faith was rooted in the mission of the Prophet

Joseph Smith. Pasteur's hope of an afterlife, for instance, was for Henry a certainty, because Joseph Smith had seen detailed visions of it. Henry didn't believe just in God, or even the Mormon Church. The foundation of his faith was belief in Joseph Smith.

That can be seen time and again in his response to questions about science and religion. For instance, here is his reply to a woman, a convert to the Church, who wondered about the theory that fossil remains on this earth might have been transported from other worlds, thus posing no contradiction to the biblical creation time line:

> Thank you for your letter of January 22nd. I was trained as a mining engineer, so the evidence seems to me to point toward an age of the earth of between four and five billion years and to the existence of pre-Adamic man. I don't think that it is reasonable to explain the observed geologic formations on the theory that they were moved from some other world. Since as Latter-day Saints we believe life exists in other worlds I have no difficulty in reconciling myself to the idea of life before Adam and to a great age of the earth. Our scriptural accounts are brief and don't seem to me to rule out these possibilities. The scriptural emphasis is on God's dealings with Adam and his descendants, and the treatment of pre-Adamic history is sketchy, no doubt for a good reason.
>
> It seems clear to me that the Lord used the Prophet Joseph to restore His gospel. This is the important thing for me. Just how He runs the world I'm obliged to leave up to Him. All I can do is find out how he does it by every means available.[6]

Henry's 1958 reply to a Church General Authority with a similar question was likewise grounded in a testimony of the Prophet Joseph:

> The geological and radiological evidence that the earth is some billions of years old is, in my judgment, overwhelming. Brother Talmage and Brother Widtsoe found no difficulty in reconciling such considerations with the Prophet's divine mission, and neither do I.[7]

Henry's fundamental faith in the Prophet Joseph Smith begs the question, "Where did it come from?" He never cited a singular, personal confirmation experience. However, he grew up hearing powerful tales of such experiences. Among those were the stories of the conversion to Mormonism of his paternal grandparents, Henry Eyring and Mary Bommeli.

MAN OF DREAMS

Grandpa Henry Eyring was born in 1835 in Germany, the son of a wealthy pharmacist, Edward, and Ferdinandine von Blomberg, a woman of noble Prussian birth. His mother, Ferdinandine, died when Grandpa Henry was eight years old. A few years later, Edward lost the family fortune in a speculative business venture (ironically, it was an experimental chemical process). Worse than the loss of the family fortune for Grandpa Henry, though, was the subsequent death of his father, Edward. At fifteen, he was orphaned and penniless.

In the years leading up to these setbacks, Grandpa Henry was a student at a private German "gymnasium," an elite private boarding school. He had enjoyed the finest education since the age of five. He studied not only mathematics and other sciences, but also the liberal arts, including Latin and French. The principal of the gymnasium was a distant relative, a grand-uncle by marriage. This man, Dr. Edward Jacobi, was also a royal chaplain and a preacher of great renown; he nurtured in Henry not only a love of learning, but also an interest in God. After the death of Grandpa Henry's father, Dr. Jacobi kept the young boy on at the gymnasium, paying the costs out of his own pocket.

At the age of seventeen, Grandpa Henry resolved to immigrate to America, an idea his father had considered as the family business was failing. In 1853, he took a younger sister and left for the United States, landing first in New York and ultimately finding employment with a druggist in St. Louis. It was there that he took the step that became his great legacy to his family. He described his first encounter with The Church of Jesus Christ of Latter-day Saints with characteristic Eyring humor:

> While in St. Louis I read at different times articles about the Mormons, representing them to be a set of thieves, cut-throats and the very off-scourings from the earth. Hearing that several companies of that people had come to St. Louis, I apprehended danger to the public safety and felt it hardly safe in the streets after night. On the morning of December 10, 1854, I happened to hear that the Mormons held meetings in a chapel corner of 4th Street and Washington Ave. Feeling a curiosity to see some of those desperate characters I went to their meeting on the evening of the same day. I arrived there rather early and discovering a bench near the door I concluded to locate myself there, thinking that if anything serious should happen I could readily make my escape to the street. After occupying that bench for a while and watching the people who were now coming in gradually I discovered that they were a friendly, sociable people who

certainly did not have the appearance of cut-throats. Upon this I took courage and actually ventured to seat myself in the gallery.[8]

Grandpa Henry enjoyed that first meeting and immediately began to explore the new religion. A coworker, William Brown, was a member of the Church and helped Grandpa with his study. He was earnest in his search for truth, and he sensed that the Church had it. However, he was unprepared to accept the notion of angelic visitations and thus struggled to believe in the revelations claimed by Joseph Smith. Fortunately, Grandpa Henry was himself a man of revelation, particularly in the form of dreams. One of those dreams came now, as he sought for a divine manifestation to be baptized.

Grandpa saw himself seated at a table with his co-worker William Brown and Elder Erastus Snow (an Apostle), a man he had never met but who would later become a dear friend. In the dream, Elder Snow talked to Grandpa for a full hour and ended his remarks with a command to be baptized, saying, "This man (pointing to William Brown) shall baptize you." Grandpa describes his response to the baptismal challenge with understatement: "On the 11th day of March 1855 about 7:30 A.M. I was baptized by Elder Wm. Brown in the west part of St. Louis in a pool of rain water."[9] (The average morning temperature in St. Louis at that time of year is 37 degrees, which would have been the temperature of the rain water.)

A MISSION TO THE INDIAN TERRITORIES

Within a few months, Grandpa Henry embarked as a full-time missionary to the "Indian Territories," present-day Oklahoma and Arkansas. He was "full of zeal, anxious to enter the vineyard of the Lord and at that time felt as though I would like to devote my whole life to the preaching of the word."[10] In fact, he would do essentially that, serving several other full-time missions and living much of his life in places determined by leaders of the Church, including the great prophet-organizer Brigham Young.

As in the case of Erastus Snow, Grandpa first encountered President Young in a dream. In 1860, having served with some success but great tribulations in the Indian Territories, he wrote,

> I had now been about 4½ years on the Cherokee Mission and felt somewhat desirous to know when I would be released from my labors. Not being able to hear anything from the Presidency of the Church, I called upon the Lord in prayer, asking him to reveal to me his mind and will in regard to my remaining longer or going up to Zion. The following dream was given to me in answer to my prayer. I dreamt I had arrived in S.L. City and immediately went to President Brigham Young's office, where I found him. I said to him: "President Young I have left my mission, have come of my own accord, but if there is anything wrong in this, I am willing to return to finish my mission." To this he replied: "You have served long enough, it is all right." Having had dreams before which were literally fulfilled I had faith to believe that this also would be and consequently commenced at once to prepare for a start.[11]

Concluding his mission, Grandpa Henry joined a company of pioneering Saints near Omaha, with whom he proceeded to Utah. Though the westward trek was arduous for many, Grandpa's report suggests none of that. He said: "I enjoyed myself excellently while crossing the plains, walking nearly the whole distance, and to me it was more like a pleasure trip than a toilsome pilgrimage."[12]

The key to his happiness was the companionship of a young Swiss woman in the company, Mary Bommeli. Grandpa Henry wrote, "On my journey across the plains I became acquainted with her and we had many pleasant and useful conversations with each other while walking together in advance of the train."[13]

WOMAN AT THE LOOM

Mary Bommeli was also a new Church convert. The story of her conversion and emigration to America was as inspiring as Grandpa Henry's. It was retold a century-and-a-half later by one of her great-grandsons, Henry Bennion ("Hal") Eyring:[14]

Mary was born in 1830. The missionaries taught her family in Switzerland when she was 24. She was still living at home, weaving and selling cloth to help support her family on their small farm. When the family heard the doctrine of the restored gospel of Jesus Christ, they knew it was true. They were baptized. Mary's brothers were called on missions, going without purse or scrip.[15] The rest of the family sold their possessions to go to America to gather with the Saints.

There was not enough money for all to go. Mary volunteered to stay behind because she felt she could earn enough from her weaving to support herself and save for her passage. She found her way to Berlin and to the home of a woman who hired her to weave cloth for the family's clothing. She lived in a servant's room and set up her loom in the living area of the home.

It was against the law then to teach the doctrine of The Church of Jesus Christ of Latter-day Saints in Berlin. But Mary could not keep the good news to herself. The woman of the house and her friends would gather around the loom to hear the Swiss girl teach. She talked about the appearance of Heavenly Father and Jesus Christ to Joseph Smith, of the visitation of angels, and of the Book of Mormon. When she came to the accounts of Alma,[16] she taught the doctrine of the Resurrection.

That caused some problems with her weaving. In those days, many children died very young. The women around the loom had lost children in death, some of them several children. When Mary taught the truth that little children were heirs of the celestial kingdom and that those women might again be with them and with the Savior and our Heavenly Father, tears rolled down the faces of the women. Mary cried too. All those tears falling got the cloth wet that Mary had woven.

Mary's teaching created a more serious problem. Even though Mary begged the women not to talk about what she told them, they did. They shared the joyous doctrine with their friends. So one night there was a knock at the door. It was the police. They took Mary off to jail. On the way, she asked the policeman for the name of the judge she was to appear before the next morning. She asked if he had a family. She asked if he was a good father and a good husband. The policeman smiled as he described the judge as a man of the world.

At the jail, Mary asked for a pencil and some paper. She wrote a letter to the judge. She wrote about the Resurrection of Jesus Christ as described in the Book of Mormon, about the spirit world, and about how long the judge would have to think and to consider his life before facing the final judgment. She wrote that she knew he had much to repent of, which would break his family's heart and bring him great sorrow. She wrote through the night.

In the morning she asked the policeman to take her letter to the judge. He did.

Later, the policeman was summoned by the judge to his office. The letter Mary had written was irrefutable evidence that she was teaching the gospel and so breaking the law. Nevertheless, it wasn't long until the policeman came back to Mary's cell. He told her that all charges were dismissed and that she was free to go, on the conditions she had stated in her letter.[17] Her teaching the doctrine of the restored gospel of Jesus Christ had opened eyes and hearts enough to get her cast into jail. And her declaring the doctrine of repentance to the judge got her cast out of jail.

Mary left Berlin, crossed the Atlantic, and had the good fortune to be in the pioneer company that Grandpa Henry and his missionary companion joined. Actually, the two missionaries were so sick with malaria when their wagon pulled alongside the others on the open prairie that they were lying down, letting the horses lead themselves; at first, members of Mary's wagon train wondered if the disheveled missionaries were dead. However, Mary helped nurse Grandpa Henry back to health, and family lore has it that they held hands as they walked across the American prairie. They arrived in Utah before summer's end and were married that winter.

Grandpa's initial duty in Salt Lake City was to seek out his priesthood leader, Brigham Young. The day after arriving, he reported to the Prophet:

> I said to him, "President Young I have come without being sent for. If I have done wrong, I am willing to return and finish my mission." He answered: "It is all right, we have been looking for you." Thus my dream was literally fulfilled.[18]

BELIEF

From Father to Son to Grandson

Like Miles P. Romney, newly married Grandpa Henry was
sent by Brigham Young to colonize in the Utah desert. After several failures elsewhere, the Eyrings were finally directed to St.
George. Also like Miles P., Grandpa Henry eventually became a
leading citizen there. The colonists in St. George especially valued
Henry's academic training. He served as mayor and president of
the mercantile cooperative. He also served in prominent Church
positions, working closely with Elder Erastus Snow, whom he first
saw in the dream he had in St. Louis. Grandpa Henry was the
recorder in the St. George Temple on the day when proxy ordi-
nance work was performed for the Founding Fathers and the great
religious Reformers. Their names in the temple record are written
in Grandpa's elegant handwriting, mastered in Dr. Jacobi's school.

Like Miles P., Grandpa Henry subsequently left his family for
a foreign mission, returning to Germany; among the children left
behind was nine-year-old Ed, Henry's father. Grandpa Henry met
no greater success there than Miles P. did in England. However,
he never faltered in his testimony of the Church restored by
Joseph Smith. He passed that testimony to Ed (who also served a
German mission). Ed in turn passed the testimony of Joseph
Smith to Henry, most famously on that day before he left for college. The words Ed spoke then are worth another retelling:

> I'm convinced that the Lord used the Prophet Joseph
> Smith to restore His Church. For me that is a reality. I
> haven't any doubt about it. Now, there are a lot of other
> matters which are much less clear to me. But in this
> Church you don't have to believe anything that isn't true.
> You go over to the University of Arizona and learn

133

everything you can, and whatever is true is part of the gospel. The Lord is actually running this universe. I'm convinced that he inspired the Prophet Joseph Smith.[19]

PRAISE TO THE MAN

Henry made the family testimony of Joseph Smith his own. In countless sermons he paid tribute to the Prophet, extolling his gifts of intelligence and inspiration. A sample of those tributes follows:

Let us consider a little the nature of true greatness in men. The people who catch hold of men's minds and feelings and inspire them to do things bigger than themselves are the people who are remembered in history. The cold person who simply propounds some logical position, however important and interesting it may be, cannot do for the Lord's children what is done by those who stir feelings of imagination and make men struggle toward perfection. On this basis, Joseph Smith stands very far up on the scale on which the Savior is paramount.

Let us next consider a few of the things that are striking in the teachings and life of Joseph Smith. Joseph grew up in a world that was narrowly sectarian. In this cramped world, he taught that man had lived eternally and would always live. This idea of a pre-existence was startling in that day, as it is in this.

Plato spoke of a pre-existence, but we learn from the Prophet Joseph that man lived before he was born; that life is a school where man is sent to learn the things the Lord intends; and that he continues on into life after death. Immortality is in the very nature of things. As intelligences, we always existed. What a tremendous influence these ideas have had! No wonder people build towns and chapels all over the world in honor of this great latter-day teacher. There will be many more wards and stakes as monuments to this great man.

Another idea that the Prophet taught was revolutionary. In place of the idea of placid membership in a heavenly choir, we have the concept of eternal progression. There is no limit to how high man, the spirit child of God, may climb. By hard work, by study, by constantly increasing in humility and wisdom through the eternities, we will approach perfection. This great idea can't help firing our imagination.

In still another way he loosened the shackles that bind men's minds. The School of the Prophets[20] was formed. He obtained the best teachers available and studied and learned all he could and promulgated the idea that the Gospel embraces all truth—that truth is to be accepted whatever its source. It is difficult to see how anyone could hear such teachings without being deeply affected.[21]

The Prophet Joseph Smith was surpassed by some in secular learning, but he was unsurpassed by anyone in his humble willingness to learn. He was genuinely teachable and was always willing to yield obedience to the promptings of the Spirit. The result was a God-given insight into spiritual matters that is having its effect for good throughout the world.[22]

Sometimes people talk about how untrained he was, and that is true. He came from humble beginnings, but he was a tremendous man. The Lord did not choose just anybody to restore the Gospel of Jesus Christ. Joseph was foreordained from the beginning. It was his high destiny and great privilege to restore again to the world the Gospel of the New Testament.[23]

In summary, I am a convinced member of this great Church which the Prophet Joseph Smith had the privilege of restoring in 1830 because of the grand ideas that he brought into the world: (1) that we lived before we came here; (2) that we progress eternally; (3) that if we live as the Savior lived, we preach a greater sermon than anything we can say.

Joseph Smith replaced the narrowness of the sectarian ideas of his day with the idea of a broad education and set an example of reaching out as far as he could into all kinds of questions. He gathered around him men who were outstanding. Prominent among them were the Smiths, the Pratts, the Youngs, the Richardses. I think of these great men who were with the Prophet daily, particularly men like Orson Pratt with his acute scientific mind, and I think that in a certain sense I have walked down the streets of Nauvoo because people who think as I do did just that. They were impressed, and they came away feeling that it was really the Lord's work. There was something to his message; it was really true; the Lord had spoken to Joseph as He did to Paul long ago. For these reasons, I feel that the Gospel is more important than anything else a man can have.

May the Lord bless us to appreciate the life of the Prophet Joseph Smith and the wonderful message that he brought to us with the restoration of the Gospel of Jesus Christ to the earth. May we live and understand it in a big way and not worry about the small things that we do not understand very well, because they will become clearer as we go on. May we have the faith, as I have, that this

Gospel has only begun to grow. The things we believe are only a part of the things that are yet to be revealed, and if we do our part, our position is sure. We will indeed be exalted in the celestial kingdom and have the blessings which the Lord has promised for the faithful.[24]

Pancho Villa and Emiliano Zapata Salazar, Mexican revolutionaries

FEAR

So far in this "Heritage" section we've seen three traits that Henry inherited from his parents and grandparents: love, ambition, and belief. Each of these traits seems to fit with the pattern of his accomplishments. We'd expect, for instance, a fellow with a knack for making friends to have been raised in a loving environment. Likewise, it goes without saying that no scientist could publish six hundred-plus papers without being ambitious. And it's no surprise that a great defender of faith would enjoy a heritage of belief.

Where, though, does a chapter on fear fit in the picture? What evidence is there that Henry was afraid of anything? And, even if he was motivated by fear, how did that contribute to his accomplishments?

Henry's three sons, Ted, Hal, and Harden, would smile at these questions, because they know the answers. They remember what their father would say when asked why he always worked so much harder than his employers required. "Because," he'd reply through slightly gritted teeth, "if the economy goes to ruin and there's only one chemist in this country with a job, it's going to be me." Henry was similarly cautious when someone sought counsel about a new job prospect. "Whatever you do," he would warn, "don't lose your health benefits."

BANDITS

Understanding why Henry was motivated by a kind of fear—and how it helped him in life—requires traveling back to 1910, the year of the Mexican Revolution. Though Henry's family was prosperously ensconced in their own Mormon colony, the country around them was a political powder keg. Porfirio Diaz, a war hero-turned-president-turned-dictator, had brought the country three decades of peace. However, the peace came at a high price. The unofficial slogan of Diaz's regime was, "Pan, o palo," ("Bread, or the stick"). Unfortunately, the vast majority of "bread" went to wealthy landowners, while common Mexicans and political opponents got "the stick." Mexico industrialized and prospered economically, but politically things couldn't last.

Revolution inevitably came, yet without clear resolution. As Henry recalled later in life, "In two years we had four presidents of Mexico, with all the turbulence and disorder that you would expect in a country where there's this kind of fighting."[1]

In fact, the revolution began in the northern province of Chihuahua, where the Mormon colonists lived. The colonists of course declared neutrality and at least had their lives spared. However, armed, unemployed revolutionaries (the colonists called them "bandits") roamed the countryside. The Mormons were often forced to contribute their property to the rebels' cause.[2] In return for cattle and food, the revolutionaries offered receipts, payable if their side won. But they also required the colonists to trade good horses for poor ones. And, in the end, the receipts proved worthless.

The rebel general in the area, a man named Emiliano Zapata Salazar, initially honored the colonists' neutrality. However, he had difficulty controlling his unruly forces. Drunken rebels often menaced the Mormons. Henry's grandmother Mary Bommeli Eyring, who still lived alone in her own home at age eighty, was threatened by such a bandit. Attempting to break down Mary's door, he demanded $100, a gun, and ammunition. Mary's life was spared only by the intervention of courageous neighbors.[3]

Bargaining for Time

The demand for guns became an unrelenting theme. In the summer of 1912 a force of six hundred rebels surrounded the Mormon colony of Dublan and demanded that the inhabitants surrender all of their guns and ammunition by 10 o'clock the next morning. This news was telephoned to the Juarez Stake president, Junius Romney (Henry's thirty-four-year-old uncle). Fifty years later, Junius recalled how he and a companion set out to negotiate with General Salazar. It was a story of daring brinksmanship that Henry knew by heart, having heard it shortly after the fact:

> Brother Harris and I immediately hitched up my team and proceeded to Casas Grandes, where we were at once surrounded by the Captain of the Guard and his companions. I told the Captain that we must see General Salazar at once, and he replied that no one could see the General until tomorrow. The General had retired for the night with orders not to be disturbed. I told the Captain that it was a matter of life and death and that we must see him immediately. I had no weapons of any kind and can only conclude that the Spirit of the Lord must have influenced him, for he took his life in his hands and escorted us directly to the General's sleeping room. When we entered, the

General aroused and demanded to know who was in the room. The Captain explained that it was Mr. Romney, and the General demanded to know what I wanted. I related the report I had received, and General Salazar acknowledged that the Captain in charge of the troops was one of his subordinates, and then he began a tirade about his actions. He said that the officer "had his orders and should not have issued any such demand, not yet!" The last two words sent a chill up my spine, for this was the first indication I had ever had that we were facing the necessity to deliver all of our guns in the Colonies or fight to retain them. As with the Captain of the Guard, I believe that the Lord must have influenced the General to reverse his own order and to leave the people and the guns alone.[4]

The colonists' reprieve, though, was short lived. The next day, they learned through a friendly Mexican informant that the rebels were only biding their time, hoping to get all of the colonists' guns without attacking American citizens. However, they were prepared to massacre the colonists, if necessary. "If this does not happen as I have said," the informant pledged, "you can cut my throat from ear to ear!"

In fact, this disclosure, though valuable, came as no surprise. The colonists sent a representative to El Paso, Texas, where a member of the Church's Quorum of the Twelve Apostles had been dispatched to be available for consultation. The recommendation of this man, Elder Anthony W. Ivins, is remarkable, unless one knows the nature of Church administration, which emphasizes delegation. Having traveled many hundreds of miles to represent the President of the Church, Elder Ivins merely passed on this message: "The course to be pursued by our people in Mexico must be determined by yourself, Romney, and the leading men of the Juarez Stake."[5]

Under Stake President Junius Romney, the colonists developed a plan of action. All of the women and children—more than 2,300—were sent to El Paso, the closest American city. Several hundred men remained in the hope of protecting their property and riding out the storm until their families could be brought back.

Henry was shipped out with the women and children, a classification to which he took offense even as an eleven year old. However, throughout his life he enjoyed telling the story of how his father, who stayed behind, bravely participated in a plot to fool the rebels and keep their best guns.

Acceding to rebel demands, the Mormon men turned over all of their older weapons. However, they secretly hid recent shipments of new guns from the United States. The secret cache of weapons in Colonia Juarez, Henry's home, was hidden in a building called the Tithing Office, at the center of town. As tensions rose, the rebels began to patrol the main street, and a large force camped in front of the Tithing House. Henry took pride in telling how his father and a brother-in-law sneaked in under cover of darkness, retrieved the guns, and spirited them away to nearby caves:

> Miles Romney[6] and Father were delegated to get the arms that they had stored in the Tithing Office and transfer them to a place called "The Stairs." They had to go to the back of the Tithing Office with the rebels camped in front and get those guns and put them on pack horses. They would have been killed if they had been discovered. That was kind of ticklish, but Father was very cool.[7]

One of Henry's sons, Hal, asked his Grandpa Ed years later

how he had pulled off such a daring deed. With typical noncha-lance, Ed responded, "It takes a good horse."[8]

EXODUS

Notwithstanding the colonists' brave resistance, their situation continued to worsen. The rebels started to loot; so staying to pro-tect property meant fighting. With a U.S. State Department announcement that the colonists were on their own in Mexico, President Romney and his fellow leaders decided to evacuate entirely. The retreat to El Paso was exhausting and fraught with danger, as Junius later described:

> After the men gathered in the mountains where we could protect ourselves, we marched to the border of the United States, miraculously protected by the Lord, pass-ing between 3,000 Federal Troops on our left and 3,000 Communist Rebels on our right. We reached the United States line, 150 miles distant, in two days' march. As we approached in the twilight, and our dust had been observed 25 miles before we reached the border, we were thought to be a band of red flag raiders such as had attacked the ranch in the past. Therefore, the officer in charge of the United States troops had stationed his men behind the rock walls of the corrals with orders to hold their fire until he should give the order to fire, but then they were to slaughter these supposed raiders. We were saved from this tragedy by the fact that one of the soldiers recognized Ammon M. Tenney, Jr., who was one of our party. The soldier shouted to the Captain, "Don't shoot, don't shoot! I know this man, Ammon Tenney[9]—these are Americans!"[10]

Junius Romney went on to acknowledge the role of Providence in the colonists' escape, and the disastrous consequences that were avoided:

> I want to tell you that no man brought us out of Mexico, and no set of men brought us out of Mexico, but the Lord, God of Israel, brought us out of Mexico. The reason that He needed to bring us out of Mexico should be apparent to any thinking person. Here we were, American citizens, and the American Government had placed a strong army there along this entire 1,500 miles of unguarded frontier to protect the lives and property of American citizens. We were American citizens, and had they massacred the people in any of the colonies, Pershing and his army would have been over there in less time than it takes to snap your fingers, and we would have been responsible for war between the United States and Mexico.

In hindsight, Junius was right. Though Pershing's army did later invade after a brutal attack by Pancho Villa on Columbus, New Mexico, the Mormons were never blamed for the conflict and associated loss of American life. Being so blamed would have added to existing prejudices against the Church.[11]

Henry also saw Heaven's hand in the exodus from Mexico. He particularly credited inspired Church leadership. He admired the delegation of authority from Salt Lake City to the local leaders, as well as the skill with which his Uncle Junius and others responded to that delegation. That thousands of colonists were evacuated with no loss of life or even serious injury strengthened his conviction that the Church was led by prophecy. He did, though, have that one bone to pick with the priesthood brethren who oversaw the evacuation:

I thought I should have stayed behind. I felt as important at eleven as I've ever felt in my life, but they shipped
me out with the women and children, which I thought
was a disgrace. It was an indication that they were not perfect in administering things.[12]

Notwithstanding Henry's preference for staying and fighting,
the trip out with the women and children was harrowing enough.
The 150-mile train ride to El Paso took almost twenty-four hours,
as the train stopped frequently to check for dynamite under the
tracks. Henry's older sister Camilla wrote a poignant record of the
journey, beginning with their last night at home:

We spent most of the night hiding things away in the
attic, under the floors and in all unlikely places. We were
allowed to take just one trunk of clothes for the family of
thirteen. I wanted so much to put in my doll and some
other treasures, but there was no room. I had always been
a great collector and had kept all my school papers, letters,
toys and everything I had ever had, and now I had to leave
them all, never to see them again.

In the morning Father drove us to Pearson in the
white-topped buggy. This railroad station was about eight
miles from Juarez. There were dozens of buggies and wag-
ons and crowds of refugees waiting for the train to carry
us to the safety of the U.S.A. A troop of bandits with guns
and bayonets was drawn up in formation at the train station. As one old lady walked by, a soldier hooked his bay-
onet through her handbag and took possession of it.

Finally we were all loaded like sardines into the cars.
We were in a third-class car with long, hard benches running lengthwise of the cars, and children and baggage
piled on top of each other.

FEAR

The trip to the border at El Paso was only about 150 miles, but the train went at a snail's pace and stopped every few miles. We were in terror all the time lest the Pancho Villa rebels might waylay us. We traveled all day and all night. Finally just as dawn was breaking we crawled slowly across the Rio Grande River and were greeted by the sight of the Stars and Stripes. I still remember the thrill that sight brought and the feeling of safety once more. A great shout went up from all the refugees.

We were met at the depot by the kind people of El Paso, who took us in automobiles—and that was a treat— out to a big lumberyard which they had improvised into shelter for the refugees. There were already hundreds there before us, and when they dumped us into this huge corral with dust a foot deep, flies swarming, and the sights and smells of that mob of humanity, it was enough to make the stoutest heart sink. They tried to arrange a stall for each family, and we piled in for the night, hanging up blankets in an attempt at some privacy.

Mother had a little money, and so the next day she scurried around to find us a lodging a little more private. She took one room in a small hotel for the thirteen of us. It was an inside room at that; no outside ventilation and July weather. There was just room to spread quilts all over the floor and manage to be one deep at least until we were asleep. In this room we ate our meals as well as sleeping.[13]

REFUGEES

When Ed arrived from Mexico several weeks later he rented a small house, in which his family and a Romney brother-in-law's family stayed. Caroline had already put Henry and his next-oldest

147

brother to work. Henry felt his share of sorrow at leaving home, just like everyone else. Having spent all of his young life riding the range, the loss he felt most deeply was his horse. He recalled the sorrow of an eleven-year-old's farewell:

> My last act when we were leaving Mexico forever in 1912 was to go out to the corral and bid my faithful saddle horse goodbye. I guessed correctly that I would never see him again.[14]

In addition to being dispossessed of all he owned, Henry was kept out of school that year in El Paso to help the family make ends meet. He would have been justified in complaining, but he didn't. In fact, he was proud of having excelled even at menial labor:

> My brother Ed and I were eleven and nine, respectively. We got jobs in department stores as cash boys. We would carry the goods and money from the clerk who had sold them to the cashier. She would wrap the goods and give us the change, and we would take it back to the clerk. So you were just serving in place of a burro to go back and forth. We would keep pretty busy. We got two dollars a week for about a sixty-hour week. We worked on Saturdays as well as the other five days. There was nothing hard about it, nor did I feel particularly sorry for myself. It seemed interesting enough. The clerks were getting ten dollars a week, and the floor walker who was in charge of a floor in Callister's Department Store would be getting twenty dollars a week. So our salary wasn't particularly out of line. With a nickel we could buy a loaf of bread or a quart of milk. So it helped. Of course, you can't

keep a good man down: before a year was up I was up to three-and-a-half a week.[15]

The family's financial situation gradually improved. However, it was decades before Ed and Caroline could sleep free from worry about financial foreclosure. Giving up on a return to Mexico, they left El Paso and ultimately settled in Pima. Henry reported their toil there:

> After a year in El Paso waiting for the Mexican situation to improve and a second year spent in Safford and Thatcher, Arizona, Father had purchased a farm by making a small down payment. Part of the farm was under cultivation. Brush was cleared from the rest by hitching two teams, one to each end of a steel rail, and dragging it across land after the mesquite had been dug up with ax, pick, and shovel. This involved a lot of hard work, but we were all healthy and anxious to get on our feet again.[16]

The reality is that Henry spent the next three decades helping his father "get on his feet again." He worked at part-time jobs as he studied, always saving and turning over all he could to his father, who had a crushing mortgage to pay. As a freshman at the University of Arizona he had a scholarship, but he waited tables anyway and sent his earnings home. He made no complaint when his father's speculative business ventures failed, as one did catastrophically in 1922 and another did in the Depression.[17] Ed was duly grateful. A family journal recollection shows how much he appreciated Henry's financial support:

> Henry attended the Gila Academy and after graduating from the high school he received a $500.00 to the University of Arizona, where he graduated in four years.

He continued his studies there, getting his master's degree in chemistry. Then he taught a year, sending all the money he could spare home to his parents, it amounting to about $1,000. Later he went to Berkeley, where he worked his own way, receiving his Ph.D. The two years before this time he taught part-time and arranged a plan for taking care of the mortgage on the home place, sending himself $900.00 and arranging for each of the children to pay $200.00 each as soon as they commenced to earn.[18]

A MULTIGENERATIONAL LEGACY OF PRIVATION

Henry had not just his own youthful experiences of displacement to motivate him, but also those of his parents and grandparents. In fact, financial ruin and forced emigration had hit every one of three generations of Eyrings and Romneys. In Henry's youth, there was the Mexican Revolution and the move to Pima. In his parents' youth, it was the Edmunds-Tucker Act, which drove them from the United States to Mexico. Henry's grandfathers also lost everything as young men: Grandpa Henry Eyring emigrated from Germany after his father's bankruptcy and untimely death, and Miles P. Romney began life as a refugee from mob-desolated Nauvoo.

It's no surprise, then, that Henry was inclined to worry about the loss of employment and health benefits. The poverty incident to refugee status motivated him, as it had generations of Eyrings and Romneys. As he said—with understatement—of the early Pima days, "The undeveloped state of the farm and a heavy mortgage provided the incentive for enthusiastic efforts to gain financial independence."[19]

Things didn't get better after he left Pima. He married just as the Depression set in, and first at Berkeley and then again at

150

Princeton he spent a full year of work knowing that he had no guarantee of anything after that. In 1931, he was the only one of four new hires to be retained by Princeton. For him, that was as powerful a reminder of the vicissitudes of life as was being driven from Mexico.

Henry acted all his life as though financial ruin were only a step away. He was loath to spend money even long after his fame and financial independence were secure. When, as a famous scientist, business took him outside Utah and a first-class plane ticket was provided, he flew coach and gave the difference back. Even as dean of the graduate school at the University of Utah, where he was widely regarded as the star of the show, he acted as though his employment was uncertain. When asked once why he continued to teach summers as dean, he replied, "It makes it hard for them to fire me." He was only half joking.

God-Fearing

That was the kind of fear that Henry inherited. Not *fearfulness,* but rather respect for powerful forces and inevitable consequences; not the negative, Freudian kind of fear, but rather something positive and healthy, as in "God-fearing." That healthy fear was no small part of the reason for his hard work and scientific success.

Righteous fear also played a role in his defense of faith. He worried more about pleasing God than he did about pleasing his fellowmen, even if that meant giving offense or losing favor with some of them. His boldness in preaching the gospel—even to those who didn't want to hear it—reflected his belief that his Heavenly Father would hold him accountable for doing so.

This fear was critical even to Henry's legacy of friendship. He believed not just in the first great commandment, loving God, but also in the second, loving his neighbor. He knew what it felt like to be treated well, as his parents had treated him. He also knew the sting of being taken for granted, as when he was deemed unfit to stay and hold the fort with the men in Mexico. His memory of those experiences motivated him to treat even the young and the unlearned better than they expected. He was afraid to slight them. By virtue of that fear, he rarely did.

Apparent Contradictions

Looking back over this Heritage section, it is an admittedly disparate, even contradictory bundle of traits that Henry seems to have inherited from his forebears and early experiences: love, ambition, belief, fear. In fact, it did lead to a paradoxical way of thinking that many people found puzzling.

Yet his paradoxical views helped him to live a happy life and do much good for others. He knew how to simplify complex things. This skill is the real reason for studying Henry: if he could do it, perhaps we can too. With that goal in mind, we move to our next section, Paradoxes.

Five-year-old Mexican ranchero

Breaking baked Arizona ground

High school graduate

The Eyring family in Princeton
(Ted is standing, with Henry, Harden, Hal, and Mildred seated)

The first annual footrace—no mercy for fallen comrades.

University of Utah cheerleading squad members turn out to support Henry in the 1971 race, shown nationwide by CBS.

False start?

No bruised shins . . . this time.

Henry's typically full office

Gesticulating to make a point to an audience in Tokyo.

Henry (center) explains a concept to distinguished colleagues, including Nobel Laureate Peter Debye (second from right).

President Lyndon Johnson gives Henry the
National Medal of Science in 1966.

Henry with his sister Camilla (right), wife Winifred, and brother-in-law
Spencer Kimball at the 1980 dedication of the Henry Eyring Building.

PART 3

PARADOXES

Behold, I send you forth as sheep
in the midst of wolves:
be ye therefore wise as serpents,
and harmless as doves.

—MATTHEW 10:16

8

MASTER OF
CONTRADICTIONS

Even those who felt they knew Henry reasonably well found him baffling. How, for instance, could a distinguished scholar talk about his work in such simple terms or mimic, as he often did in the classroom, a "drunken molecule"? Was it all just an act? And what could you make of a scientist devout in his religion but eager to study the mechanisms of evolution? Or what about those annual footraces, which he always lost; why did he keep running, even with TV cameras rolling?

Those who knew Henry really well saw the apparent contradictions but realized that he had somehow mastered them. In fact, Henry's most insightful friends recognized that it was the paradoxes that made him who he was. In 1933, when Henry was just thirty-two, his brother-in-law Spencer Kimball was asked by the Church to write a tribute to him. Spencer, who knew Henry perhaps as well as anyone, explained his wife's younger brother this way:

His success comes of the combination of keen intellect, rare ambition, Edison-like industry, perseverance and the living of a clean life. Though his scientific work is much to him, his family ties and his Church are more important. His search for the Truth has followed a religious as well as a scientific trend. Truly this young man has lived up to the immortal lines of Kipling:

> *If you can talk with crowds and keep your virtue,*
> *Or walk with kings—nor lose the common touch;*
> *If neither foes nor loving friends can hurt you;*
> *If all men count with you, but none too much;*
> *If you can fill the unforgiving minute*
> *With sixty seconds' worth of distance run—*
> *Yours is the Earth and everything that's in it,*
> *And—which is more—you'll be a Man, my son![1]*

Spencer's tribute shows that he was on to Henry's great gift. The thing that made him unique was his ability to embrace ideals that, to most people, seem opposed.[2] Just as Kipling did in "If," F. Scott Fitzgerald identified this ability to balance competing ideals as a mark of genius:

> The test of a first-rate intelligence is the ability to hold two opposed ideas in the mind at the same time, and still retain the ability to function. One should, for example, be able to see that things are hopeless and yet be determined to make them otherwise.[3]

First-rate Intelligence

Henry was such a "first-rate intelligence." He had no difficulty with apparently contradictory ideas, so long as both were founded in truth. Most of us don't like trying to do that; we prefer to simplify the world. When two ideas seem opposed, we ultimately choose one or the other, even if both may be true. To do otherwise, we rationalize, is to choose confusion and befuddlement.

Henry, though, was content with this kind of ambiguity. In fact, he liked such puzzles. In his mind, for example, science and religion weren't fundamentally at odds with one another; they just weren't fully reconciled yet. Henry reasoned that God knows all the answers and will ultimately reveal them and show how everything fits together. Rather than being irritated by the missing pieces of the puzzle and the apparent contradictions between science and religious doctrine, Henry was intrigued.

Those less patient with ambiguity were inclined to see him as compartmentalized in his thinking or even blind to obvious contradictions. They couldn't understand, in particular, how he could believe so firmly in faith while at the same time ardently advocating logic. However, for Henry the so-called contradictions were just paradoxes—truths seemingly in opposition, but true nonetheless.

Henry's ability to manage paradox began with his upbringing. He had no trouble, for example, showing loyalty to both of his father's two families, treating his "Aunt" Emma and his own mother with equal affection. What seemed an either-or proposition to most people for him simply wasn't: when it came to loving both sides of his extended family, he took a "this or that?" question and answered, "This *and* that."

Henry also learned to be comfortable with paradox from pursuing scientific questions. For instance, the fundamental discovery that launched his specialty, quantum mechanics, is that matter has a dual nature. Prior to this discovery, scientists believed that an atomic particle was like an object that we can handle, such as a baseball. The quantum theorists, however, discovered that very small particles can also act in wave fashion, much like light.

What was believed to be an either-or condition (particle or wave), turned out to be a duality (particle *and* wave).[4] It's a hard concept to conceive, but a good scientist must accept the paradox or be unable to get anything done.

Perhaps most significantly, Henry also had a dualistic view of God. He knew from Joseph Smith's testimony that man is created in the image of God the Father and His Son, Jesus Christ, and that they have bodies of flesh and bone. However, he also believed that their influence is as expansive as the universe; he had as evidence of that both the inspired writings of Joseph Smith and also his own scientific observations, which showed divine order everywhere. Like Joseph Smith, Henry had no difficulty with the paradox of an individual, personal God who *also* exerts limitless influence.[5]

THE SIMPLICITY OF COMPLEX THINKING

Henry's ability to manage this kind of paradox allowed him to tackle complex things as though they were simple. Where others might get their minds "wrapped around the axle" of a paradoxical situation and never make any progress, he would say, "Yes, these two facts seem contradictory. Let's assume that they are both true and see if we can find the missing pieces that reconcile them."

Of course, he wasn't always conscious that he was attacking paradoxes this way. He was so comfortable with paradox that he often didn't recognize it as such until after he'd found the missing puzzle pieces that explained the apparent contradiction away. Thus, he might find the chapters that follow a bit amusing. One can almost hear him ask, "What's all the fuss about?"

Still, Kipling and Fitzgerald had a point: the ability to reconcile apparently competing truths is a test of genius. It is also crucial to being productive and happy in this complex world.

Even if he wasn't consciously aware of it, Henry had that ability, and it's worth studying. We'll do so by looking at six paradoxes of behavior that he seems to have mastered.

The first three paradoxes involve desirable attitudes that aren't entirely antithetical, but that tend to work against one another in most of us. In other words, it's hard to have a lot of one and a lot of the other at the same time. The challenge lies in getting them both together. Those competitive companion sets are

- Confidence and Humility
- Discipline and Creativity
- Freedom and Obedience.

The next three paradoxes are a bit different. They involve not two desirable traits in tension, but rather one good trait that is hard to get without a less-desirable companion coming along for the ride. For example, Henry had a genius for reasoning, but he didn't have to know all the reasons for everything, at least not immediately. In particular, his patience with religious matters allowed him to faithfully and happily pursue those questions that can be answered in this life, without worrying about the unanswerable ones. In other words, he valued the reasoning process without having to know all the reasons. We'll explore three paradoxes of this type:

- Reasoning, More Than Reasons
- Fundamentals, Not Conventions
- People, Not Public Opinion

And the inhabitants [of the world]
are begotten sons and
daughters unto God.

—DOCTRINE AND COVENANTS 76:24

9

CONFIDENCE AND

HUMILITY

One of the more intriguing things about Henry was that he could be confident without being cocksure. Listen to the surprising mix of confidence and humility in his remarks to a group of Church members gathered at Brigham Young University in the 1960s:

> Do we understand everything about science? Of course we don't. A substantial part of what we teach is baloney. But it is part of our religion that we do not understand things completely. The Lord gives us here a little and there a little, and as time goes on, it is going to get better. So I am not going to spend two minutes to try to prove that everybody in the Church always says things exactly correctly because it would not be true, and I am not here to provide any half-baked argument to support the scriptures. They do not need it. If they did, my support would not

help much anyway. I think that my religion is on a basis of just looking at how this thing works, of being humble enough to pray and trying to live up to the spirit of the Gospel and actually feeling the Spirit of the Holy Ghost. I think anybody can feel the Spirit of the Holy Ghost if he is humble, humble enough to pray, humble enough to really want to, and to live in accordance with the teachings of the gospel. So I do not worry in the least about problems like which one of my ancestors was a monkey, if any of them. However the Lord did these things suits me fine. There is nothing I can do about it anyway. It is all over, and I am just exactly like I am however He did it. And so for the life of me I am never able to worry along with the people who think science is a threat to their religion. It just is not. It could not be, and if it is, you had better fix your religion or your science, or both.

Let us go on with a few other things which I think are interesting. "Where are we going?" I just said that at least I do not have sense enough to worry. I never was happier and never believed my religion more. It is really true. It will stand up under any kind of thing that comes along, and if it does not, I will fix it so it does. So I am just a big boy trying to get along, and I expect to go to Temple Square in the hereafter.[1] My wife is less sure than I am that I will make it, but I am counting on nothing less than the celestial kingdom.[2]

The apparent contradictions in what Henry is saying here are almost too many to count. He gladly admits, for example, that his wife thinks he's less than perfect (and maybe even a bit of a schmuck), but he is absolutely sure of earning passing marks from God. He admits imperfections in both scientific understanding and fellow Church members, but he obviously supports the essential soundness of both. He exudes confidence about what he doesn't know. It all sounds a bit schizophrenic.

THE CHILD OF A SMILING HEAVENLY FATHER

Henry, though, didn't have a split personality; there was just a single voice in his mind. And the voice spoke one phrase that explained both Henry's confidence and his humility. The voice said, "You are a child of God."

Actually, in Henry's case, the conviction that he was God's son came not so much from a voice as an image. He was a visual thinker; imagining things that he couldn't see helped him understand them better. When he did chemistry, he pictured individual molecules in his mind's eye. The same thing was true when he prayed:

> I am a visual thinker, both in my science and in my religious life. When I pray, I "see" God in my mind's eye. It helps me get down to specifics if I'm speaking to Him face to face. It's not a detailed impression—I couldn't tell you whether we are indoors or out. I really notice only His eyes. They are looking at me, and He is smiling. When you think how big the universe is and how many more interesting things must be happening than anything I could possibly have to say, you must admit it's nice to have the feeling that you have God's full and complete attention, whenever you pray. He doesn't have to speak. Somehow my meandering thoughts seem to arrive at a better solution than I had come up with until then.[3]

Just as the discoveries of science gave Henry confidence in imagining molecules invisible to the human eye, the doctrines of

The Church of Jesus Christ of Latter-day Saints emboldened him to imagine a personal, loving Heavenly Father. The God who appeared to Joseph Smith was all powerful, but He came in the form of a resurrected man. The doctrine of a God similar to a mortal father resonated with Henry, who idolized and loved his earthly father, Ed, so much. Believing what Joseph Smith saw, he found it natural to envision his Heavenly Father not as an incomprehensible, unapproachable force, but rather as someone like his own "Papa," a loving friend with smiling eyes. As he said,

> One of the many things the Restored Gospel has done is to emphasize, as the scriptures have always done, the deep personal concern of God for His children.[4]

> Clearly the Bible portrays the Creator as one who enormously transcends mortal man in His unimaginably great qualities, but not one who has dissolved in a mystical infinity unrelated to His children. Rather, we worship the kind Father who knows His children and loves them.[5]

A Student of the Creator's Greatness

Of course, Henry's view of himself as God's son didn't lessen his respect for the Creator. Being a scientist, he knew better than most of God's tremendous power relative to man's. He often made this point with a joke contrasting his real estate interests with the Creator's:

> God, whom we worship, understands all of the things that go on in a universe which extends more than two billion light years in each direction. I like to compare the universe with my holdings. The comparison is instructive. My wife and I have a lot which is sixty feet across the

front, one hundred feet deep, and extends straight up to the limits of space, so far as I know. Clearly, this qualifies me to speak on the broader aspects of the universe. Actually, man rooted to his little plot of earth can only stand in utmost awe of the all-powerful Arbiter of the universe.[6]

That same sense of his relative smallness comes through in his response to a man who wrote him about a scheme for "dismantling Evolution once and for all." This fellow wanted to call a worldwide seminar on evolution and have LDS scientists gather evidence contrary to the theory. Henry wrote this gentle reply, which is rich with insight about God's wisdom relative to our own:

> As a devout Latter-day Saint the important fact for me is that the Lord is directing the affairs in His Universe, not exactly how He does it. Whether or not some organic evolution was used or is operating seems to me to be beside the point. He is infinitely wise. I just work here. If He told me in detail how He works I'm sure I wouldn't understand much of it. The effort spent on the crusade you envision would be better spent trying to understand a little better how God works. Sorry if we see things a little differently.[7]

DIVINE POTENTIAL

Yet Henry's view of himself as a son of God made him not just humble, but also confident. He recognized that being the literal offspring of a Father in Heaven meant having the capacity—and the destiny—to become like Him. This sense of divine heritage inspired Henry with great confidence in himself and his fellowmen:

173

I believe that every brilliant conquest made by man is but a manifestation of the divine spark which sets him apart from the rest of creation. Man is in the image of God, destined to go on learning and perfecting himself throughout eternity.[8]

To illustrate this point, Henry often told the story of Newton's triumph in discovering the laws of motion and gravitation, which allow the prediction of eclipses and the launching of satellites. He noted how these once unimaginable feats are now taken for granted:

Astronomers predict exactly when an eclipse will occur. Using this knowledge, men make great preparations, assemble expensive scientific equipment and move to the ends of the earth when told that an eclipse is imminent. They get their cameras ready to take the pictures, open the shutter at the right moment and the eclipse begins at the predicted instant. If the eclipse were ever so little off schedule, this would make headline news around the world. Here we are treated to two miracles: first, fabulously exact laws exist; and second, man has the genius to unravel these mysteries and reduce the existing order to codified laws which he then manipulates in the service of mankind.

We need to understand that the Creator of the universe is great beyond anything imaginable, but it always adds to this deeper understanding of the Gospel to see that we are able to partake at least to some degree of His greatness and shape an orderly world to our needs.

It is a remarkable human achievement to launch a satellite in the sky and, to a small degree, become a partner in creation. This fits into our idea of eternal progression.

We believe that eventually the children of God will increase in wisdom beyond any assigned limit.[9]

Though Henry knew his own limitations, the prospect of limitless potential as a son of God inspired him with confidence. New acquaintances immediately saw it in him. Glenn Seaborg, a Nobel laureate and accomplished executive, said of Henry:

> He was a very clear lecturer. He made things sound understandable, perhaps deceptively so. You had the impression after he explained something that you understood it. He was very alert, articulate, almost exuding intelligence.[10]

Likewise, Kenneth F. Pitzer, a fellow chemist and former president of Stanford University, observed,

> Henry was friendly, enthusiastic, and extremely self-confident.[11]

Even Henry admitted that his confidence bordered on excess. Commenting on why he wrote and published so many research papers, he said,

> I suppose it's some kind of egotism. I like to understand what molecules do, but I also like to tell about what I know.[12]

In reality, Henry's confidence wasn't a matter of egotism. He knew that in the partnership between himself and his Father in Heaven he was carrying the light end of the load, by a lot. Yet knowing that he had such a partnership made him confident that, if he did his best, Heaven would make up the rest and things would turn out right.

Happy Muddler

This idea of divine partnership led to what he called his "happy muddler" strategy of scientific research. His confidence in God's help allowed him to face one failure after another without worry, knowing that success would ultimately come. He explained the "happy muddler" philosophy this way:

> As a youngster I expected the profound man to be a careful, reserved man. This is sometimes true, but he also may be a lively, volatile person. Apparently a good mind makes errors like a poorer one, but simply thinks faster, oftener, and longer, so has more good ideas.[13]
>
> There are unsuccessful bright people who are so over-critical that they cannot even stand their own creativeness. Being critical slows down creativity because when you first get an idea, it generally does not come full-blown like Athena from the mind of Jove. If you are horrified because it is not perfect to begin with, you may abandon it. To be a successful scientist, it is often useful to be a happy muddler.[14]

Henry's graduate research students saw this happy muddler strategy at work every day. He literally deluged them with questions to pursue, apparently unconcerned for their likelihood of bearing fruit. In fact, churning out as many ideas as possible—no matter how wacky—was the lynchpin of Henry's research discovery strategy. One of his students described the process of bringing order to the gaggle of new ideas this way:

> Each morning he would come to work bubbling over with new ideas. Most of his ideas were wrong, and it was the responsibility of his graduate students to find the

logical errors or the reasons why the ideas were not work-able. However, there remained 5 to 10 percent of the ideas which were inherently interesting and provided a useful concept of the gross way in which phenomena occurred. Thus each day we had a very practical demonstration of winnowing and sifting of ideas. The ability to recognize which approaches were blind alleys was most important.[15]

Henry applied the "happy muddler" strategy not just to par-ticular research problems, but to his whole career. He explained that to an interviewer who asked him whether, if he had his career to do over again, he would make any changes. Henry replied,

> I wouldn't know how to go back and do things any differently than I did before. That's the pitiful thing, because one thinks that one has learned something. I think the stumbling along that I've described in choosing a profession had a broadening effect that was quite worth the cost. If you do the job well, the very best you can, the opportunities will open up. I never had any very definite goals other than to do whatever job I was doing to the best of my ability. I've always had the feeling that if I did that well, I would somehow muddle through, as the English are famous for saying. The best advice I could give to young people would be just that—do the best you can with what you have about you. The future will take care of itself.[16]

ON THE LOOKOUT FOR SILVER LININGS

Henry actually lived that philosophy of optimism. Even in the tough times, he kept believing that doing his best would be enough. As a result, he saw the silver linings in many clouds even as they hung low overhead. That was true, for instance, of the Indiana auto accident that nearly killed him and his family. Rather than resenting the pain and the lost time, he saw the forced inactivity as an opportunity to polish his ART paper. In hindsight, the weeks of hospital convalescence proved valuable beyond all expectations, given the scrutiny the paper would receive. Even without the ability to foresee such a benefit, though, he had faith at the time that good things could come from his bad situation, as long as he gave it everything he had.

Another critical moment of optimistic perseverance, or happy muddling, came on the day he arrived for his precious year of research in Berlin. He had selected Michael Polanyi as his back-up mentor, knowing that his preferred choice would be traveling overseas when he was scheduled to arrive. As it turned out, Polanyi himself was gone when Henry got to Berlin—on the same overseas expedition as the other man.

Henry had every reason to be incensed at Polanyi's apparent failure to honor a commitment. Worse yet, there was talk of sending him home because his American government grant required supervision of his studies. Henry, though, didn't let any of this bother him. He diplomatically ignored the threats to send him home. And, while patiently waiting for Polanyi to return, he threw himself into an exploration of the institute's facilities. He recalls his philosophical reaction this way:

> So I was really then left without anyone to work with directly, but of course there were libraries and everything else one could use, and one could get acquainted with the Kaiser Wilhelm Institute, so I busied myself with these. [17]

Henry's confident optimism kept him in Berlin when he might otherwise have given up and gone home; that in itself was a victory of character. However, the real achievement wasn't just in staying, but in making the most of his time when there seemed to be nothing to do. In fact, his efforts in the institute library soon paid a huge, unexpected dividend.

When Polanyi finally returned from Princeton, he wanted Henry to start work on a particular research problem he'd been thinking about. However, the necessary laboratory equipment was already tied up by other research teams. Faced with this new roadblock, Henry again stayed upbeat. As he pondered other research topics, he recalled something he had read in the library while waiting for Polanyi. It was a paper on experiments involving simple reaction rates. Henry shared the paper with Dr. Polanyi. Together, they saw a way to apply the paper's findings to more complex reactions. That insight, born of Henry's time alone in the library, was the seed for what later became ART.

NOT TO WORRY

The humble confidence that carried Henry through good times and bad was a blessing not only to him but to those who encountered him. In particular, people faced with doubts about the compatibility of religion and science took courage from his confidence. Some of those doubts about science and religion are still poignant. For instance, in the early 1960s, Henry discussed with a group of Church members the then-revolutionary experiments that were the forerunners of today's attempts to create life in the laboratory. He assured his audience that it would be a long time before anybody stirred up a vat of chemicals and made a man step out. Then he put the crowd's fears in perspective. More than forty years on, his humble observations inspire as much confidence (and laughter) as they did then:

I do not know just how soon or when we will know more. I am sure the Lord is not particularly frightened at his clever children. I am sure that He thinks they are pretty dumb. So people who think He is jealous have quite different ideas of how great He is than I do. I think that all of the things that we think are clever, that we might do, must be so trivial to Him that I am sure that He is not jealous. Do not worry about it. I mean, do not hold off on any bright ideas that you have for fear the Lord will be worried about you overtaking Him. I think it will be safe.

There is another point of view that I like to think of. "How did the Lord make the world?" I think that He is very, very clever. Some people would have you believe that He did it more or less with a shovel—that He just sort of made it in a way that they understand. They will tell you all the details. I doubt that they know.

The Lord is very, very clever, and the smartest things that we can think, I am sure, do not even begin to touch the magnificence of His understanding of this wonderful world that we live in. It is tremendously big. I have emphasized that time and again. I guess I would like to say again how big it is. Most of us know. We have already looked out two billion light years. Two billion light years is a long way. Let us multiply the numbers together again. The velocity of light is 186,000 miles a second. Then if you go that fast for two billion years, you would be surprised how far you have gone. It really is a long way. We know history; we know what happened.[18] We do not know what is happening out at the edges of space now, or even what happened a billion, nine-hundred million years ago. We will know that in the future. But we know what happened there two billion years ago, and things were about like they are now in this neighborhood. So the show has been going on for some time, and I think it will go on about as long as it wants to.

Here is another question that is interesting to me. "How long is the show going to last?" How good a situation do we have? Should we sell our homes because the sun is going to burn out? There is a problem with that idea. The best answer that scientists can give is that the sun is perhaps 5 billion years old, and it ought to be good for twice that length of time. It may get cranky at the end and burn up and act silly, but it ought to go pretty good for that long. So I am going to keep the little place I have in Salt Lake on that basis. I do not think I want to sell it.

How does the sun operate? Well, the best we understand is this: the sun is about half hydrogen, you remember. Four hydrogen atoms go together to make helium, which is a little bit lighter than the four hydrogen atoms from which it is made. The difference in weight appears as the heat of the sun. That is the furnace, then, that we are working with. About half of it is left. It is in good shape, and whoever was smart enough to put the thing together in the first place can add more wood if he wants it to go on longer; so this is under control. I would not let it worry me.

Henry never did worry about things beyond his ken. Especially when it came to God's precise plans for the universe and His children's lives, he had the humility and faith to wait for things to become clearer later. He really was a happy muddler. That philosophy helped him in everything he did. It allowed him to be one of the world's more creative scientists. It also made him

181

an unusually effective advocate of both science and faith. He wasn't driven, as most people are, to declare the game over and either science or religion the victor; rather, he argued for patience as the game played itself out and for faith that both science and revealed religion would ultimately win. Finally, being a happy muddler made him a pleasant friend, especially to the legion of student researchers he invited to muddle along with him.

Henry was able to embrace the happy muddler strategy because it sprang naturally from what he learned as a boy—that he was a child of God and needn't fear any truth. His father, Ed, taught him that, both in word and loving deed. It was easy for such a child to be both confident and humble.

Teach ye diligently and my grace shall
attend you, that you may be instructed more
perfectly in theory, in principle, in doctrine,
in the law of the gospel, in all things that
pertain unto the kingdom of God, that are
expedient for you to understand;
of things both in heaven and in the earth,
and under the earth; things which have
been, things which are, things which must
shortly come to pass; things which are
at home, things which are abroad; the
wars and the perplexities of the nations, and
the judgments which are on the land; and a
knowledge also of countries and of kingdoms.

—DOCTRINE AND COVENANTS 88:78–79

DISCIPLINE AND
CREATIVITY

Henry knew how to "stay on task." He taught his sons the way to recognize when they had worked long enough. He would exhort them, "You've got to learn to work until your ears ring."

Henry worked that hard himself. One of Henry's graduate students recalled the high price of keeping pace with his mentor:

> Professor Eyring's capacity for work was enormous. He worked Saturdays and would have worked Sundays if it were not for his religious convictions. Lectures were held on Saturdays and on holidays. Henry believed in honoring George Washington's birthday by working. I recall having to attend his statistical mechanics lectures on the Friday after Thanksgiving, 1959.[1]

Easily Interrupted

Ironically, though, even in the midst of deep thinking, Henry was easy to interrupt. His second wife, Winifred, testified to that: "I call him many times during the day and he always sounds like it's a great pleasure for him to be disturbed."[2] His students and colleagues at school bore similar testimony. For instance, a needy student who walked into his office without an appointment could get his undivided attention for an hour. Likewise, fun-loving research assistants found it easy to divert him with storytelling and games such as the one where they pitched erasers across the laboratory like horseshoes. The interesting thing is that Henry took the diversion as seriously as he did his science.

An example was the way he responded to calls for help from motorists stranded near Princeton's Textile Research Institute, where he was the director. The institute, located on the shore of a lake, offered beautiful scenery, but the roads were bad. Frequent summer rains turned the dirt roads to mud, and visitors to the institute often got stuck. Upon learning of such an emergency, Henry would have his research assistants drop whatever they were doing to join him in a rescue mission. He enjoyed the challenge of digging a car out of the mud as much as pondering a chemical research problem.

Not all of his colleagues shared his zeal for such hard, relatively menial labor. One of them, a fellow named George Halsey, wanted to quit in the middle of a particularly trying rescue mission. As another student on the scene reported, Henry showed Halsey, the would-be mutineer, little mercy:

> One day a delivery truck from the Pennsylvania Railroad became stuck. The driver was evidently unconcerned. This only meant that he would receive overtime. Henry brought all of his students out to rescue the driver. While the driver was lying on the grass, Henry was

laboring with a shovel attempting to dig out the truck. Halsey saw no sense in this and said, "Henry this is pointless. The driver doesn't care. I am not going to work at this." In anger, Henry picked up the shovel and said, "George, if you don't go home immediately, I am going to hit you with this shovel." Naturally, Halsey left. However, within an hour, he received a call from Eyring who said, "George, let's get back to work on our paper."[3]

This story illustrates Henry's gift for diving deeply into vastly different tasks: he was as interested in the bonding of atoms to one another as in the bonding of a tire to mud. He could attack a problem as though it were the only one in the world and then switch to something else at a moment's notice. That was true even when it was time for sleep: he could be in the midst of a complex calculation and switch it off like the light next to the bed. As he said of such a problem saved for the next morning,

> I wake up in the night, but I don't really lose sleep over it. I don't worry about it. But I have a funny mind that doesn't let go of it.[4]

Somehow, Henry's "funny mind" was both disciplined and also capable of going in new directions on the spur of the moment. His graduate students knew about those spur-of-the-moment ideas only too well. They saw a new bunch every morning; it was their job to identify the few good ideas among the many creative but flawed ones.

Trained to Work Hard

Where did Henry's mix of discipline and creativity come from—and how did he manage to balance it? Knowing the challenges of his youth, the discipline side of the equation isn't hard to understand. Henry learned hard work from his father as they sweated to clear arid land in Arizona. Under those inhospitable conditions, discipline was the price of survival.

He also had great examples of disciplined labor throughout his scientific career, beginning at Berkeley. Speaking of G. N. Lewis's lab there, he said,

> I found it to be a very congenial atmosphere for study and living. I'd grown up on the farm in Arizona. I was used to hard work. I actually finished my PhD degree in two years. This meant working long hours. I typically went to the laboratory about 8:00 in the morning and seldom left before 10:00 P.M. or later. By working holidays and other days, I really had in that two-year period done pretty much the work that would be accomplished in a much longer period. Any able person could, through hard work and dedication, complete a degree following the example set by Lewis and his associates in a shorter period than was usual.[5]

In addition to G. N. Lewis, Henry spoke admiringly of the work ethic of the other great researchers who had mentored him. He credited their personal examples of hard work with the success of their laboratories and the other scientists who worked there:

> I learned that great research laboratories are built around great men. G. N. Lewis, G. E. Gibson,[6] Farrington Daniels, Michael Polanyi and H. S. Taylor were a few whose influence was felt most.
>
> Professor Taylor always did much more than was expected of anyone else. Nothing is so effective as example. That great research laboratories are built about

an inspiring leader is partly due to the leader's own productiveness but even more to the fact that he attracts other productive people.[7]

GETTING TO THE BOTTOM OF THINGS

In Henry's world of cutting-edge research, just as on the farm in Arizona, disciplined effort was a way of life. He knew that he had to get to the bottom of things no matter how much effort it took. He believed, for instance, in never using a mathematical formula without knowing why it worked; before he trusted the formula, he had to derive it mathematically from the more-basic formulas on which it rested. Hugh Taylor paid tribute to Henry's tendency not to accept what was written in a textbook just because it was written in a textbook:

> He tends to discover the facts of science for himself rather than to read what others have found. For Eyring, a scientific fact becomes a fact when he has discovered it and discovered why it is a fact.[8]

Henry's rule of deriving his own equations wasn't a matter of feeling competitive with the scientists who had discovered them in the first place. It was, rather, that he knew the benefits of probing a problem to its most fundamental level. He explained his get-to-the-bottom-of-it philosophy this way:

> I have sometimes been lazy about going to the bottom of some mathematical proposition needed in my research and have spent considerable time figuring out ways of getting along without the information. The inevitable outcome of such a course is that the particular miserable

189

question keeps recurring and recurring until you finally dive in and clean the matter up once and for all. You then wake up surprised to discover yourself on a peak with vast vistas in all directions, and you wonder why you didn't pay the honest price in the first place.[9]

Henry's statement about "paying the honest price" and being rewarded with "vast vistas in all directions" is important. It reveals a connection between discipline and creativity. Through experience, Henry had learned that the hard work required to fathom a complex problem often produces the unanticipated benefit of new, creative insight. In this sense, the apparent paradox of discipline and creativity is an illusion that the truly disciplined mind ultimately sees beyond.

Henry taught that principle to a colleague whom he asked to help with a tough math problem. They had done similar problems before, spending hours making tedious calculations with slide rules. This time, though, Henry proposed tackling a type of problem that was significantly more complex. His young colleague protested, arguing that they wouldn't live long enough to finish. Henry replied, "That's true if we don't learn anything while we are working on the problem."[10] They dove in together, and indeed found a quicker way.

This story demonstrates how the seeming paradox of discipline and creativity is resolved by having the proper definition of "discipline." If by discipline one thinks of doing things by the book, that is indeed a threat to creativity. If, on the other hand, discipline means getting to the bottom of things—understanding the logic behind the book—that kind of discipline is the wellspring of creativity, the starting point for new insight.

CROSSING DISCIPLINARY BOUNDARIES

Henry knew the compatibility of the right kind of discipline and creativity not only by virtue of a lifetime of working to get to the bottom of things, but also because of a unique doctrine of Mormonism. Through Joseph Smith, the Lord challenged the nineteenth-century Saints to seek knowledge "diligently":

> Teach ye diligently and my grace shall attend you, that you may be instructed more perfectly in theory, in principle, in doctrine, in the law of the gospel, in all things that pertain unto the kingdom of God, that are expedient for you to understand.[11]

Significantly, in addition to teaching the need for deep, disciplined study, through Joseph Smith the Lord also advocated an unusually broad search for truth. He spoke of knowledge of all sorts:

> [T]hings both in heaven and in the earth, and under the earth; things which have been, things which are, things which must shortly come to pass; things which are at home, things which are abroad; the wars and the perplexities of the nations, and the judgments which are on the land; and a knowledge also of countries and of kingdoms.[12]

Joseph Smith himself personified insatiable curiosity and thirst for truth in all fields. Though he received no formal education beyond the second grade, he spent his life studying a vast array of subjects: history, astronomy, law, and linguistics, to name just a few. In this respect, the Prophet's approach provided Henry with a vision of discovery contrary to the academic dogma of the mid-twentieth century. The academic world that trained Henry thought of knowledge in terms of distinct domains, or "disciplines." Chemistry, for instance, was one discipline, and physics another. Though both of these sciences deal with the nature of things at the atomic level, they were viewed in Henry's day as different (so much so that chemists initially had a hard time accepting the potential usefulness of quantum mechanics, a theory from physics). In other words, a good, disciplined scientist was expected to keep his thinking within the academic discipline.

Joseph Smith's teachings convinced Henry that his search for truth ought to be broader, that he could learn things in one knowledge domain that would shed light on unanswered questions in another. God, he knew, didn't have His knowledge divided up into "disciplines." Why, Henry reasoned, should he?

Much of Henry's creativity thus flowed from ignoring the traditional, by-the-book kind of discipline. Like Joseph Smith, he sought truth everywhere it could be found. Crossing disciplinary boundaries gave him a creative advantage: approaching things with the perspective of a newcomer, often he could see things that the experts had overlooked. Boundary crossing also gave him the advantage of being in the vanguard of scientists who pioneered the convergence of traditional disciplines. Molecular biology, for example, emerged during Henry's career as a blend of traditional chemistry and biology. With his versatile Absolute Rate Theory and penchant for boundary-crossing, he was well positioned to play in this new field. His contributions included new insights into the dynamics of cancer, a subject that drew his attention when his wife Mildred developed the disease. In the end he couldn't cure her, but he published useful research on cancer and many other medical issues. His milestone five-hundredth paper, for instance, was entitled "The Dynamics of Aging."

Henry also ranged across academic disciplines outside of work, studying history, religion, and philosophy. His sermons on the subject of science and faith reflect broad expertise in those subjects. He also learned two foreign languages (Spanish and German), as well as the "language" of business, which he picked up in frequent consulting engagements.

In addition to all of this formal learning, Henry was an informal student of people. Strangers willing to answer his first ice-breaker question would soon find that they had told him their life's story. Mildred got this treatment (which she called "the third degree") the first time they met: "In ten minutes he had all the fundamental information about me—family, schools, church, etc. I've heard him use it with thousands of people since then." When it came to asking questions of strangers, Henry lived a principle that he often preached: "You can learn something from everyone." As a result, he didn't have to make a formal study of a subject such as the internal combustion engine; all he had to do was take an interest in the fellow pumping his gas.

"DEEP INTEREST"

For Henry, the distinction between discipline and creativity—let alone any kind of paradox involving the two—didn't exist. He was curious about everything and uninhibited by traditional disciplinary boundaries; that was one source of creativity. A second source was his discipline in getting to the bottom of things which likewise led to creative insights. Discipline and creativity worked together, inseparably.

To him, it was all just a matter of what he called "deep interest." He prided himself in getting lost in his thoughts, whether they were thoughts of chemistry or thoughts of a delivery truck mired in mud. In either case, you had to lose yourself in it. He often talked, for instance, about "living" among molecules. He described what it meant to be so mentally engrossed:

> It really means getting acquainted with the molecules as if they were your friends and knowing what their nature is and what they will do. It is like a detective story.[13]

It is interesting to consider what qualifications make for scientific intuition. The familiar story of the lost race horse is instructive. The lost horse was sought for all day by the entire town, unsuccessfully. On the second day the village fool went out and in an hour returned with the horse. In response to inquiry as to his procedure, he explained that the first day he sat and thought what he would do were he a horse. On the second day he went to the point where he himself would have gone. The horse was there. If one wants to become a chemist one in effect becomes a molecule. In the process, he almost thinks of himself as one and he gets to know them as he would know his friends. And if he is to be creative, he walks down the street and mistakes one of his friends for a molecule on occasion. I mean to say that surely the understanding of the molecular world, the physical world, is only to be had at the price of deep interest.[14]

Henry often told a story about Albert Einstein to illustrate this "price of deep interest." They met once in Princeton with representatives of the U.S. military during World War II to discuss explosives. Henry describes the conversation they had on a lunch break:

> After a very pleasant morning in discussion with Professor Einstein, we walked together at noon through

what had been a rose garden but was now planted with a field crop. I plucked a sprig and asked Professor Einstein what it was. He did not know. We walked a little farther and encountered the gardener sitting on his wheelbarrow. His reply to same query was, "It is soybeans." Even for a first-rate mind, what gains attention is not just propinquity[15] but interest. Professor Einstein's mind was too busy with more important things.[16]

Usually when Henry told this story, he ended it with the quip, "Einstein didn't know beans."

Henry applied the test of deep interest when he selected graduate students. He was asked once, "Can you tell whether someone is going to be a good chemist when you meet him?" He replied with his definition of a promising candidate:

There are some factors to look for. One is whether he reacts quickly. You can talk with him and tell whether he sees things and grasps ideas. But he has to be more than bright if he is going to be a good scientist. He also has to be interested. That takes longer to discover, but you can work with him for a little while and find out. Unless he just gets lost in his work and feels that knowing molecules is like knowing people, he probably won't get far. If he is a time server, if he just likes to work eight hours and then go do something else, he won't change the world.[17]

One of Henry's three sons remembers being revealed as such a "time server." In the Eyring household the price of room and board for college-age sons was majoring in physics. Henry felt that physics, even more than chemistry, was the best preparation for employment, because it required a firm grasp of applied mathematics. Henry's second son, Hal, dutifully majored in physics, but not with much enthusiasm. He frequently sought his father's help with homework, as anyone living under the same roof with a math genius would. He later recalled how one day his father challenged him.

> My father was at a blackboard we kept in the basement. Suddenly he stopped. "Hal, we were working this same kind of problem a week ago. You don't seem to understand it any better now than you did then. Haven't you been working on it?"

Hal admitted that he hadn't, and got this response from his father:

> "You don't understand. When you walk down the street, when you're in the shower, when you don't have to be thinking about anything else, isn't this what you think about?"
>
> When I told him no, my father paused. It was really a very tender and poignant moment, because I knew how much he loved me and how much he wanted me to be a scientist. Then he said, 'Hal, I think you'd better get out of physics. You ought to find something that you love so much that when you don't have to think about anything, that's what you think about."[18]

The Costs of Deep Interest

Henry lived this principle of finding a life's work that grabs your attention even when you don't have to think about it. He thought about science almost all of the time, even away from work. Wherever he was—walking to and from the university, relaxing at home after dinner, sitting in church—he could turn scientific ideas over in his mind as though standing before a blackboard. An opened envelope from the day's mail or any other scrap of paper was a potential notepad.

In fact, Henry's ability to be present at home in body while his brain was elsewhere was a great family joke. One oft-told story had him sitting in the living room, pencil and paper in hand, while conversation went on around him and a radio blared in the next room. Everyone assumed that Henry was oblivious to the distractions. Without warning he shouted, "Will you turn up the radio? I can't hear it in here."

Though Henry's three sons found such stories entertaining, his wife Mildred was somewhat less amused. For instance, one year she bought tickets to the symphony. Henry willingly went, but couldn't resist writing equations on the program. Mildred noticed, and that was the Eyrings' first and last year as symphony goers.

Mildred, more than anyone other than Henry himself, bore the cost of his devotion to science. Fortunately, she knew from the beginning what she was getting herself into. The two of them met in 1927 at the University of Wisconsin. Mildred was an assistant professor and head of the women's physical education program at Utah; when she and Henry met she was in Madison for just one year of graduate work. Having seen her at Church gatherings in the fall of 1927, Henry took a while to ask her out; they didn't have their first date until Christmastime. However, once committed to courtship, Henry moved with typical determination and speed. They were married the next August.

Mildred often said that she entered marriage knowing that chemistry would always be Henry's first love. Their brief courtship established that fact. Most of their dating occurred on the lakes around Madison, in a canoe that Henry bought specially for the purpose. It was as close as Henry ever came to conventional romance. However, once the engagement was set, he sold the canoe. (He undoubtedly reasoned that there wouldn't be another summer for them in Madison, and that the smart move was to sell before the end of canoeing season; he was, after all, still paying the mortgage on the farm in Pima.)

In any event, Mildred was nobody's fool; she didn't marry Henry with dreams of romantic canoe rides. Though she couldn't foresee the fame he would achieve, she knew from the beginning how chemistry dominated the thoughts of her husband-to-be. She knew that his career would determine where they lived and how much time they would spend together.

A MAJOR INTERRUPTION

Notwithstanding long hours at work (and distractedness at home), Henry was a devoted husband and father. He and Mildred raised three sons, Edward (Ted), Henry Bennion (Hal), and Harden, each of whom earned doctoral degrees and served faithfully in Church assignments. Particularly at one critical moment, Henry made a significant sacrifice for the sake of Mildred and the boys.

It was 1946, and Henry was at the height of his success at Princeton. Back in Salt Lake City, the University of Utah had just appointed a new president, Ray Olpin. The university granted primarily undergraduate degrees, but President Olpin had a bold growth strategy that included a full graduate program. Unbeknownst to Henry, hiring him was the lynchpin of that strategy. Throughout his life, he loved to tell how Olpin and Mildred successfully conspired to conscript him to Utah:

> Mildred was a native of Utah, and we were anxious that our sons marry in the Mormon faith. I was indeed heavily influenced by my wife's feelings on this decision to

leave. There is an interesting human story if we can take a minute for it. Women are very interesting. They state that men are smarter than they are. When President Olpin of Utah made the offer, my wife, Mildred, left the decision up to me. Deep down I know that she thought the cards were stacked in favor of our leaving for Utah and had decided that I would go. On the other hand, as I observed the change, it meant that I would have to start the Graduate Program at Utah from the very beginning.

I was in a most favorable position at Princeton. My salary was very satisfactory. I had nine good graduate students who performed outstanding scientific work. I therefore decided against the move. Since she said that she wanted me to decide, I wrote my letter of regrets to Utah.

The next day she asked me what I had decided, and I replied that I had decided that we shouldn't go. She was crushed. She said little, but wrote a note to me and asked me not to read it until I got to my laboratory at the university. I can't repeat it verbatim but she implied that she had lived in exile, away from Utah, for nineteen years. She would, of course, continue if it was necessary, but she said that she had never been so disappointed in any decision in her life. Of course I had actually been on the edge of making the move, and her note was decisive. The challenge of returning to Utah and to a new environment academically, building up a program, was exciting. I contacted Professor Hugh Taylor, the Department Head at Princeton, and told him of my change in plans. We were, of course, very good friends, and he implied that he was aware of the possibility of my change of heart. He did point out several obvious factors. Princeton had more money than the University of Utah. I said I understood that, and even the offer of a special professorship did not change my mind. He asked permission to talk to my wife about the situation, which, of course, was more than agreeable to me. This he did, telling her that I was making a sacrifice; that as the years went on, I'd be tremendously disappointed as a person who did research well and administration badly. He implied that I would eventually end up being quite unhappy. Her response was that she'd take that chance.

Actually, it has all turned out tremendously well. I was already established so that I got research money the same as I would have gotten at Princeton. I was able really to go without any disadvantages. We did set up a strong program at the University of Utah. I am sure that many have interpreted my action as one of great personal sacrifice. I think that that would be the wrong picture. I deserve no credit as a person who makes great sacrifice. I always do the kind of things that I like to do.[19]

In fact, there was a sacrifice. Leaving Princeton probably meant closing the door on the Nobel Prize. However, Henry liked telling the story of Mildred's letter and his decision to go to Utah because it symbolized the balance in their marriage: each granted to the other the things that mattered most. Mildred got her sons back to Utah, and Henry got to keep his chemistry. The Nobel Prize was a nonessential.

Moreover, Henry found creative ways to make the most of the situation in Utah. With more graduate students there than he'd had at Princeton, he actually published more research, burnishing his scientific reputation notwithstanding the lack of the Nobel. Also, being in Utah put him in close proximity to the leaders of the Church. Had he stayed in Princeton, they wouldn't have developed such great personal confidence in him. Without the move to Utah, there would have been no Henry, Champion of the Faith.

DEEP DEVOTION

Henry again showed his colors as a husband twenty years later. In 1969, Mildred was dying of cancer. In the years before her passing, he did what he could from the office, collaborating with medical professors at the University of Utah Hospital in seeking a cure. Then, in the latter stages of Mildred's disease, he took up a bedside vigil. The time he spent living at the hospital was more than a symbolic gesture. He knew that he also had the beginnings of cancer. He waited to seek treatment, though, until Mildred was gone.

One of Henry's sons recalled the day of his mother's death and how his father continued to serve her even after her departure:

> The afternoon my mother died, we went to the family home from the hospital. We sat quietly in the darkened living room for a while. Dad excused himself and went to his bedroom. He was gone for a few minutes. When he walked back into the living room, there was a smile on his face. He said that he'd been concerned for Mother. During the time he had gathered her things from her hospital room and thanked the staff for being so kind to her, he thought of her going into the spirit world just minutes after her death. He was afraid she would be lonely if there was no one to meet her.
>
> He had gone to his bedroom to ask his Heavenly Father to have someone greet Mildred, his wife and my mother. He said that he had been told in answer to his prayer that his mother had met his sweetheart. I smiled at

that too. Grandma [Caroline Romney] Eyring was not very tall. I had a clear picture of her rushing through the crowd, her short legs moving rapidly on her mission to meet my mother.[20]

Henry's nephew Edward Kimball enjoyed an exchange with him that captures the essence of his simultaneous devotion to science, family, and faith. Henry replies to Edward's first question with a reference to Edward's father, President Spencer W. Kimball:

Edward: Is there anyone, outside science, you particularly admire?

Henry: I admire your father. He is a remarkable man. He seems to me a selfless person who has found something to serve that is bigger than himself. I think that is always a great thing.

Edward: He works at the Church much as you work at chemistry.

Henry: The same way. He forgets himself in it. He is a great man. I know others. I know many people in the Church for whom I have that kind of feeling, but none that I know that are more devoted than your father and my mother. My mother had that same quality of selflessness.

Edward: What is most important to you?

Henry: I think the gospel and my family and friends. And I enjoy science. I am interested in it like some people get interested in a game, or in making money. It is fun to try and understand how things fit together. Life is to me an exciting game, and the concept of eternal progression which the gospel teaches gives meaning to it all.[21]

*There is a law, irrevocably decreed in
heaven before the foundations of this world,
upon which all blessings are predicated—
and when we obtain any blessing
from God, it is by obedience to that
law upon which it is predicated.*

—DOCTRINE AND COVENANTS 130:20–21

FREEDOM AND

OBEDIENCE

Henry always spoke his mind. He particularly liked to share his opinions about the fundamental doctrines of the Church. That was true even in the presence of the senior Church leaders. He knew many of them intimately, as neighbors and relatives. But there were times when he ought to have been more deferential, connections notwithstanding. That is illustrated in a story of a personal faux pas that he loved to tell. He recounted it once to his nephew, Ed Kimball, the son of Church President Spencer W. Kimball:

> I got a letter from Richard L. Evans[1] to come down to a two o'clock meeting for the new magazines,[2] along with a great many other people. I was visiting your parents and I said, "I am going to a meeting for the magazines." Your father said, "I am going, too, at nine o'clock." I had forgotten in the meantime that mine was for two o'clock and

assumed it was the same meeting. My secretary was not there that morning, and I was a little bit late, so I hurried down to the Church Office Building. When I got there, I went in and said to the receptionist that I was supposed to go to a meeting. He said, "Well, isn't it this afternoon?" I said, "No, it is this morning." And so he took me in and there were four Apostles—your father, Marion Romney, Brother Evans and Brother Hunter—and the magazine editors. I was quite surprised that there was no one else from the Sunday School but I thought, well, they must regard me very highly, and so I just sat down. Your father shook my hand, so did Marion, and everyone—I knew them, you know—so I sat down. The discussion went around and I was willing to offer my views quite freely. However, Brother Evans said, "Your turn will come in a few minutes."

When they got around to me, I told them that the Church magazines never would amount to a damn if they did not get some people with independence in there who had real ideas and would come out and express themselves. If they were going to rehash the old stuff, they would not hold the young people. I gave them quite a lot of fine advice and I damned a little when I wanted to and when I got through, Brother Evans said, "I do not know anyone who characterizes the idea of independence any more than you do; are you applying for the job?" I said, "No, I am not applying for the job, but I think I have given good advice." Everyone was very nice to me.

I did not have any feeling, even after I had been there, that there was anything wrong, and thought that they must have a high opinion of my wisdom. When I got back to my office, my secretary asked, "Where have you been?" I said I had been down to that Church magazine meeting. She said, "That is this afternoon at two o'clock."

What is so funny is not that I made a mistake, but that I was so insensitive as to not realize it. I did not go to the two o'clock meeting. I felt that I had done my work. Brother Evans got up in that meeting and, I am told, said that they had had a meeting in the morning and that very useful advice had been supplied by Brother Eyring. He did not say that I had not been invited.

I am amazed at the graciousness of the brethren in making me feel I belonged, when any one of them might have been annoyed. They are a most urbane group. On my part, there was no holding back; I just tried to help them all I could.[3]

Though Henry laughed about his mistake, he really had crossed the line of decorum. Swearing in meetings with the Brethren was a serious breach of etiquette, even if you were invited to be there. Fortunately, they understood that Henry's unconventional language was a throwback to the days of plowing up mesquite in Pima, when the mules sometimes needed special verbal encouragement.

FAITHFULLY OBEDIENT

The real reason that the Brethren forgave Henry's insubordination is that they knew his heart. No one exceeded Henry in obedience to the direction of Church leaders. Throughout his life, he would drop what he was doing in response to their calls to serve. That was true whether the assignment was to give a sermon on science and religion, to train Sunday School teachers, or to pull weeds on a Church welfare farm.

He didn't simply fulfill these often inconvenient assignments without complaint; he also did so with good humor and discretion. For instance, in his sermons on science and religion it must have been tempting to say that he was speaking with the formal authorization of the Brethren. In fact, President David O. McKay and his counselors in the First Presidency assigned him repeatedly to represent the Church in science-and-religion discussions. Among faithful Church members, it would have added great weight to his arguments to say, "I speak regularly at the request of the First Presidency, and they're supportive of my views." The temptation to cite the Brethren's backing would have been especially great when well-intentioned Church members criticized his scientific views as evidence of weak faith or even heresy.

However, Henry never defended himself or his arguments by invoking the Brethren's authority. Doing so would have been a breach of their confidence; they had privately encouraged him to speak up, with the implicit understanding that he would be speaking only for himself. He discretely stood on his own authority and took his lumps, because that was part of the job. He might cuss to make a point with the Brethren in private, but when they gave him an assignment, he spared no personal expense to carry it out.

THE PLAN OF SALVATION

Henry's combination of always speaking his mind and always following orders surprised many people; it seemed contradictory. However, to him there was no contradiction between individual freedom and obedience to valid authority. In his mind, freedom and obedience weren't at odds. In fact, they were inextricably linked. That is because he believed in something called the doctrine of agency and accountability. He believed, in other words, that man has God-given freedom to choose, but that moral choices have inevitable consequences. Thus, he saw obedience to divine law as the best possible exercise of his freedom to choose.

This belief of Henry's is rooted in our Heavenly Father's plan of salvation for His children. The plan is to allow men and women to choose their actions, whether consistent with eternal principles of welfare and happiness or not. Anticipating mankind's wrong choices and the misery that would inevitably follow, Heavenly Father appointed a Savior, Jesus Christ. The Savior would bear away mankind's misery on conditions of individual repentance and obedience to divine commandments. Those commandments would be communicated to men's otherwise veiled minds by prophets and by personal inspiration.

This plan was presented to all of Heavenly Father's children before this world began. A persuasive leader named Lucifer proposed an alternate approach. Lucifer argued that the misery inherent in Heavenly Father's plan could—and should—be avoided by constraining individual choice. In the end, Lucifer's proposal was rejected by the majority, who recognized that choice—or "agency"—is essential to learning and growth and is worth preserving even at the risk of misery. Support for Heavenly Father's plan of agency and accountability undoubtedly hinged on the Savior's offer of redemption: men would be held accountable for wrong choices, but He would stand ready to redeem them, on condition of obedience. Those who followed the Savior on earth would be rewarded with a return to the presence of the Father and with eternal progression.

In many of his sermons on science and religion, Henry elaborated on this plan by which the world operates, explaining why freedom of choice and obedience are both essential to progress and happiness:

We believe that as intelligences we have always existed. In a pre-existent state we became the spirit children of our Father in Heaven. When the Council in Heaven was held,[4] we elected to accept earth life as a period of growth and development and probation. We were born into the world having our free agency; i.e., with the right to choose to do either good or evil.

Death is not the end but only brings a transfer of our activities, and in due course our spirits will be clothed with a resurrected body. Our position in the hereafter will depend on our conduct here, and we can continue to grow more perfect in goodness, wisdom and knowledge throughout the eternities.

Earth life has its great significance as the bridge between these two eternities. In undertaking any journey, the destination we reach depends on the road we take, how well we make our plans and how vigorously we carry through.

The Gospel is the Lord's plan for the journey. Because we have our free agency, we can accept or reject it. Finally, even if we accept the Gospel plan, we can carry through in a way that will get us into the celestial kingdom[5] or we can reap an eternity of vain regrets for what might have been.[6]

DIVINE RESTRAINT

Henry often talked about the fateful choice between agency and compulsion presented to us before we came to this earth. He was particularly impressed that an all-powerful God would offer men complete freedom, knowing in advance that they would abuse it:

In the great council in the premortal life, a tremendous decision was made that man was to have his free agency. This brings with it many interesting problems, since the Lord's children often make unwise decisions with tragic results. War and catastrophe are taken by some people to be evidence against the existence of God, or at least His unconcern for the evils that overtake man. I think this should be thought of in a completely different light.

Lucifer promised to bring salvation to every soul, whether the person to be saved deserved it or not. Dictators have been operating in the same way from time immemorial. Never has there been a more concerted effort to take away free agency than in the modern communistic world, where about one percent of the population rules through force and terror. God's non-intervention in human affairs is not a sign of His absence or His disinterest. Rather, it exemplifies one of His greatest gifts—free agency, which enables us to work out our individual salvation. If Lucifer were ruling the world, no one could doubt his presence.[7]

Sometimes well-meaning people mistakenly describe dictators as "wanting to play God." Nothing could be further from the truth. Instead, insofar as dictators exercise unrighteous dominion, they are anti-Christ.

Latter-day Saints are cautioned with these words:

" . . . When we undertake to cover our sins, or to gratify our pride, our vain ambition, or to exercise control or dominion or compulsion upon the souls of the children of men, in any degree of unrighteousness, behold, the heavens withdraw themselves."[8]

A RESPECTER OF FREEDOM

Henry cherished individual freedom, both his own and others'. He knew that allowing freedom of choice is the best way to foster learning. He often quoted the Prophet Joseph Smith, who, when asked how he managed to govern the Saints in Nauvoo so well, answered, "I teach them correct principles and they govern themselves."[9]

Henry also appreciated the trust and respect for freedom inherent in his father's counsel before he went off to the University of Arizona. In a nutshell, Ed's challenge to his eighteen-year-old son was to seek the truth and live it. Later in life Henry commented on the wisdom of this minimalist counsel, which gave guidance without prescribing conduct:

> My father's advice left much maneuvering space. A ship in port may snap if tied up too tightly, but never gets far out of line riding at the end of a good anchor which leaves it free to maneuver. A too narrow dogmatism has always, and will always, defeat itself.[10]

Henry saw respect for individual freedom as essential not only to raising faithful children but also to assuring the advance of science. In his 1948 nationwide *Church of the Air* address, he said:

> The Christian doctrine of the worth of the individual has largely made possible the freedom under which science has flourished. It is a matter of great concern to men of science that liberty over the earth is being restricted, and as liberty becomes restricted, untrammeled research will narrow. I am grateful that I have lived in a time when a man could do largely as he chose to do and in a land where he could map out his way and follow it. I consider

it one of the greatest blessings that has come from our Christian civilization, and I believe that it has made us a great people.[11]

While cherishing his own freedom, Henry respected the freedom of others, even if it meant deferring to them in some things. He was particularly famous for his laissez-faire style of academic administration. Rather than trying to direct the affairs of the graduate school at the University of Utah, he let those beneath him run the show. He described the philosophy behind his trusting approach this way:

> There are two philosophies of administration. In one as much power as is appropriately used is left with departments for their decision. In the other rules and regulations are handed from above. We worked happily and efficiently under the first system. I am not aware of any serious division arising at any time in the twenty years I served as dean. I remember twice when President Olpin[12] was consulted on the conduct of the graduate school. I asked him how he thought things were going in the graduate school. He said he had more interesting things to think about. I interpreted that as a vote of confidence. On another occasion President Olpin asked if I would like an assistant dean to help with administration. I said no but he needn't bother tell me if a replacement seemed necessary, since I would find out in a few days anyway. He smiled. The people I worked directly with and the administration made my twenty years as dean exceptionally pleasant, and much was accomplished.[13]

Henry's administrative strategy was to delegate many operating responsibilities to department chairs, fellow academics who reported to him. Even greater delegation of authority went to his secretaries. Henry called them the "real deans" of the graduate school. He enjoyed telling several stories about the power that his secretaries wielded. One was of how his first secretary, Priscilla Winslow, set the administrative style for the graduate school. Having come from Princeton, Henry was inclined to implement procedures at Utah similar to Princeton's. However, Ms. Winslow had been an administrative secretary at Harvard. Consequently, Henry would say, "The graduate school turned out to be like Harvard's instead of Princeton's."[14]

In another oft-told story, the university's finance office returned a check to his office for having an incorrect signature. The university required financial documents to be signed by deans only. However, because of Henry's frequent work-related travel (he was away from campus an average of one day in four), he violated this rule as a matter of habit, delegating the signing of checks to his secretary. The problem in this case was that he had actually signed a check himself, and the finance office didn't recognize his signature. He quickly got his secretary's signature, and the finance people were satisfied.

Henry relied so heavily on his secretaries that he didn't even trust himself to choose their successors. When one of his secretaries was ready to retire, her final duty was to select the next "real dean" of the graduate school.

"Obedience Is the Price of Freedom"

Notwithstanding his penchant for delegation, Henry took his own administrative responsibilities seriously, as much so as his research. When he wasn't on the road he faithfully attended administrative committee meetings. The administrative procedures of the graduate school may have been Priscilla Winslow's, but the strategy was Henry's. He drew the people and the money, and he set the standards of effort, that lifted the school to national prominence.

For Henry, it was a matter of principle to attend meetings and perform other duties that he easily could have shirked. "Obedience," he would often say, "is the price of freedom." As an illustration, he claimed that his reason for teaching more than a full load of classes year after year was that it freed him from worrying about the minimum teaching requirement. Exceeding the minimum, he reasoned, left him worry-free and able to think about other things.

Henry's belief in obedience was rooted in the same principle of agency that inspired his love for freedom. He saw obedience as the source of freedom:

> Obedience to Gospel principles can make a man master of himself, and thus of his own destiny; there is no greater freedom than that. Nothing of importance is ever accomplished by man except by obedience to correct principles. Obedience is the price of freedom.[15]

As with so many deeply held beliefs, Henry cited Joseph Smith for showing this connection between obedience and freedom:

> I want to recall a remark which the Prophet Joseph Smith made and which people sometimes forget: every blessing you get in this life is predicated on some law.[16] If you want some particular blessing, the Lord has arranged this very exact world so that you get the blessing only if you work for it.[17]

Henry taught that the freedom-obedience connection applies not only in the lives of individuals, but also to the fate of nations:

There is literally no end to scientific truths and devices. But, unfortunately, possessing them does not solve our problems. We dare not slacken our pace until a world order is somehow achieved which recognizes and preserves the rights of the individual soul. The world is truly girding for Armageddon. Only if man recognizes the dilemma and matures spiritually can we avert disaster. This has long been foretold in the scriptures. Now even the dull must see it.

But this is no time for despair. It is our great opportunity. If we and enough others continue unfalteringly in search of truth in all fields and live as the Gospel teaches, threatening as the future seems, we will ride out the storm. However, nothing but our best is good enough.

As suggested in these passages, Henry was a patriot, grateful for the blessings of the rule of law in the United States of America. His deep commitment to the law of the land stemmed in large part from having seen the breakdown of law in Mexico. Being forced to flee his home and all he owned, he said,

I learned the advantages of a stable government. The very basis of civilization is rule by law. When men start picking and choosing which law they will nullify, the choice of anarchy is just around the corner. Every thinking person must honor and sustain the law. In this great country an orderly procedure is provided for changing an unpopular law. To proceed any other way is to court national disaster.[18]

Obedience at Home

Henry got help practicing the principle of obedience at home. In his youth, Caroline and Ed set the example and required obedience of their children. Later in life, Henry's marital companions helped him in the same way. He often gave credit to Mildred and Winifred for keeping him in line with Church doctrine. Mildred, for instance, held the line on tithing:

> By my wife, Mildred Bennion Eyring, our three sons and I have been schooled in uncompromising integrity— "Tithing is one-tenth." One doesn't forget easily testimony lived in the home.[19]

Mildred's schooling of Henry in obedience wasn't limited to formal Church commandments. She was also a strict taskmaster when it came to his eating habits. He once joked with a group of physical education students about how Mildred taught him obedience to laws of dietary health:

> I don't know anything that will pay quite the dividends as being sensible about looking after your body. I think that I was very fortunate in this respect. I married a woman who happened to be in charge of physical education here at the University of Utah when I married her. I met her at the University of Wisconsin, where I had gone as a young instructor and she had gone for a year's leave of absence. She has very many qualities, and I would like to tell you one.
>
> When we were married, I'd always thought I needed to eat two eggs. I grew up on the farm and worked hard, and I thought that I ought to have at least two eggs, and she just quietly cut it down to one, and I thought that it

was an indication that she didn't love me that I'd get treated that way. I waited a little while and pointed it out to her. I said that it looked like a degree of harshness that was hardly called for, but she was adamant, and by that time my stomach had shrunk so that one egg is all I want now. I can't get back to the two; in fact, I don't eat any.

The other thing that I found out with this partner of mine, she can say the most caustic things when I get over-weight, which I am prone to do, and it's really been a great help. I think that one lives longer, and I think all of us agree, if we just control our weight. There isn't any single thing that will make us more acceptable in appearance and make our health better than just not overeating. I attribute at least such health as I have, and I think I have been very fortunate, to having gotten married to this very svelte woman who has got a sharp tongue, one that I respond to. I can stand quite a bit of abuse and still eat heavily, but there's a degree that you can't go beyond, and I recommend to any of you that are not married to pick a partner like that who will hold up a mirror to you whenever you start getting overweight. I believe that that is as important a thing as one can have happen to them.[20]

Respect for Church Authority

Henry was equally good at submitting to the direction of Church leaders. As in the case of Mildred's admonishment, he welcomed priesthood counsel, even from leaders whose imperfections he knew firsthand. He enjoyed the benefit of growing up in a home where Church leaders were honored, not just for their positions but as individuals. "I never heard a criticism of the Church in our household in my life," he said.[21] In fact, early experience taught him a deep reverence for priesthood leadership. In particular, he saw the Church in action as the Saints were driven from Mexico and never forgot the courageous, noble conduct of its leaders:

> When the civil government disappeared, the void was filled by our Stake President, Junius Romney, and our bishop, Joseph C. Bentley. The orderly evacuation under the direction of Church authorities of almost 5,000 colonists in July, 1912 followed a pattern in many ways reminiscent of Nauvoo and reminded me that Church concern extends to all the problems of its members. These early experiences left no doubt in my mind of the efficacy of the Church in action. It was indeed a way of life and was already part of me.[22]

Henry remembered one particular example of his Uncle Junius's courage and forbearance, of his leading gently even when the situation seemed to call for dictating to the colonists. The setting was another meeting with the rebel general Salazar, one just before that terrifying night when Junius woke the general to negotiate with him:

> Uncle Junius Romney was summoned to Casas Grandes, where Salazar was headquartered. There was a long talk back and forth, but Salazar told Uncle Junius that if he didn't issue an order that the Saints should turn in their arms, he was going to take them by force. He said, "You're not going to leave here until you give that order." President Romney said, "I can't give that order. We don't work that way. I can tell them what you say, but I can't tell them what to do."[23]

After a long standoff, Salazar finally relented. He sent Junius Romney, under guard, to hold a council with his fellow Saints. As mentioned earlier, by counseling together they came up with the plan to give the rebels their old guns, while secretly retaining the new ones. In hindsight, President Romney's refusal to make an "executive decision" on the spot led to a better strategy for protecting the Saints; in council together, they came up with a plan that President Romney might not have conceived on his own, under the pressure of Salazar's gaze. However, telling Salazar that he couldn't command the colonists was more than a mere negotiating tactic. It was really true: like Joseph Smith, Romney knew he had the authority to counsel, but not to command.

Obedience to Imperfect Leaders

Henry spoke often of his confidence in the leaders of the Church. For instance, to anyone who asked why he sometimes dozed in Sabbath meetings, he would answer: "It's a sign that I know the Church is in good hands."

In fact, Henry knew enough Church leaders personally to see their human frailties and imperfections. Far more than most Church members, he was in a position to critique the character and actions of the senior leadership. However, his confidence in them was firm. He saw their weaknesses, but he wasn't bothered. He knew he could trust his ecclesiastical leaders to lead with wisdom and love. He knew that because the Lord Himself had so entrusted them. As he said,

> At best, men are faltering and imperfect. The Savior stands alone as the perfect example. The Gospel is indeed the plan which the Creator of the universe has devised to guide His children and bring them back to Him. Through the ages, He has chosen from among His worthy sons

prophets to act as guides to His children. Today, The Church of Jesus Christ of Latter-day Saints is presided over by good and wise men who instruct and counsel those who have the wisdom to listen.[24]

Henry was often approached by Church members who assumed that, because he had taken scientific stands contrary to those of some leaders, he might be an ally in criticizing them. These would-be conspirators were always disappointed—or, if they were open to being taught, they had their views changed. Henry recalled one such episode:

> After a talk, which covered various aspects of man in the cosmos, a young man in the audience stood up and said, "Well, Dr. Eyring, they tell me that what you do is put your religion in one compartment and your science in another. Isn't that inconvenient? For instance, I want to propound a question to you. Joseph Smith is reported to have said that there are people living on the moon." He continued, "Now, Dr. Eyring, we know there is no oxygen on the moon, so that couldn't possibly be true. What do you say to this question?"
>
> I answered about as follows: "I especially appreciate being asked that question, because it is easy to answer, and I like easy questions better than hard ones. As a Latter-day Saint, like any other honest man, I am obliged to accept only the truth. I simply have to investigate whether men live on the moon. I am reasonably certain they don't, but anyway, we'll know by direct exploration.[25] If we don't find them there, they don't live there. As a Latter-day Saint my problem is as simple as that.
>
> "I want to add a few more thoughts. Many times men of importance have statements attributed to them they

never made. I think that if J. Golden Kimball[26] said all of the things he is credited with saying, he would have had to talk even more than he did, and he did very well.

"Now, what about the Prophet Joseph Smith? I don't know whether he said men live on the moon or not. But whether he did troubles me not in the least. A prophet is wonderful because he sometimes speaks for the Lord. This occurs on certain occasions when the Lord wills it. On other occasions, he speaks for himself, and one of the wonderful doctrines of this Church is that we don't believe in the infallibility of any mortal. If in his speculations the Prophet thought there were people on the moon, this has no effect on my belief that on other occasions, when the Lord willed it, he spoke the ideas that the Lord inspired him to say. It is for these moments of penetrating insight that I honor and follow him."[27]

I have no objection to Joseph Smith's making any number of mistakes. Of course he did, and I like it. I like to see some of the brethren make mistakes, because then I think that the Lord can use me, too.[28]

Perhaps I can say it another way. The Church would have been perfect if the Lord had not let the people into it. That is where the mistake seems to have been made, but we understand this too. The Church is part of his wonderful plan to work with you and with me.[29]

THE TRAP OF CRITICISM

As these statements make clear, Henry was eager to forgive even Church leaders their imperfections; it gave him hope that Heaven would forgive his sins as well. He also saw the danger of becoming distracted with others' imperfections when he still had many flaws of his own to work on. He offered this warning about criticizing the weaknesses of others:

> When you start looking around and deciding whether the Church is true because one of the brethren does not do quite what you think he should, I can tell you a better place to look. See what you yourself are like. Maybe that is why you think the gospel is not true. If I can keep Henry Eyring doing what he ought to do, I am sure the Gospel will seem wonderful.[30]

Henry stayed focused on "doing what he ought to do," and the gospel did indeed seem wonderful. He always followed the counsel of his Church leaders and always benefited from it. He felt especially blessed by accepting assignments from Church leaders to serve. He encouraged others to be similarly obedient in accepting Church callings:

> The faithful Latter-day Saint who has been taught to accept the calls that come to him through proper channels and who discharges these responsibilities faithfully has access to the inner "peace of God, which surpasseth all understanding." There is no greater gift than this.[31]

Henry enjoyed the peace of God, thanks in part to his mastery of the apparent paradox of freedom and obedience. Obeying freed him from worry.

"SILKEN THREADS"

Obeying also brought another blessing: it gave him deep insight into the nature of his Heavenly Father. In particular, Henry understood the logic behind the seeming paradox of an all-powerful God who honors faltering mankind's agency. It is hard to imagine a more enlightening explanation of God's paradoxical treatment of His children than the one Henry offered in these lines:

> In the great Council in Heaven, already referred to, two plans were offered—one whereby the minds of men would be compelled to accept the truth. There would be no choice. Man would make no error. The other plan was set forth by God. In His plan, man would have his free agency. He could decide between the Church of God and all other ways operating in the world.
>
> God rules from heaven. He does it with such silken threads that some think he has lost the reins. Some people do not even know that He exists. Others wonder whether He exists. I have often thought that a condition like this could never have come about if a dictator such as Hitler or Stalin were ruling.
>
> God is so gentle, so dedicated to the principle that men should be taught correct principles and then govern themselves—that they should take responsibility for their own mistakes—that His children can actually question whether He exists. To me, that in itself is one of the testimonies that He exists. I cannot think of anything which more wonderfully typifies His mercy, His kindness, His consideration for us, His concern for us, than that He does it all with bonds that are like the strongest steel but are so gentle that you cannot see them.[32]

*Whatever principle of intelligence
we attain unto in this life, it will rise
with us in the resurrection.
And if a person gains more knowledge
and intelligence in this life through
his diligence and obedience than another,
he will have so much the advantage
in the world to come.*

—DOCTRINE AND COVENANTS 130:18–19

12

REASONING,
MORE THAN
REASONS

Some paradoxes take a this-*and*-that form; for instance, Humility *and* Confidence, Freedom *and* Obedience. The paradox lies in accepting two apparently contradictory ideas. Henry's mastery of such this-*and*-that paradoxes made him seem unusually broad-minded, very flexible in his thinking.

However, on some matters he could appear inexplicably narrow-minded and inflexible. In those cases, he exhibited paradoxical thinking of a different sort. He could take two superficially similar ideas and say, "This, *but not* that." A prime example was his view of the limits to logic. He was among the most logical thinkers ever; he could posit a theory for almost anything. However, there were some matters that he was simply unwilling to speculate about.

In this respect, he would often disappoint scientifically

minded people. Most of them, for instance, loved his willingness to explore the mechanisms of organic evolution. But they were disappointed if they expected him to declare evolution to be the definitive means by which God prepared Adam's body to receive a spirit. He enthusiastically studied the possibilities and even the probabilities of evolution. He even published a paper saying that, given the chemistry involved, it would have taken about one billion years for the first life to form from nonliving elements. Yet, notwithstanding this scientifically rigorous speculation, in the end he wouldn't take a stand on how God did it. One of Henry's scientific colleagues, a member of the Church, wrote once to thank him for his unequivocally equivocal position on evolution:

> When I was in Salt Lake one time, I was discussing some problems of early man with you in your office. I then asked: "How do you believe it was?" You replied, "I believe whichever way it turns out to have actually been."[1]

Insoluble Problems

Withholding final judgment of evolution was just one example of Henry's paradoxical love of *reasoning,* which came without a need to know all of the *reasons* behind things. In fact, he would demonstrate to anyone who asked that certain questions are unanswerable by the human mind. He often made the point with unsolvable math problems:

> If you insist on knowing pi^2 exactly, you are asking for the impossible, since the series never ends. Thus you can know the answer to as many places as you please and therefore to any desired degree of accuracy, but the question, "what is the exact value?" would take an eternity to answer. The statement that we can never know everything

about the Gospel is thus a mathematical certainty, since here is one truth which has no answer in finite terms. There is an endless number of such questions without an exact answer. "What is the value of the square root of 3?" is another example. Still another is the question, "How much exactly will you ultimately know?" Some questions take literally forever to answer. We recognize an essential truth from these simple examples in mathematics. By diligent study—in the example above by using a computer—we can get a better and better idea of the true picture. But to ask for the *whole* picture is meaningless—we can't get it in a finite time.[3]

Unlike Henry, most people dislike the unknown. We view reasoning as the painful price of getting answers to our questions. Having figured something out, we are glad for the certainty and are happy to stop the search. In fact, distaste for the unknown and the hard work of reasoning may tempt us to prefer a hasty, even faulty answer to having none at all.

Henry didn't have that problem. He loved reasoning; new riddles were like unopened birthday gifts. He also hated sloppy logic. He would rather muddle through a problem to a solid conclusion than cut quickly to a weak one. If a solid answer couldn't be obtained with the information available, he was happy to wait until more data could be had. He was a passionate thinker who didn't worry about unanswerable questions.

AN ETERNITY OF LEARNING

This seeming contradiction was, like so many others, rooted in Henry's faith. He recognized that the inability to answer many complex questions is a natural consequence of being a child of an omniscient God. He also believed, though, in eternal progression. He had faith that, being a son of his Heavenly Father, the uncertainty was only temporary and no reason to give up hope. He knew that understanding would inevitably come as a consequence of never-ending learning:

> Things which must be trivially simple to the Lord are often inscrutable mysteries to us. This provides an interesting perspective on eternal progression. There is apparently no end to learning and no end of things to learn.[4]

The thought of "no end of things to learn" excited Henry. Rather than being discouraged by the prospect of an eternity of problem solving, he found it rejuvenating:

> One never really grows old as long as there are higher peaks still to be climbed. If each day brings a new challenge with an opportunity to pit one's best efforts against a hostile environment, life remains as interesting and stirring at sixty as at twenty. "Ah, but a man's reach should exceed his grasp, Or what's a heaven for?"[5]

SPIRITUAL EXPERIMENTATION—"TRY THE THING"

When it came to reasoning, Henry's reach was boundless. That was true of questions of science as well as those of religious doctrine. Even in matters where faith had given him a sure testimony, he was eager to experiment and to confirm his faith via logic. His father, Ed, set the precedent for that with his precollege counsel. In one of many retellings of the story of their conversation, Henry quoted Ed this way:

> This religion that we have is only truth. It is not anything else. So don't get nervous. Don't get worried about anything that you learn. Go and study geology and biology and organic evolution and anthropology and

everything else that you like. The more the merrier. If there is anything I have told you that will not stand up, it is not the gospel. We do not want it anyway. Let it go. The truth is all that we are standing for.

The Prophet Joseph Smith really had revelations from the Lord. The Lord spoke to him. He gave us this great religion. Every Mormon and every Gentile can see that, by golly, the thing works. And that was the test the Savior gave for it.

Try the thing; see if it works. If you can't see it that way, then you probably can't see it anyway. It really does work.[6]

Recalling this story on another occasion, Henry said, "I was taught early that the Gospel, being true, is priceless, but also that because it is true it is immensely sturdy—not fragile."[7]

The principle of spiritual experimentation to which Ed referred—and on which Henry continually relied—is found in the New Testament. The Apostle John recorded an exchange between the Savior and a group He encountered in the temple at Jerusalem. Hearing Jesus teach powerful doctrine, "*the Jews marvelled, saying, How knoweth this man letters, having never learned? Jesus answered them, and said, My doctrine is not mine, but his that sent me. If any man will do his will, he shall know of the doctrine, whether it be of God, or whether I speak of myself.*"[8]

Henry recognized the Savior's challenge to test His doctrine as an application of the scientific method. A scientist discovers the laws by which the world operates by formulating a hypothesis. The scientist then conducts experiments to see whether the hypothesis holds up; if so, the hypothesis is taken as correct.

Citing the Savior, Henry challenged would-be believers to

apply the same method of testing to religion that he did to science:

> The gospel commits us only to the truth. The same pragmatic tests that apply in science apply to religion. Try it. Does it work?[9]

> To people who ask, "Oh, as a scientist, how can you be a devout Latter-day Saint?" I say, "Nonsense. My religion is on the same basis as my science. It works. It really makes people better. It is an organization that is tremendous. Everybody is the Church. You have a part in it; I have a part in it. You could not have more unlikely material than some of us, and yet the Lord chooses to work with us and try to make something of us. You can't do better than that."[10]

Henry spent his lifetime experimenting according to the Savior's direction in John. He lived the principles of the gospel, and he enjoyed the fruits thereof—not only personal peace and happiness, but also personal conviction that the gospel must be true because "it works."

EXAMINING THE CREATOR'S HANDIWORK

Having proven the gospel by living it, Henry naturally sought to explain *why* it worked. That was the nature of the scientist in him. He was especially interested in seeing what the physical world might teach him about his relationship with his Heavenly Father. As he explained:

> For one who feels compelled, as I do, to accept the existence of the Master Architect, it is important to

examine His handiwork for the light it throws on Him and on His program for His children.[11]

Henry's scientific approach to learning about his Heavenly Father served him well, especially when it came to studying the physical realm. As he observed the workings of the universe, he saw signs of God's power and love for mankind everywhere, and that buttressed his faith and fueled his enthusiasm to learn more. As he said,

> There is probably no better way to deepen faith in the Gospel than to try to think out how this magnificently complicated world came about. Only a profound scholar of the physical sciences is able to calculate the utter improbability of any universe arising by chance. There is, however, a deep meaning running through all that touches our lives. The gospel is to be found not only in the scriptures but in every detail of the world, if we can but read it.[12]

Henry would never have applied the label "profound scholar of the physical sciences" to himself. However, thanks to his background in reaction theory (ART), he could in fact show the infinitesimally small probability of a universe such as ours arising without divine intervention. He did so this way:

> An interesting calculation illustrates the complete improbability of a hot sun arising by chance. We suppose that in order again to become hot the sun must accumulate an amount of heat equal to that it gives off in its lifetime. This must be accumulated from its surroundings, which we shall assume in the heat death[13] drop to a temperature of 700 degrees Centigrade. Then, using the

straightforward theory of chemical reaction, we find that the length of time in years equal to at least one with a hundred thousand, billion, billion, billion, billion, billion zeroes must elapse before a hot sun has a "fifty-fifty" probability of occurring again by chance. This is almost no chance at all! Surely our hot sun did not arise by such a chance fluctuation. The Creator accomplishes His purposes by much more subtle means.[14]

Every piece of information of this kind reveals new facets of the cosmic design and increases our awe of the Supreme Intelligence operating through the universal reign of law.[15]

"You Do Not Ever Prove Anything"

Of course, Henry recognized that mathematical calculations and scientific observations didn't prove anything about religion. However, he knew that the same thing is true in science. As he explained, in science—just as in religion—the most compelling "proofs" ultimately rest on basic assumptions, or postulates, that cannot be proven beyond doubt:

Actually, you do not ever prove anything that makes a difference in science or religion. You set up some basic postulates from your experience or your experiments and then from that you start making deductions, but everything that matters is based upon things you accept as true.

When a man says he will believe in religion if you prove it, it is like asking you to prove there are electrons. Proof depends upon your premises. In Euclidian geometry, you learn that three angles of a triangle total 180 degrees and that two parallel lines never meet; the whole argument proceeds very logically. But there are other kinds of geometry. In elliptical geometry, parallel lines do meet. If you go up to the North Pole and draw two parallels of longitude, they will hit the equatorial plane at right angles. That makes 180 degrees, plus the angle at the pole. And the lines are perfectly parallel at the equator, and the fellow that does not know they are curving will find that two parallel lines meet. It is perfectly good geometry. It is two dimensional on the surface, but it is curving in a third dimension. Analogously, we do not know whether or not this three dimensional space we live in is curving in a fourth dimension. You can build your logic perfectly, but whether your postulates apply to the world you live in is something you have to get out of either experiment or experience.

Every proof in science depends on the postulates one accepts. The same is true of religion. The certitude one has about the existence of God ultimately comes from personal experience, the experience of others, or logical deductions from the postulates one accepts. People sometimes get the idea that science and religion are different, but they are not different at all. There is nothing in science that does not hinge on some primitive constructs you take for granted. What is an electron? I can tell you some things about the electron we have learned from experiment, and if you accept these things, you will be able to make predictions. But ultimately you will always get back to postulates.

I am certain in my own mind of the truthfulness of the gospel, but I can only communicate that assurance to you if you accept my postulates.[16]

RELIGIOUS POSTULATES AND LOGIC CHAINS

Henry's fundamental religious postulate was the existence of God. He was sure that our remarkably ordered universe did not arise by chance; everything from the vastness of space to the precision of atomic vibrations convinced him of that. He knew that there had to be a Supreme Intelligence. From that foundational postulate he could spin out compelling logical chains. Among them was this one about the gospel, or God's plan of salvation for His children:

> The more I try to unravel the mysteries of the world in which we live, the more I come to the conception of a single overruling power—God.
>
> The conception of a God ruling the universe and concerned with how it works is impossible for me without the corollary that He should be interested in man, the most remarkable phenomenon in the world. Being interested in man, it is natural that He would provide a plan for man's development and welfare. This plan is the Gospel of Jesus Christ.[17]

A similar chain of deductive reasoning supported Henry's belief in scripture and prophecy as key elements of the plan of salvation:

> Man has perfected the art of communication to the point where he can direct a satellite to photograph Mars and later have it relay the picture back to earth. There seems to be virtually no limit to man's possibilities of communication of space exploration. Considering such human achievements, it is reasonable to suppose that the only limitations God places on His communications with

man are those which are necessary to best carry out His divine purposes. Accordingly, I am led to accept revealed religion as something which is expected.

Since the Bible gives the best available account of God's dealings with man in ancient times, I find it natural to accept it as the prophetic record of these events. But since the Bible has passed through human hands, it is inevitable that it should reflect human fallibility as well as divine inspiration. It should be accepted for what it is—a divine message of inspiration and hope to struggling humanity. It outlines the divine plan by which man may return to his immortal state where he may grow endlessly in wisdom and understanding of the mysteries that are at present veiled to him. Since the need for prophetic guidance still exists, I find it natural to believe it is still present in the contemporary world, and so I accept as modern scripture the prophetic writings of today. All prophetic insights, recorded and spoken, give the believer consolation as well as encouragement to live the good life that eventually will be weighed in the balance at final judgment.[18]

Henry's logical analyses also confirmed his faith in the afterlife and in the ultimate perfectibility of man:

To accept the idea that the human personality ends with death is to accept life as a futile, meaningless gesture. God would be less compassionate than many good men if life ended at the grave. Broken, uncompleted lives are the best possible reason for a hereafter in which the scales of justice are balanced by a just God. To believe otherwise is to attribute to God a lack of sensitivity that we find regularly in good men. Such a supposition is incredible to me.[19]

The purpose of living is to grow in wisdom and goodness, and this growth is possible only because God gives man freedom to choose. This freedom necessarily gives man the opportunity to make wrong choices as well as right ones. Our opportunity to grow would cease if freedom of choice were withheld. However, the banishing of error while still preserving human freedom to choose will be the inevitable consequence of an increase in understanding and in goodwill. It is reasonable, therefore, to look forward to a free society in which sin will have all but disappeared.[20]

Bold Reasoning

Henry didn't stop at logical analysis of such fundamental doctrines as the existence of God or His communicating through prophets and scripture. His reasoning sometimes took him to the limits of imagination (and sometimes to the limits of official Church doctrine). For instance, based on a noted astronomer's estimate that the universe contains 100 million planets on which life might exist, Henry reasoned,

> It is accordingly natural to conclude that the universe is flooded with intelligent beings and, presumably, always has been. Any unfolding of intelligences that may eventuate on this earth only repeats what has happened previously elsewhere.[21]

To the controversial question, "Are we going to create life?" he responded with this reasoning:

> You know, it would be a pity if you could prove that it could not be done. It would really be downright

embarrassing, because *I* am already here. It must have been done. Life has been created and I suspect, therefore, that it can be done again. It is just a matter of knowing how. Some people think that they would apostatize if somebody came out with a report that life was created— that somehow it would violate some principle in the gospel. I wish that any of you who feel that way would show me which one it is. We believe that the Lord did create life. We believe that we are His children. We believe that if we learn enough, someday we might be creative, too. However, do not worry about it. Nobody has gotten a tub yet and mixed in some chemicals and had a man step out of it. That is not here yet.[22]

Henry was even bold enough to reason about sacred processes. One of those was the translation by Joseph Smith of ancient records, such as Egyptian papyri. Speaking to secular scholars' doubts about the relation of those records to the scriptures that the Prophet wrote, he said,

> Since God didn't need human records to know what is in the scriptures, and since the Prophet wrote under inspiration, external aids must have had their great importance in getting the Prophet into a frame of mind to communicate with the Divine Sense which enlightened his understanding. In this way, any human limitations in the records are transcended, and the faithfulness of the recorded scriptures hinges on only the Prophet's sensing of Divine Will. This is not to say that God does not use human tools in promulgating His purposes. He does, but He obviously can communicate directly with man when it advances the Divine purposes.[23]

As has been noted so often, Henry accepted without reservation that Joseph Smith was the Lord's prophet. He never questioned any doctrine or principle taught by the Prophet. Yet his belief in reasoning and the steady advance of understanding was so firm that he aspired to build on the Prophet's legacy, just as scientists build on the work of their predecessors. In fact, he believed that Joseph Smith would have wanted it that way. To a friend, a senior Church leader, Henry wrote,

> When one contemplates how different our understanding of religion must be from the Creator's omniscience, one realizes that nothing but growth, reinterpretation and generally widening horizons is appropriate in fields of religion.
>
> If we interpret the world precisely as the Prophet Joseph did, we are entirely unworthy of his tremendous precedent-breaking example. The Church, from its topmost councils to the man in the street, is at its best when it is undergoing thoughtful change. "Fundamental Principles" are never well enough understood by mortal man that they can't be said better.[24]

A PARENT'S RESPONSIBILITY TO REASON

Henry particularly preached the importance of study and reasoning to parents, whom he knew would play the central role in their children's education and development of faith. He gave many of his science and religion speeches with parents in mind, hoping to aid them in their task. He argued that all parents—mothers and fathers alike—have to know enough science to credibly answer their children's questions, especially questions related to faith. The power of his simple message comes through in the transcript of his 1964 "Science and Religion" speech at a BYU Leadership

Week devotional. To his assembled audience of parents, mostly mothers, he said:

> I would like to talk about why we should concern ourselves with science. I think most of you should care for very good reasons. The influence that you have on your children and grandchildren depends very much on how well you understand the world. It is surprising how much they will listen to you if they think you are talking sense, and how little attention they will pay to you on the things that you talk nonsense on, that you do not even pretend to know very much about. So it is important to everybody, and certainly to every leader, to be as widely acquainted with the things going on in the world and to understand what people are thinking and saying as clearly as he can if he wants to influence other people. I think that each of you has a definite obligation to understand something about science in this world, because it is very much to the fore. . . .
>
> There are lots of things, of course, that science does not know, but to me the saddest thing I see is people who feel that science threatens them religiously. It could not possibly threaten us religiously, because the same God who "made" our religion, that same God is making the universe. Science might threaten our *understanding of* religion. I am not doubting that—that some of us, including me, have such a faulty understanding of our religion that almost anything might threaten it. But the thing that is important about that is if we want to influence our sons and daughters, we must get our religion in the kind of shape that it cannot be threatened by anything that science discovers or does not discover.

What is true about the Gospel of Jesus Christ—not what you understand and think, which is partly nonsense, no matter who you are—but what is *really* true is all that we are committed to. That will stand any kind of treatment or anything that you can imagine. You do not have to worry in the least about anything the professors will teach at Brigham Young University or the University of Utah or any other university. . . .

Actually, I would like to end on this note: You could not live in a more exciting time. We have the true gospel, the gospel that the Lord revealed here, to learn, to guide us, to understand where we came from, and where we are going. We live in a time when science is the most exciting it has ever been. You have heard the figure that ninety-five out of every hundred scientists that ever lived are living right now, and science is moving faster than it has ever moved before. Every day you can read something exciting in the paper. If you do not keep up, you will be an old fuddy-duddy. You will not have any influence with your kids, so you have to come to Leadership Week just to learn, so they will not think you are a dummy.

That is really true, you know. We owe it to ourselves to understand the world we live in—science, music, and art. I am crying now because I haven't the slightest conception of what music is. I like it in a kind of way if they do not keep at it too long, but I really do not understand it. I am ashamed of that, but not enough to do anything about it. But if you do not know things, and if you will not learn, and if you will not try to understand things, you will not have any influence. You will not be leaders.

We do have to know science. We have to know everything about the world, and more than that, if you are afraid that science is going to knock the gospel over, you really haven't got your religion in shape. There isn't anything to worry about between science and religion, because the contradictions are just in your own mind. Of course they are there, but they are not in the Lord's mind because He made the whole thing, so there is a way, if we are smart enough, to understand them so that we will not have any contradictions. Let us struggle to do that. May the Lord bless us.[25]

THE DANGERS OF SPECULATION

Yet even as Henry preached the importance of thinking and learning, he warned against unjustified exercises in reasoning. He knew that logic only went so far in spiritual matters, and he cautioned against unfounded speculation:

> People ask me, "Well now, have you converted anybody?" And I say, "Well, I doubt it, but I'm thankful that no more people have apostatized than have on my account. At least I try to live as well as I can, and I try to get the main points first." I try to see what the gospel really depends on. I try to keep from worrying about the kind of things I am not sure about. If I start arguing about them, I'll get it half wrong and maybe nearly all wrong— because I don't understand them. These matters are unfinished. They will be clarified in due course.[26]

Knowing that some matters are "unfinished," Henry avoided speculating about questions that he couldn't firmly answer, particularly when the answer didn't bear on his spiritual progression. Organic evolution was such a matter: scientifically interesting, but

243

not relevant to whether a fellow ought to attend church or pay his tithing.

In fact, Henry disdained those who grew too confident of their wisdom and its value to the world. He probably offended, for example, an acquaintance who suggested in a private conversation that the Church was lucky to have the support of learned men such as themselves. His confidant made the mistake of using the words "we intellectuals." Resentful of being so classified, Henry sternly replied, "Don't ever call me an intellectual—I just do chemistry."

He particularly didn't want to be classed among those whose scientific insights produced arrogance relative to matters of faith. He was critical, for instance, of eighteenth- and nineteenth-century scientists who grew overconfident of the predictions that Newton's laws allowed them to make. Able to forecast physical phenomena such as lunar eclipses with perfect precision, some scientists reasoned that every human thought and action was similarly predictable. This line of reasoning led them to believe in strict predestination. It also cast doubt on the role of God and divine influence in men's lives. A noted scientist and philosopher of this school, Pierre La Place, was once questioned by Napoleon about God's involvement in the creation. La Place is reported to have replied, "I have no need of that hypothesis."[27]

Henry enjoyed pointing out how such overconfident scientists got their comeuppance with the arrival of quantum mechanics and its unpredictably roving electron. Scientific philosophers had drawn false conclusions about the predictability of human behavior—and caused much religious confusion in the process—all based on bad scientific assumptions about the laws of nature. Citing this example, Henry warned against such scientific speculation:

Scholars are continually learning more about the world we live in. In spite of this, when they go beyond what they can strictly prove, they are just like the rest of us. They are guessing.[28]

Interestingly, Henry was equally critical of well-intentioned but logically unsound speculation in favor of religion. He took issue, for example, with the attempts of Thomas Aquinas to explain the universe in scientific terms consistent with then-prevailing religious doctrine. Aquinas was a medieval churchman and philosopher who, in Henry's words,

> undertook to weave all knowledge into a single consistent scheme to support his religious convictions. He leaned heavily on Aristotle and wove what is now very bad mechanics into some of his proofs for the existence of a Creator. The result is a philosophy shot through with palpable error. Perhaps the believer never does more dis-service to religion than to support the truth with bad arguments. The impatient listener, perceiving the obvious errors, often "throws out the baby with the bath" and turns away, even from true religion.[29]

THE BABY AND THE BATH

"Throwing the baby out with the bathwater" is a metaphor Henry used often to describe his fear of attempts by the religious faithful to explain away scientific discoveries contrary to their faith. In particular, he worried that young people wouldn't buy simplistic efforts like Aquinas's to resolve the apparent inconsistencies between science and religion. He expressed that concern many times, including once in reply to a Church General Authority who sought his opinion of a recently published article in a Church magazine. The author of the article was an LDS religious educator who had cursorily studied some science in preparation for writing an emotional defense of faith. Henry wrote,

> I would think the best way of countering the influence of those who would deny the central influence of God in the affairs of men is to marshal the positive evidence for order and design in the Universe. Once this is accepted, the precise means God used in working out his design is reduced to mere detail—interesting but not of overriding importance. The detailed workings of the immensely complicated Universe are at best incompletely understood. For the layman to get embroiled in scientific detail is to put himself in an immensely unwise position. A good man can scarcely serve the truth worse than to defend it by ill-conceived arguments. He is very apt to confirm those whom he attempts to dissuade in their plan to "throw out the baby with the bath." This author will, in my opinion, alienate those whom he would like to help.[30]

Henry gave the same warning to overeager defenders of faith in a speech called "What Are the Things That Really Matter?":

> There is no harm in attempting to resolve apparently conflicting points of view, providing one is not taken in by one's own sophistry. There are few ways in which good people do more harm to those who take them seriously than to defend the gospel with arguments that won't hold water. Many of the difficulties encountered by young people going to college would be avoided if parents and teachers were more careful to distinguish between what they know to be true and what they think may be true. Impetuous youth, upon finding the authority it trusts

crumbling, even on unimportant details, is apt to lump everything together and throw the baby out with the bath.[31]

"IT WAS EVER SO"

Henry's warning against overzealous reasoning in defense of faith was founded not only in personal experience, but also in his knowledge of history. He knew the history of science and its impact on religion. The philosophical storms of the twentieth century may have been severe, but they were not unprecedented. Religious believers had faced challenges from science many times before; the true believers always came through stronger, as he said:

> With each new discovery, the skeptic finds less need for God, while the devout Latter-day Saint sees in it one more evidence of His overruling hand.
>
> It was ever so. The Bible speaks of the four corners of the earth. In the time of Columbus, there were those who thought a flat earth was a religious necessity. When it turned out to be round, Christ's teachings were found to be just as consistent with the new view as with the old. Later, when Galileo verified the theories of Copernicus and said the earth moved about the sun and so could no longer be considered the center of creation, there were bigots ready to burn him at the stake. When the smoke of battle cleared away and men looked at matters calmly, it became apparent that nothing essential had been lost. A lot of human philosophy disappeared, but it turned out to be unnecessary.[32]

History helped Henry see that while new discoveries might flood the scene, discovery itself was nothing new. He knew that discoveries of science could never threaten religion, no matter how seemingly ominous.

TRANSCENDENT FAITH

It wasn't just a knowledge of history, though, that gave Henry confidence in the sure position of religion. Rather, it was simple faith, transcending all logic. As much as he loved to reason, his faith was preeminent. He shared the view of the great mathematician Gauss, who said this of the limits of human reasoning:

> There are problems to whose solutions I would attach an infinitely greater importance than to those of mathematics—for example, touching ethics, or our relation to God, or concerning our destiny and our future; but their solution lies wholly beyond and completely outside the province of science.[33]

Commenting on the religious faith of Gauss and other great scientists, Henry remarked, "Apparently the best minds, like the humblest, when confronted with the problems of the ultimate meaning of things, must and do walk by faith."[34]

That is why Henry could reason so ambitiously without ultimately needing to know all the reasons: his faith in an omnipotent God put his science and reasoning in perspective. He wasn't just willing to concede God's superiority, he reveled in it. He knew that, in due time, a loving God would reveal the reasons behind all things. Until then, he was as happy as a little child to just believe.

That was clear in everything he said about science and religion, but it was particularly evident in his responses to those inquirers who wrote letters asking him to address their doubts. For instance, to Sister Gerber, a Church member who worried about explaining evolution to her nonbelieving friends, he wrote,

As a devout Latter-day Saint it seems to me that the important thing is to know that God organized the World. He did it! How he did it is very imperfectly understood and is something we can only speculate about.[35]

Throughout his life, Henry bore testimony of the transcendent power of faith. He was grateful for his science and his ability to reason. Reasoning supported his belief in God and His plan of salvation for humankind. However, Henry's testimony rested ultimately on faith and the spiritual inspiration available to all. He put it this way:

As exciting as this modern information is, and as clearly as it seems to parallel our religious thinking, still the fact remains that the problems of where we came from, where we are going, and the purpose of it all must ultimately be answered from the divine source open to Abraham and to all men—and from this source only.

The mysteries of the universe lead most men to worship the Supreme Intelligence who designed it all. However, the great blessing of the gospel is the additional avenues it opens up for developing this faith into a perfect knowledge. Now, as always, sure knowledge of spiritual matters can only come by faith, by prayer and by living it in such a way as to have the companionship of the Holy Ghost, as is promised to all the faithful.[36]

And thou shalt declare glad tidings, yea,
publish it upon the mountains, and upon every
high place, and among every people that
thou shalt be permitted to see.

—DOCTRINE AND COVENANTS 19:29

13

FUNDAMENTALS, NOT CONVENTIONS

In whatever he did, Henry believed in and practiced sound fundamentals. An equation couldn't be trusted, for instance, until he'd taken it apart and discovered how it worked. Likewise, a defender of faith had better distinguish between fundamental doctrines of his religion and mere personal opinions. Attention to fundamentals mattered.

At the same time, many who knew Henry well thought him a bit of a wild card. In particular, many of his fellow scientists wondered about his unorthodox approach to research. He was almost roguish in his attack on problems. Having found a new research question, he would chew on it intensely until discovering the essence of the answer. Then, with the details of the problem still left to be worked out, he was on to something else. Henry described his unconventional approach to scientific discovery this way:

I perceive myself as rather uninhibited, with a certain mathematical facility and more interest in the broad aspect of a problem than the delicate nuances. I am more interested in discovering what is over the next rise than in assiduously cultivating the beautiful garden close at hand.[1]

THE FRANS HALS OF SCIENCE

This roving style stood in stark contrast to the traditional scholarly approach, which is to pursue a discovery until every "i" has been dotted and every "t" crossed. Even scientific admirers thought Henry unconventional. Nobel laureate Peter Debye, for instance, compared him to a pre-impressionist painter: "His contributions to science are like the paintings of Frans Hals," Debye said. "He paints with a bold, broad brush."[2] Given that Hals is considered second to Rembrandt among Dutch painters, Debye's statement must be taken as complimentary. However, in a scientific world committed to precise realism, it said something that Henry was likened to an impressionist painter.

In fact, though Debye was a friend, he may have been among those who felt that Henry showed a bit too much disregard for scientific convention. When Henry spoke of "assiduously cultivating the beautiful garden close at hand," he was referring to the standard practice of research scientists. The conventional wisdom is that, if you're going to make new discoveries in science, where countless thousands are trying to do the same thing, you had better focus your efforts. Even the most accomplished scientists may spend an entire career in that one spot, attempting to advance the frontier of knowledge only across a narrow arc.

It was undoubtedly irksome, then, to see Henry ranging without a care over the whole scientific frontier. He seemed to have no regard for traditional academic boundaries. He felt he had every bit as much to contribute to a discussion of biology or medicine, for instance, as to one of chemistry. His Absolute Rate Theory (ART) allowed him to do that because it provided new insights into almost all chemical processes, not just those traditionally studied by chemists.

He compensated for his lack of knowledge of a particular academic field by partnering with specialists. These collaborators would describe to him phenomena in their fields. Even without understanding all of the underlying science, Henry could then use ART to explain what was going on. Of course, with so many problems to be addressed and so many collaborators to be had, it was no surprise that, having cracked one of those problems open, Henry left it to them to work out the details. Meanwhile, he was off to explore new frontiers.

In reality, he wasn't an unfocused researcher. Nearly everything he did built on his knowledge of ART. And he was always deepening that knowledge. For instance, in the late 1930s, when a new kind of mathematics called "group theory" appeared, he took pains to become an expert in the new technique. One of his Princeton colleagues recalled Henry's surprising proposal to write a paper on the subject:

> He said, "I know nothing about group theory. Why don't we learn about it by writing a paper?" So he wrote a paper and put our names on it.[3]

There again, though, Henry was violating convention: you aren't supposed to write scientific papers on subjects you don't know anything about. It must have chafed the specialists.

To Henry it seemed natural. He had seen one of his mentors, Michael Polanyi, do the same thing. Polanyi was a true Renaissance man. Formally trained in medicine, he taught himself chemistry well enough to be considered among the world's best; then, later in life, he became a renowned scientific philosopher, writing, as Henry did, of the role of faith in science.

Roaming the frontiers of knowledge was also the style of Joseph Smith. In the formal sense, Joseph had not studied beyond the second grade. Yet he tackled all subjects with equal confidence, heedless of convention or criticism.

THE GREAT FUNDAMENTAL TRUTH

The Prophet Joseph was Henry's great example of dismissing convention especially in one field, the preaching of the gospel. Joseph spent his life retelling the story of how, at age fourteen, he saw a vision of Heavenly Father and His Son, Jesus Christ. He was ceaselessly persecuted and ultimately martyred for his testimony of the vision. However, as he said, there was no choice but to share the marvelous news of what he had seen:

> I had actually seen a light, and in the midst of that light I saw two Personages, and they did in reality speak to me; and though I was hated and persecuted for saying that I had seen a vision, yet it was true. . . . I knew it, and I knew that God knew it, and I could not deny it."4

Henry didn't see firsthand what Joseph Smith did. However, he had a personal conviction that Joseph Smith had told the truth about seeing the Father and the Son, and he felt compelled to share his conviction just as though he had witnessed the vision himself. It was a fundamental truth—in fact, *the* fundamental truth of our time—and there was no excuse for not telling it. He believed that it was his obligation to share the gospel. He often expressed that conviction, as in this summary of the Church's doctrine of missionary work:

The Savior, after His resurrection, made clear to his disciples their responsibility to carry the Gospel to every creature. In the last chapter of the Gospel according to Mark, the Savior's injunction is recorded in this way:

"Afterward he appeared unto the eleven as they sat at meat, and upbraided them with their unbelief and hardness of heart, because they believed not them which had seen him after he was risen.

"And he said unto them, Go ye into all the world, and preach the gospel to every creature.

"He that believeth and is baptized shall be saved; but he that believeth not shall be damned.

"And these signs shall follow them that believe; In my name shall they cast out devils; they shall speak with new tongues;

"They shall take up serpents; and if they drink any deadly thing, it shall not hurt them; they shall lay hands on the sick, and they shall recover." (Mark 16:14–18.)

The Lord, speaking through the Prophet Joseph Smith, has made it equally clear that it is our responsibility to develop in others a determination to live the Gospel. In the Doctrine and Covenants we read:

"And the voice of warning shall be unto all people, by the mouths of my disciples, whom I have chosen in these last days.

"And they shall go forth and none shall stay them, for I the Lord have commanded them." (Doctrine and Covenants 1:4–5.)[5]

FULL-TIME MISSIONARY

Taking the Lord's command to preach seriously, Henry became a natural, zealous missionary. It was in this that he became

a real breaker of scientific convention. All of his scientific colleagues knew that he was a religious man because he never passed
up an opportunity to tell them so. That was true whether the
gathering of scientists was large or small. He frequently told the
story, for instance, of an impromptu poll he conducted among a
dozen of the world's preeminent scientists. He recalled the discussion these scientists had over dinner:

> One of them turned to me and asked, "How many of
> these people believe in a Supreme Being?" I said, "I don't
> know; let's ask them." There was no objection. I said,
> "Now, let's put the question as clearly as we can. How
> many of you think that 'There is a Supreme Being' best
> represents your point of view, and how many think that
> 'There is no Supreme Being' best represents your point of
> view? Let's not have a long discussion about what we
> mean, but just choose between these two propositions."
> All twelve said they believed.[6]

Henry was every bit as bold about discussing religion before
large groups of scientists. For instance, in the year he presided over
the American Association for the Advancement of Science, the
country's most prestigious scientific association, he wrote a presidential message to his fellow one hundred thousand members. His
message included overtly religious references like this one:

> Space travel is here, and man has, at least in a small
> way, taken the beginning step in the discovery of new
> worlds. To the religiously inclined, like myself, this is just
> one more step in an eternal progression.[7]

Particularly later in life, Henry was interviewed often about
his scientific accomplishments. Whenever the situation allowed,

he went beyond discussion of science, offering journalists lengthy, detailed statements of his faith. This one in a science magazine was typical:

> With my devoutly religious feelings, I know I am never alone in the world. I think you could not describe my feelings any other way. I'm convinced that this life is meaningful and that it wouldn't make sense without a continuation after death. For me, the idea of living again is a reality. This feeling of not being alone gives meaning to life. I feel that there will eventually be justice. This belief allows understanding of the gallantry of men who, for instance, stay at their posts in time of disaster, such as when a ship is sinking. Or those who help lift the burdens of other people at great sacrifice. This aspect of life has a meaning that I think transcends any other kind of meaning. I try to live up to my ideals even though I fail at times. I tremendously admire those around us who have this sense of duty. In the vastness of the universe we are not alone, but are really looking to a higher Power. Religion is a living, real thing for me. I don't see how it is possible to be happy without it. The idea that one is a brother to one's neighbor and the obligation that we have to lift the burdens of those around us is more important than material things. Happiness is more a function of worthwhileness than the possession of material things.[8]

In addition to speaking this way to large audiences, Henry also testified of his beliefs to colleagues one at a time. He stayed in touch, for instance, with former scientific collaborators and wasn't shy about discussing religion with them. His files include a 1968 letter from Nobel laureate Eugene Wigner, his friend from decades earlier in Berlin and Princeton. From what Dr. Wigner wrote, it is evident that Henry had sent him a complimentary copy of *The Faith of a Scientist:*

> Dear Henry,
>
> Let me thank you most sincerely for "The Faith of a Scientist" and for the cordial dedication therein. I appreciate both and wish to congratulate you on having written this book. Much of what you say needed to be said very much.[9]

Natural Testimony

Though his constant preaching was unconventional in the extreme, Henry wasn't conscious of crossing the boundary between professional and private life when he discussed religion with his scientific colleagues. It wasn't a matter of being daring or unconventional. His faith was so strong—so fundamental—that for him the boundary simply didn't exist. His son Hal described the phenomenon this way:

> Once I read a talk he had given to a large scientific convention. In it, he referred to creation and a Creator as he talked about his science. I knew that few, if any, in that audience would have shared his faith. So I said to him with wonder and admiration, "Dad, you bore your testimony." He looked at me with surprise on his face and said, "Did I?"
>
> He had not even known that he was being brave. He simply said what he knew was true. When he bore testimony, even those who rejected it knew it came not by design but because it was part of him. He was what he was, wherever he was.[10]

Of course, Henry's mixing work and religion prompted good-natured ribbing from some of his scientific colleagues, who easily recognized themselves as the targets of proselytizing. For example, in 1975 Henry received this letter from the editor of a professional journal whom he met the year before in Oshkosh, Wisconsin:

> You may recall, I marveled at how well preserved you are, and attributed this to your Mormon faith, which prohibits all vices that are harmful. I commented that since I didn't partake of vices like smoking, alcohol, coffee, etc., that I was probably a Mormon. And you said, "Well come on out and we'll baptize you."
>
> Well, lo and behold, I was watching the TV news the other night and doggone if there was Dr. Eyring in some sort of a decathlon competition with the president of Arizona State University. And I'll be further doggoned if Dr. Eyring didn't emerge the winner!
>
> Congratulations on your athletic prowess! Certainly another grand testimony for the tenets of the Mormon faith.
>
> With this evidence for the righteousness of your ways, you better get that water of baptism ready for me![11]

Henry was playfully teased about his religion even in public. For example, when he gave a lecture entitled "The Structure of Water" at Harvard, his host introduced him with this jest: "Dean Eyring is limited in the substances he can study: as a Mormon, he's restricted to looking at water."

THE GIFT OF THE BOOK OF MORMON

Though he preached all his life, Henry actually never served a full-time proselytizing mission. When he was a young man, the

Church precluded from service men with mortgage responsibilities such as those he was helping his father carry. And, because Henry never retired from the University of Utah, he and Winifred never served together as missionaries, as many retired Latter-day Saint couples do. However, with all of his public and private statements on behalf of the Church, most made voluntarily and on personal time, no one saw him as shirking missionary service.

In fact, some people knew Henry for a kind of missionary service that went beyond his preaching about science and religion. In the last decade of his life, Henry systematically gave away copies of the Book of Mormon. Following procedures established by the Church, he purchased copies of the Book of Mormon and pasted his picture on the inside front cover, along with this typed statement:

> I was born in Mexico and speak Spanish. I am the author of "The Absolute Reaction Rate Theory." I have taught at the University of California, Wisconsin, Princeton, Arizona, and Utah. I was the Dean of the Graduate School of Utah.
>
> My three sons were bishops in the L.D.S. Church at the same time. We know the gospel is true and the Book of Mormon is the word of God. I give you this book to read. Please feel free to write to me. I would like to discuss the gospel with you.

Hundreds, perhaps thousands, of such personalized copies of the Book of Mormon were distributed. Many recipients of Henry's gift took him up on his invitation to correspond. His files contain dozens of thank-you letters. More than a few were written in Spanish. All express gratitude and interest in learning more about the Church. Some letters indicate ongoing correspondence with Henry, such as this handwritten one, received in 1975:

It was very, very thoughtful of you to write to me while I am studying LDS teachings and history with Elders Johnson and Porter. They are indeed fine young men—wise beyond their years.

I have always stood somewhat in awe of the Mormon Church—but am finding it to be much easier to understand as I study more. The concept of modern prophets and revelation is quite different than the doctrine of the Protestant church in which I was raised, but with meditation perhaps I can come to accept it. Of course, I must say that very humbly, for it is certainly the Church which has the power and authority to weigh and judge and accept me rather than vice versa!

Your letter was all the more welcome since it arrived just after I returned from Missouri, where I had been called by the passing of my mother. I am very glad to be able to say that my faith was strong enough to carry me through that sad time with the realization that it is only a temporary, if indefinitely prolonged, parting. The Mormon doctrine of pre-existence, fore-ordination, and future eternal existence are a great comfort in such times of testing.

In addition to being popular in Spanish-speaking countries, Henry's gifts of the Book of Mormon were well received in Japan. One young missionary there wrote asking for a specially customized copy for a research scientist he was teaching. The missionary described this distinguished researcher's special need:

He listens to our lessons really good, and asks good questions, but as a scientist with a practical mind, he's having a hard time accepting the concept of a living God, and revealed religion, and especially the fact that God can bless him with a testimony.

We had a meeting with him last night, and after the discussion let him read a small part of the last conference issue of the *Ensign,* where President Tanner[12] quoted from one of your books, and was quite surprised at his reaction. He asked to be excused and left the room, and then came back with the Japanese translations of two of your books.

Because of his respect for you as a scientist, if you don't mind, I'd like to ask you to share your testimony with him and his family by writing a short testimony in this Book of Mormon, addressing it to him personally, and especially by mentioning the fact that the Lord will answer his prayers. Naturally, I'm sorry to cause any inconvenience, but would be sincerely grateful for your help.[13]

Henry responded quickly to this request, as to many others like it. He seems to have saved every letter of thanks and every report from a missionary who received and placed one of his Books of Mormon. It's impossible to know the full impact of Henry's missionary efforts. However a representative of the Book of Mormon placement program—clearly someone who knew Henry well enough to speak playfully with him—wrote this note, attaching the names of two contacts:

Dear Missionary:

These two people have your Book of Mormon. Write and convert them.

I remember you said your daughter[14] was going to Italy on a mission. Please send me a check for $60 and I will send her 100 of your books. I do not know how many converts have come from your books. I know of eleven. Your help and support are appreciated very much.[15]

FUNDAMENTAL DUTY

Of course, not everyone who heard Henry's testimony of Joseph Smith and the Book of Mormon immediately converted. He liked to tell the story, for instance, of how his preaching didn't seem to impress Albert Einstein much. One day, as they rode together in a car, Henry made the case for the Mormon doctrine of the afterlife, in which all people will be resurrected. Einstein heard the theory of humans being resurrected and replied, "What about dogs?" Flummoxed by this unexpected question, the best Henry could offer was his belief that the Supreme Being would take due care. "I'm a little weak on dogs," he said, "But I'm sure that He is sensitive to all needs." Afterward Henry confessed, "I don't think Einstein was overwhelmed by my answer."

In addition to falling mostly on deaf ears, Henry's incessant preaching to his scientific colleagues couldn't have pleased all of them. It may have even cost him some recognition of his scientific achievements. However, he never noticed any such cost, and he wouldn't have cared in any event. He considered preaching the restored gospel a fundamental duty, convention be hanged. In fact, he knew that his sacrifices were meager relative to those of others who had stood up for the truth. He particularly admired nonbelievers who, merely for conscience' sake, defended the fledgling Church even at the peril of their lives. One of those was a man named Alexander Doniphan, to whom Henry paid this tribute:

> Latter-day Saints hold in grateful remembrance the names of men who in modern times shielded the oppressed Saints from the vengeful destruction of the

oppressor. High on this list stands the name of General Alexander W. Doniphan. General Doniphan was three years younger than the Prophet Joseph Smith and faithfully served as his legal counsel in Clay County, Missouri. During the Missouri persecutions, General Doniphan commanded militia under General Lucas, a bitter enemy of the Saints. The latter, by a ruse, had taken the Prophet and others of the brethren prisoners, convened a court martial, and sentenced them to death.

About midnight of Nov. 2, 1838, General Lucas wrote:

"Brigadier General Doniphan—Sir: You will take Joseph Smith and the other prisoners into the public square of Far West, and shoot them at 9 o'clock tomorrow morning. (Signed) Samuel D. Lucas, Major General Commanding."

General Doniphan replied:

"It is cold-blooded murder. I will not obey your order. My brigade shall march for Liberty tomorrow morning at 8 o'clock; and if you execute these men, I will hold you responsible before an earthly tribunal, so help me God."[16]

Henry noted the nobility of General Doniphan's action and the price he was willing to pay to protect Joseph Smith:

Alexander Doniphan, who was only thirty years old when this happened, always remained faithful to the Saints, became a hero in the Mexican War, and served two terms in the United States Senate. In May, 1874, General Doniphan visited Utah and spent some time with President Young. The man who had saved the life of the Prophet was naturally a welcome guest in Salt Lake City. The utter destruction of Jackson County, foretold by the

Prophet Joseph, had made a deep impression on the general.[17] Doniphan was a tolerant, courageous, good man who believed in justice, even when following his conscience might have ruined him.[18]

Henry may have thought of Alexander Doniphan in those moments when speaking of the Church to his scientific colleagues seemed impolitic. Doniphan risked being court-martialed for defending Joseph Smith. All Henry had at stake was a bit of scientific reputation. That was a small price to pay for doing a fundamental duty that he owed to God, to the Prophet, and to his fellowmen. He said it this way:

> Those who understand the Gospel have the special responsibility of sharing this understanding with others. The special message we have comes out of Joseph Smith's mission. Revelation has the same place in the Church now as anciently. When man has used his faculties to do what he can for himself, he can look to a higher source for inspiration and help. As Paul spoke of the law as being schoolmaster, so we think of the Church as a school to guide us along the road to eternal progression. It is the divinely inspired best way, and as such, is of paramount importance. Joseph Smith restored this best way.[19]

Every man seeking the interest of his
neighbor, and doing all things with an eye
single to the glory of God.

—DOCTRINE AND COVENANTS 82:19

14

PEOPLE, NOT
PUBLIC OPINION

For being such a "people person," one who made friends so easily and treated everyone so well, it's remarkable how little Henry worried about what people thought of him. Criticism in particular didn't matter. Unless he thought a complaint was justified, he just ignored it.

That philosophy came through in his answer to a question from his nephew Ed Kimball, who asked, "Do you ever publish papers that you are later embarrassed about?" Henry replied,

> Not that I *am* embarrassed about, but perhaps that I *should* be embarrassed about.
>
> I have published over five hundred scientific papers, frequently with collaborators. I have written nine books, also with collaborators. And I have been editor of about twenty annual reviews of physical chemistry and co-editor of eleven volumes of physical chemistry. No, there is no

paper I am ashamed of, because at the time it was written, it was the best we knew. I have no apologies. Each paper was the best I could do at the time. That I was not born smarter is really not my fault. Maybe as important as anything in whatever success I have had is the ability to go ahead continually without worrying about whether other people like what I do. If an idea is wrong, it will fail; if it is right, nothing can stop it.[1]

KINDNESS TO STRANGERS

At the same time he was brushing off critics, though, Henry would show unusual—even undue—deference to those who sought his help. He was kind to everyone, strangers included. That was true even when they were making unreasonable requests. Time and again, for example, he was solicited by crusaders with ill-conceived schemes to defend religion against science. Letters he wrote in response show remarkable respect for these deluded strangers. One proposed this scheme:

Dear Dr. Eyring:

I am writing to ask your help. I'm putting a book together and need some guidance. My book, by way of explanation, is not for members of our church, but is written to all our brothers and sisters in the world, and particularly to young people who are so pliable, but do not know about the Plan of Salvation. I am very sneakily teaching it to them without mentioning "Mormon Church" or "Restored Gospel." But I am bringing them just up to that point—and hopefully leaving them with a truth-seeking attitude and desire to know more.

Now, here's where you come in. In my chapter on the Creation, the main concept of which is to teach the fulfilling of the measure of our creation, I need a little help. I of course run into evolution. I read up on it—various things, and understand that fossils are found back in Cambrian and Pre-Cambrian periods—and that's fine with me. It's also fine with me that there is limited change within species. All this does not conflict with the Bible, but when we come to "fossil *man,*" I am at a loss as to any possible explanation.[2]

The letter goes on like this at length. The writer asks Henry for answers to a long list of scientific questions. It finally ends with a request to reprint a chapter of *The Faith of a Scientist* in the writer's proposed book.

Henry responded to this unsolicited letter, as was his custom. In this instance, though, his reply was a bit longer than usual, and there was a special sensitivity to it. The letter shows how gently he could say "no" to a bad idea. Rather than dismissing the writer as scientifically unqualified and her proposal as ill-conceived, he offered only thoughtful explanation:

We are not told who Adam's father was. To me the important thing is that Adam is the spirit child of God. He came into this world when he received a mortal body. The Fall consisted of becoming subject to death, and everyone born into the world is subject to death and so partakes of this fallen state with Adam. Finally, through the atonement we will all receive a resurrected body.

Whether Adam's father lived on this earth or some-where else would seem of secondary importance to me. Adam was the one whom God recognized as presiding over the first dispensation and as such, with Eve his wife, became our first parents.

If God did or did not use organic evolution to prepare

the bodies to house His spirit children I remain unconcerned. I think the scientific evidence on organic evolution, like everything else, should stand or fall on its merits.
Being trained as a geologist, it answers many otherwise
difficult problems for me, and I find no conflict with it
and the Gospel.

I don't own the copyright to my little book, but it will
probably be best for you to put ideas of yours which parallel mine in your own words anyway.

Kindest regards.[3]

Henry's combination of insensitivity to critics and deep concern for strangers makes one wonder. How could he care so much
about people but so little about their opinion of him? The answer
is most easily understood a piece at a time. First, let's take the
imperviousness to criticism.

"THE LITTLE BOY WITH TWO MAMAS"

Henry learned to ignore negative opinions early. As a young
refugee from the Mexican colonies, he bore the insults of strangers
who gawked at his odd family. He recalled how, when he was a
refugee in El Paso, his department store coworkers mocked him.
They soon found that young Henry Eyring didn't embarrass easily:

The clerks called me the little boy with two mamas. I
always tell everything I know. So if they wanted to know
about our family, I would tell them. I didn't care. I had no
feeling that I had anything to hide. I didn't care much
whether they liked it or not. They thought our family was
interesting.[4]

El Paso had few indigenous Mormons. Thus, it was natural for the locals there to point fingers at a large polygamous family. However, the Eyrings continued to be an oddity even in Arizona, where they settled in a largely Mormon community. Henry described how they still stood out in Pima:

> We lived up there on a hill. Mormon and Gentile[5] knew that we were a big family. We were able students in school. We weren't very rich when we were starting there because we had bought our farm on time. But I never was humble to the point where I felt discriminated against.[6]

When pressed by an interviewer on the matter of outright discrimination against himself and his unusual family, Henry was dismissive—even a bit combative:

> I never noticed anything. You've got to know me. I didn't concede anything to anybody. I was ready to fight if anyone wanted to. I didn't like to fight, but if anybody wanted to push it, they could always get a fight. That kind of a person if he minds his own business is treated like anyone else is treated. I was always head of my class in school. The Catholic teacher said that somebody had asked her how she felt about teaching the Eyrings. She said she wished the rest of them were as smart.[7]

Henry maintained pride in his atypical family even as he moved away from predominantly Mormon Pima to the University of Arizona. As a college student he often brought non-LDS friends home to visit, where they met both of his father's families. He knew that they'd find the family duplex startling, but he didn't care. In fact, he was proud of his large, branching family tree:

I'm not a humble man, so I had nothing to hide. If anyone wanted to know how many wives my father had, I would always tell them. I still do. I also like to tell people that I've got 240 first cousins. I tell it all. I don't have any feelings of inferiority to anybody.[8]

THICK-SKINNED SCIENTIST

Immunity to criticism, forged in Henry's youth by anti-polygamy prejudice, proved to be a great asset later in life. In his scientific career, for instance, his lack of concern for criticism was tested time and again. Undoubtedly the greatest test came in his early thirties, when the *Journal of Chemical Physics* rejected his crucial ART paper, the one that effectively launched his career. He'd been careful to choose that journal over all others, knowing that it was the one friendliest to mathematical theories of chemistry. He also hoped that Harold Urey, the journal's editor, would be favorably disposed to his work, being already familiar with it.

The *Journal's* rejection, then, came as a great disappointment. Adding insult to injury, the reviewer of Henry's paper essentially said that the fundamental concept behind ART was bogus. Henry was fortunate to have been blessed with thick skin. And he was doubly blessed to have supportive, influential friends. Without them, he later observed, thick skin alone might not have been enough:

> If I'd been younger, I guess I would have been crushed by this review. Actually, Hugh Taylor and Eugene Wigner, a famous Nobel Laureate whom I had known in Berlin, upheld the paper. It would be hard to find a more competent reinforcement. There is a lesson here in that if one believes in one's judgment, one goes ahead. Criticism is not going to hurt you if you are right. I think there are

very able people who cease to perform because of criticism. As I recall, Newton was very disturbed by the fact that Hook[9] was such a severe critic. At times, Newton turned away from science and, as a matter of fact, in his later years did other things than science. The greatest people can apparently be too sensitive.[10]

STRAIGHT TALK

Perhaps it shouldn't be surprising that Henry expected others to take criticism as stoically as he did. He wasn't afraid of offending anyone with straight talk, provided he thought they needed to hear what he had to say. He always told people what he'd want to know if he were in their shoes.

That was true, for instance, of his position on education. Throughout his life he preached the importance of education to making a living in the modern world. He used examples of the increasing power of machines to illustrate the point that an uneducated person is in a very tough spot:

> A man using his mind can direct a machine which can do an amount of work a thousand slaves could never accomplish. For a few dollars a man can telephone to the ends of the earth, or if need be he can fly non-stop to any spot on earth. The untrained mind with only physical strength to offer has become economically valueless in competition with a machine. By the same token, anyone who can see a little more clearly how to use the tremendous forces at our bidding can multiply his strength beyond limit. Calculating machines are now being built which can make calculations faster than a small army of brilliant humans. If one must compete with the machine,

one is lost. If one can really master machines, one's value is beyond price.[11]

He sometimes made the same point more graphically, at an even greater risk of offending some of his listeners. That was the case with his address at BYU's 1964 Leadership Week. Having described recent developments in science, he said this about the value of education:

What does it mean? I will tell you what it means. It means that we are going to do everything more and more using our heads and less and less using our arms. Any young man or woman who is so ill-advised at the present time, if their mind is good enough to let them, to not go to the Brigham Young University, or one of the other state universities, and get training is a very brave person. I mean, it is almost guaranteed that unless they are much smarter than the people who go to college and get the training that way, they will have a subservient position in the community. Society needs us to go ahead and get training if we possibly can, if we are able to.

I would like to use again the analogy that I have used so often about how much you are worth if you will not make decisions. I just love to tell it. (As I always say, I have heard this thing many more times than you have, but let's tell it again.) You have twenty tons of coal (I think that is the way I generally start) and a ten-foot fence. When I was down in Pima I could have thrown that over the fence— and I can still do it—twenty tons in a day. Now, twenty tons of coal weighs at 2,000 pounds per ton, so twenty times 2,000 is 40,000, and if you lift it ten feet over the fence, that is 40,000 times ten. That is 400,000. Is that right? And you don't belong to a union, you remember, so you can work for six days a week. That is 2,400,000 foot-pounds. Do you know how much that is worth? It is worth about a penny in power. It is a kilowatt hour. A kilowatt hour is 2,650,000 foot-pounds, and this is only 2,400,000.

If you do not have anything but muscles, brother or sister, the only thing we can do is send you to the fish hatchery. You are not worth anything. We can only afford to pay you about a penny a week. So, if you will not make decisions, if you will not take responsibility, if you will not come to Leadership Week and learn something, by golly, you are not worth having—and the only reason that we don't feed you to the fishes is because we are good religious Latter-day Saints, and we think you will change your mind.[12]

Models of Kindness

Henry may have offended some people with his hyperbolic talk of the fish hatchery. However, they couldn't doubt his motives. He was driven to help people. Concern for the welfare of others was—just as much as disregard for negative opinions—programmed into him in his youth.

He often recalled, for instance, the lasting impact of a visit from his Sunday School teacher, Priscilla Allred. She came to his home when he was stricken, at age four, with typhoid fever:

Miss Allred was an attractive young lady, and I was proud and happy that she cared enough to visit me. She spoke to me cheerfully, and after a brief visit with my mother and me, went on her way. But something important had happened to me. I had been a vital part of a fine teacher-student relationship that I have never forgotten. I learned that day how important it is to care about people even when they are small and may not seem very important.[13]

Another hero of Henry's youth was his high school science teacher, Alma Sessions. Like Miss Allred, Alma Sessions went out of his way to help Henry, in the process shaping not only his professional career but also his outlook on people:

> The "hero" of the Academy for me was a Mr. Alma Sessions. He had been a star on the basketball team at the University of Arizona. He was an electrical engineer who had returned to the high school with great enthusiasm. He believed in involvement in the real sense. For instance, he took us into the field where we surveyed a place for building a dam. He had actually built his own telescope and shared his excitement in all these endeavors with us. He knew of my love for mathematics, although I was actually in his science classes. I recall one day his saying, "You like this sort of thing; you should be an engineer." He was well aware that curricula very well done at the University of Arizona was and still is in mining and second in electrical engineering. Mr. Sessions recommended that I take one of these. I admired him and respected his judgment. I decided that if I took electrical engineering I'd surely electrocute myself, but I might survive mining. I went to the University of Arizona and registered in mining.[14]

Of course, Henry's preeminent role-model of loving condescension was the Savior, Jesus Christ. In moments when Henry's patience was tested to the limit, it was the Savior's doctrine and example that helped him respond charitably. In a sermon called

"Developing in Others a Determination to Live the Gospel," Henry noted the power of the Savior's example of humility and love:

> The greatest of all teachers:
> " . . . called the twelve, and saith unto them, If any man desire to be first, the same shall be last of all, and servant of all.
> "And he took a child, and set him in the midst of them, and when he had taken him in his arms, he said unto them,
> "Whosoever shall receive one of such children in my name, receiveth me: and whosoever shall receive me, receiveth not me, but him that sent me."[15]
> And a little later,
> "But whoso shall offend one of these little ones which believe in me, it were better for him that a millstone were hanged about his neck, and that he were drowned in the depth of the sea."[16]

Henry concluded,

> In love and humility the Savior touched men's hearts. May the Lord help us in our humble way to do the same.[17]

FAMOUSLY FORGIVING

Henry wasn't perfect, but in his humble way he tried to exemplify the Savior's love of others. He was famously forgiving, for example, of the alleged weaknesses of his fellow Church members. He often repeated a witticism to this effect:

> Some people have pointed to some member of the Church and said, "Now Dr. Eyring, that's one of your

brethren, and he's not what he ought to be." My answer is this, "Well, you ought to see what he would be like if it weren't for the Church."[18]

Henry was also generous to his students. He was a stern taskmaster, especially in the laboratory. However, his students felt his respect for them. One of them wrote this appreciative tribute:

> One aspect of Dr. Eyring's personality that was particularly appealing was his thoughtfulness toward all who came in contact with him, regardless of their station in life. He has written of "how important it is to care about people even when they are small and may not seem very important." I myself observed numerous occasions in which he practiced this principle. He once remarked on the importance of being good to people you pass "on the way up," because you will want them to be good to you when they pass you on their way up and you are on the way down.[19]

More than just treating colleagues respectfully, Henry could be surprisingly forgiving of their weaknesses. His son Hal recalled observing a late-afternoon discussion between his father and a graduate student. It was obvious even to a casual observer that the student was underperforming. After the fellow left, Hal asked, "Dad, why didn't you let that guy have it?" Henry replied, "The world knocks them down. I try to build them up."

LOVE OF GOD AND OF ALL MEN

Henry's genuine concern for everyone was an asset not only in his scientific collaborations, but also in his work on behalf of the Church. For example, when in the late 1960s the editors of

The Instructor magazine launched their series of faith-building articles by recognized scientists, Henry took the lead in smoothing the occasional ruffled feathers. Many of the scientists who were asked to contribute to the series, though firm in their faith, had difficulty writing for a general Church audience. Some wrote in the same technical style they used for science journals. Others wrote provocatively, in ways likely to stir up controversy. Both types of problems had to be addressed and resolved, even at the risk of giving offense.

One author's article on genetics presented a particular challenge. In the view of the editor of *The Instructor,* it was too technical, too provocative and, to top it off, too long. The editor drafted a two-page letter suggesting a detailed list of changes. Among the editor's many potentially offensive suggestions was the recommendation that the author read two style guides, *The Art of Plain Talk* and *The Art of Readable Writing.*

Fortunately, this letter was preempted by one that Henry had already written. His simple suggestions were book-ended by the kind of praise that his mother, Caroline, might have given:

Dear John:

I like your article very much. I think if you could add a paragraph relating it to the Gospel by bearing your testimony that it would greatly enhance its usefulness to *The Instructor.* Perhaps also in such paragraph you could lay out a little more how ideas of inheritance play a very important role in the family and Church. I greatly appreciate your help in our enterprise.[20]

Henry's love even for those he disagreed with ultimately won their affection. That was true of the man that some considered his rival in questions of science and religion, Joseph Fielding Smith. In 1955, they exchanged pointed views both via letter and also face-to-face. Their opinions were diametrically opposed, and anyone who knew where each man stood assumed that their relationship was confrontational. But Henry always downplayed the supposed confrontation. In fact, he described the key discussion, in President Smith's office, as friendly. President Smith likewise noted the amicable tone of their interactions. After receiving one significant letter from Henry, President Smith described it to a friend this way: "It was conciliatory and rather gentle, and he conceded to me the right to my views, but failed to answer any of the challenging questions which I sent him."[21]

It wasn't hard for Henry to get along with President Smith, notwithstanding their differences of opinion on scientific matters. He considered President Smith a brilliant man and sustained him as a prophet. He placed the capstone on their friendship with a personal tribute written at President Smith's passing. He eulogized his old friend this way:

> As many people have remarked, President Joseph Fielding Smith was a man without guile. He presented every question exactly as he saw it and accepted the consequences of his position whether this was pleasant or unpleasant. Everyone who knew him even remotely knew that he was against sin, but it is only less generally well known that he loved the sinner. This can be illustrated by a personal experience of the author.

Henry then recounted his discussions with President Smith about the age of the earth (thereby implicating himself, with typical self-deprecation, as a "sinner"). He closed his tribute with these words:

> Wholesome is another word strikingly exemplified by President Smith. Riding in military jets (early, when they

280

didn't always land appropriately), being an honorary officer in the National Guard, playing handball well at sixty, and yet being outstanding as Church Historian and the leading authority of the Church on doctrine bespeak the whole man. Even more important, President [Smith] exemplified devotion to duty and other Gospel principles in his own life as few others have done. It is curious that this kindest of men should sometimes have been thought of as austere and as living in a world apart. Unfortunately, the frequent price that must be paid for excellence is to be misunderstood. To me and to a host of others, President Smith's kindness, his devotion to duty and to Gospel principles will remain a beacon for all, shining across the years.[22]

The respect for a friend manifest in this tribute was, in Henry's case, universal. He loved people. However, he loved God more. Thus, he didn't worry about others' opinions of him, and he wasn't afraid to disagree on matters of principle. Because his love for others came through, few who disagreed with him ever considered him a foe. For those as committed to the truth as he was, it was just a matter of time before firm friendship set in.

PART 4

TESTAMENT

Henry, the race completed

THE KIND FATHER
WHO CREATED
IT ALL

Henry died of cancer on the day after Christmas, 1981. He kept working until nearly the end. He taught undergraduate classes that fall semester, and he traveled on business to Texas just a few weeks before his death. His research continued. He was collaborating on three books at the time of his death, and fourteen papers bearing his name were published after his passing.

Henry's energy and enthusiasm were prominently on display just a year earlier, when the University of Utah named its new chemistry building after him. Addressing an appreciative group of friends and dignitaries, he quipped, "I thought you were supposed to be dead before they named a building after you. But I guess they looked at me and decided I was near enough that it would be okay to go ahead."[1] However, he contradicted his own insinuation that his strength was fading. Responding to the many tributes paid him at the ceremony, he said, "It's kind of like attending your own funeral. But don't think for a minute that I'm going to commit hari-kari in order to make it seem more appropriate—I've got too much to do."[2] He underscored his intention to stay at his work with self-deprecating humor: "I'll keep working as long as I can find my way to the chemistry building and somebody there will let me in. Now that my name is on the building, it should be a lot easier."[3]

Even from his hospital bed the following year, he kept doing science. His son Ted, a fellow chemist, recalled visiting his father near the end. Henry excitedly reported, "I've thought of a new way to teach calculus that is much easier to understand."

The final weeks of life, though, were excruciating. The pain of the encroaching cancer was unbearable, and the medications administered to alleviate it clouded his mind. At times he reverted to Spanish, the language of his boyhood. He often spoke of his "Papa," Ed. Those who sat with Henry through the nights could tell from his words that he looked forward to seeing his father again. Sometimes it wasn't clear whether he was speaking of Ed or of his Father in Heaven.

TIME TO COMPLETE SOME THINGS

Henry's neighbor, Church Apostle Neal A. Maxwell, ministered frequently to him during the final months. On several occasions, Elder Maxwell gave Henry priesthood blessings. His wife Winifred's journal entry of July 17, 1981, records the substance of one of these blessings:

> Elder Maxwell pleaded fervently with the Lord to give Henry another season; Neal pleaded a number of times for time for Henry to complete some things.[4]

In the ensuing five months Henry's work continued about as before, with the exception of time lost to chemotherapy treatments. He was typically productive, but there were no unusual achievements. Perhaps, though, Elder Maxwell had a different vision when he sought the blessing "for Henry to complete some things." For instance, there is a story of his serving one last time on the local Church welfare farm, where crops are grown by volunteers and given to the poor. Henry's son Hal tells the story this way:

> Dad was the senior high councilor in his stake, and he had the responsibility for the welfare farm. An assignment was given to weed a field of onions, so Dad assigned himself to go work on the farm. He never told me how hard it was, but I have met several people who were with him that day. I talked to one of them on the phone, and he said that he was weeding in the row next to Dad through much of the day. He told me the same thing that others who were there have told me. He said that the pain was so great that Dad was pulling himself along on his stomach with his elbows. He couldn't kneel. The pain was too great for him to kneel. Everyone who has talked to me about that day has remarked how Dad smiled and laughed and talked happily with them as they worked in that field of onions.
>
> Now, this is the joke Dad told me on himself afterward. He said he was there at the end of the day. After all the work was finished and the onions were all weeded, someone said to him, "Henry, good heavens! You didn't pull those weeds, did you? Those weeds were sprayed two days ago, and they were going to die anyway."
>
> Dad just roared. He thought that was the funniest

thing. He thought it was a great joke on himself. He had worked through the day on the wrong weeds. They had been sprayed and would have died anyway.

When Dad told me this story, I knew how tough it was. So I asked him, "Dad, how could you make a joke out of that? How could you take it so pleasantly? He said something to me that I will never forget, and I hope you won't. He said, "Hal, I wasn't there for the weeds.""[5]

This inspiring story is known not just to the relatively small group of fellow laborers there that day in the onion patch with Henry. Hal, Henry B. Eyring of the Church's First Presidency, later told the story in a public address entitled "Waiting upon the Lord." Having recounted the story, he drew from it this moral:

Now, you'll be in an onion patch much of your life. So will I. It will be hard to see the powers of Heaven magnifying us in our efforts. It may even be hard to see our work being of any value at all. And sometimes our work won't go well.

But you didn't come for the weeds. You came for the Savior. And if you pray, and if you choose to be clean, and if you follow God's servants, you will be able to work and wait long enough to bring down the powers of Heaven.

I was with Dad in the White House in Washington, D.C., the morning he got the National Medal of Science from the President of the United States. I missed the days when he got all the other medals and prizes. But, oh, how I'd like to be with him on the morning he gets the prize he won for his days in the onion patches. He was there to wait upon the Lord. And you and I can do that, too.[6]

Thanks to Hal's telling this story publicly, it is known to countless members of the Mormon Church. They wouldn't have the benefit of it had Henry not been blessed by his friend Elder Maxwell to "complete some things."

In those final months Henry also made what appear to be, in hindsight, important preparations for the life to come. As his physical suffering intensified, the burden was great both for him and for those who sat with him through the agonizing nights. One of those watchers, his wife Winifred, recalls how, in a moment of intense pain and pleading, he cried out, "Why has God done this to me?" With the dawn, he shared the insight that came in answer to his racked prayer: "God is testing me. He wants only strong men in his kingdom."[7] Elder Maxwell approved Henry's final efforts in this funeral epitaph: "He taught us to live well, and in the end taught us to die well."[8]

STILL TEACHING

It's tempting to wonder what Henry has done since he got to the other side. Certainly he's been busy. If there are celestial chemistry classes, he has no doubt been enrolled and earning A's. But he probably has more important things to do. The vast majority of people there never learned in this life what he knew about God. They still need to hear and decide to accept the truths that he can teach them. Most likely, he is teaching a "full load" in the next world, just as he did in this one.

Assuming that his personality and teaching style are the same (seemingly safe assumptions), he's having great success among ordinary folk. Here on earth he had a gift for making people feel intelligent and important. There was a kind of magic to meeting Henry Eyring and feeling his respect for you. There could be no denying his intellectual greatness, so you had to believe that, if he showed you respect, you must be respectable. He treated even novice students as though they were smart, and that made them feel smart—whether they could understand chemistry or not.

Henry's respect for others helped him build not just their confidence in themselves, but also their faith in God. Because of his simple manner, he could speak of the Creator in a way that was both understandable and encouraging. His unusual combination of insight and humility made it seem that God might not be so far off after all, that a conversation with Him might be pleasant and fun. More than his science, that was Henry's great talent and his gift to this world. By treating people as though they were important, he built their love for themselves. And by testifying simply of a caring Heavenly Father, he built their love for God.

DIVINE COMMUNICATION

He was especially good at encouraging those who couldn't imagine communicating with God, who struggled to see a smiling face when they prayed. He recognized that not everyone was a visual thinker, as he was. Thus, he taught of the multiplicity of ways in which God can communicate with his children, and they with Him. Among the modes of communication, he said, are holy writ and the beauty and precision of the physical world. He admitted that these messages aren't easily read, but that each of us can learn. In a sermon called "Communication," he made the point this way:

> The Gospel, in all its beauty and perfection, is effective only as communicated. In each generation, the Gospel needs people like the Apostle Paul to proclaim it for all to read and to hear. His epistles have brought faith and hope to millions. They fairly vibrate with the faith and ardor of this great apostle. Not all of our great

religious leaders, however, have been blessed with this gift of communication. How many of us, like Moses, when commissioned to lead Israel from bondage, say, "It is too difficult—for I am slow of speech"? Exemplifying, in a superlative degree, the overcoming of this barrier to communication is Miss Helen Keller. A short time ago, *Life Magazine* carried a picture of the 73-year-old, smiling Miss Keller with her hand pressed against President Eisenhower's face, following his reactions by touch. She has been without sight and hearing for seventy years. One can scarcely imagine more complete isolation. Yet, with the help of her teacher Ann Sullivan and others like her, Miss Keller did the impossible and learned to communicate her thoughts better than many who have no special handicap.

Communication of information involves both a sender and a receiver. The Gospel flows out from the Creator of the World, who sees the end from the beginning. It flows out to all who are able to receive it. Too many of those who are blind and deaf to this flow of information foolishly deny the existence of the Creator. How much wiser they would be if, like Helen Keller, they could overcome blindness and deafness and reach out and touch Him.

Written in the many languages of the world are all sorts of messages which escape us completely because we don't speak that particular language. We have not found the appropriate Rosetta Stone. The Creator of the Universe has implanted a message in every created thing. Tennyson expressed the idea of the interrelationship of things beautifully in the following words:

Flower in the crannied wall,
I pluck you out of the crannies.
I hold you here, root and all, in my hand,
Little flower—but if I could understand
What you are, root and all, and all in all,
I should know what God and man is.

Geologists search for the meaning to be read into the piled-up strata of the earth much as a historian might turn the pages of an ancient, damaged manuscript. The astronomer seeks the answer to his questions in the depths of space. Still other men concentrate on the scriptures alone. The wise man searches all these and other sources, knowing that all are communications from the same divine source and certain that, if followed far enough, all will guide him back to the Divine Presence.

The scriptures give us a clear understanding of the concern of the Eternal Father for His children. In both ancient and modern scriptures, man has received Divine communications which establish the religious pattern for those who heed it.[9]

THE ROLE OF PROPHETS

Henry admitted the difficulty of relying solely on physical and scriptural records to gain a testimony of God. That is why he preached so frequently and fervently the need for modern prophets such as Joseph Smith. He had a visual metaphor for the crucial role of prophets in this life:

The world may be likened to a great building filled with people who are unable to reach the windows high above the floor unless they are willing to make an almost superhuman effort. At the other end is the one-way entrance. Here we see the infants enter, mature, labor, and grow old, and most of them never make the struggle to reach the windows where they could catch a glimpse of the otherwise invisible world that surrounds them. Instead, they talk with each other and, not finding anyone who has actually looked through the windows, they decide that probably there aren't any after all and that the stories handed down of great men who by their struggle have glimpsed a world beyond are the inventions of knaves or fools.

In spite of this doubt, though, the stories live on. Some of them tell of prophets who have struggled to a window and actually talked a few moments to the kind Father who created it all. He is very busy with His other children who have already come from this and the other buildings into the garden. He smiles at His brave sons and gives them words of encouragement to take back to His other children. He tells them how to organize a school to prepare them for the life to come.

There is at least one school which believes that its great men can still climb to the window and get the necessary instruction—that the curtains have not been drawn. I am thankful to a kind Providence that I've been allowed to go to that school. This is one very important reason for being a Latter-day Saint. When the silent and inevitable messenger calls us into the garden, let us not go unprepared.[10]

Henry followed his own advice about trying to communicate with God. Thanks to a lifetime of heeding the counsel of living prophets, as well as studying the words of God as written in scripture and the physical world, he was prepared for the call of "the silent and inevitable messenger." Now he's a missionary on what he once called "the Temple Square in the hereafter," spreading the word there.

HOLDING COURT

It's hard to know what teaching style he's using. He certainly took varying approaches here in this world. In writing, he could be pithy and even poetic. That is the style of each sermon in his book, *The Faith of a Scientist.* It is exemplified in this beautiful passage:

> A very few sentences suffice to outline the simple philosophy that guides me. This magnificent universe operates according to an over-all plan. The Planner is so great that He can be, and is, interested even in me. Because of His interest, man is here according to a plan which is in accord with the divine purpose. Since it is obvious that individuals are born under unequal circumstances and ordinarily fail to receive justice in this life, it is natural for me to believe in an immortality which achieves this justice. Since an all-wise God can communicate with man to man's advantage, such communication is to be expected. The Church of Jesus Christ as restored through the Prophet *is* this communicated plan which leads to eternal progress. Believing in this over-all destiny, I can still achieve it only by an infinitude of decisions made one at a time.
>
> If I were you, I would get this master plan in mind, believing that if all the little things are done well, one by one, the big things will take care of themselves.[11]

Of course, in addition to Henry's poetic style, there was the informal, spoken style of Henry, "the character"—witty, verbose, confident almost to the point of irreverence. It seems unlikely that he holds court in the hereafter in that style, the way he used to for audiences here. Perhaps, though, he's got them laughing a bit in the next world, too. In any case, a fun way to end this story of his life is to imagine that we are in the audience one 1970s night at Brigham Young University. The subject, as usual, is science and religion. He concludes his lengthy, unscripted remarks with this testimony of a loving Heavenly Father's plan for His children:

> I would say the Church is this educational institution that equips us to go on this long journey that all of us are going on, and are on now, and will continue on even after we die. Of course it can be done better by people helping us and people helping each other, so that you can take advantage of other people's experiences and you don't have to make all the mistakes over again, and so I expect an organization.
>
> All right, what kind of an organization do I expect? Well, this is the thing that I would say, that when God wants to, obviously He can communicate with you. I mean, there isn't any question about that. If He wants to, then this Wisest Being in the Universe can talk to you, can tell you whatever He wants to, and He can put it into your mind or He can punch the right nerve if He wants to and you can think the right thought. Even I can see how you can do that. Don't use the argument that, since I wouldn't be able to do it, obviously God couldn't. That has a fallacy in it, because I would admit to begin with that you are not as smart as God, and I would say you haven't proven anything to me.

So this Wisest Being in the Universe, just take this for granted, obviously He can communicate with you. Then the fact is that, if it will serve His purpose, He does so, and so for me I'm expecting the sort of thing that happened to Paul on the road to Damascus. Here was a scoundrel who could stand by and watch Stephen stoned—a good man, but had the worst ideas you could think of, a harsh man. On Paul's going down to Damascus to pick up some other Christians and punish them, the Lord says, "Well, this fellow"(well, I don't know what the Lord said, but I'll tell you anyway). The Lord says, "Well, this fellow is in trouble and he's doing harm," and so He just cracked down on him a little, and old Paul comes to and turns right around and becomes the greatest missionary of all time.

What kind of man was Paul? I would say that there are two things about him that are certain. First, he was extremely able. You couldn't do the missionary work and write all those epistles that he did and do all the work that he did without being a first-rate mind. Secondly, the man was himself absolutely convinced of this experience. He may have been wrong. He may have had epilepsy. He may have been crazy as a loon, but I'd like to be crazy the same way. He was really effective. This man was absolutely convinced. Even to the point of dying for the conviction that this thing happened. Well, I wasn't there, but I have history and I'm convinced that he was right, and so now I'm tremendously religious. As soon as I make that conclusion, I'm off to the races, because God actually has shown Himself there.

I would say exactly the same thing about Joseph Smith. The great thing that had been lost through the years from the time of Paul and the Apostles and the Savior's coming to the earth, the great thing that had been lost was the idea—the actual revelation—that God could communicate with man.

Why can't God communicate with you? Well, you're so smart that you can't listen, and in fact that's the greatest problem that He has with any of us. I've always used the example since I taught fifteen years at Princeton where it was very popular to say, "You can tell a man from Harvard, but you can't tell him much." I think that's the biggest stumbling block that most people have in religion, and I think that was the trouble with Einstein. All men, especially those that are very able, are so often right in their dealings with people in their specialty that they forget that some other things are not their specialty and that somebody else may be doing better. But it's very difficult for people of that kind to realize that other people may have something to tell them, or God, or any other person, and so they can't listen.

The great thing about Paul is that after he got batted over the head he could listen. And it's a good deal the same as the story of the mule: you had to bat him over the head to get his attention. Well, Paul was about like that. He did get it straight through his head.

The Prophet Joseph Smith, I would say, was almost exactly like Paul. He was a very able man. Joseph Smith was tremendously able, as you judged what he did. I mean, there isn't any question in my mind about whether he was able—the kind of men that gathered around him and listened to him, and were impressed, and built their whole lives around him; the way the gospel got on; the tremendous concepts that he had of eternal life and of a pre-existence and a continuing on through the eternities, and this being just a tremendous journey. And he's tremendous. But he also was convinced. Whether you say Joseph Smith saw somebody or he didn't, as far as he was concerned, everything indicates that he was absolutely convinced.

These things happen, just like Paul was convinced. Well, maybe both of them were epileptics. But I don't believe it, and I don't think that's the best explanation. I have to decide for me, but I'm convinced that the best explanation is their explanation. That is because I think they were very able. They were perceptive people, and the other thing is that I am expecting that kind of thing. You understand that I'm thinking that whenever it serves God's purposes to communicate with human beings, He will. I can't imagine anything else. Wouldn't it be strange if the world wasn't going the way He liked it and He had perfect ability to tell somebody to straighten up and get into line and it would go more nearly the way He liked it? Suppose somebody was like that and cared about the world. You just have to believe that He cares, and if you believe that He exists, why, obviously whenever it serves His purposes this is going to happen. So this is something I expect.

The model I've built of the world—which may be completely erroneous, but at least the model that I have built of the world—is a natural thing. So of course I expect it. Now, I think that the great message that the Latter-day gospel has for the world is just that message of communication. That is, a lot of churches say that the canon of scripture was full—in the time of John the Book of Revelation finished things. Well, that doesn't make sense to me. I mean, certainly people were as confused about what life is, about eternity, and about religion as they were in the time of the Savior, so we needed just as much as before. I would be very surprised if this Being in my mind, in this model of the universe that I have, wouldn't think that it was a good thing to have revelation, and that He does it every time that it suits His purposes, and one of the things that was necessary was to find people that would listen. Joseph Smith was of course tremendously able; he was also a person of good character who, when he knew what to do, would do it. But he also could listen, and so then the gospel for me is this very beautiful picture.

And maybe it doesn't prove anything. You see, in a sense, the way the world looks to me doesn't look that way to you; you'll come to some different conclusion. But I can't make any sense out of these experiences. I would say, added to that, that I have actually tried what the Savior said and prayed, and, as far as I'm concerned, have had answers to prayers. And so then that is the same kind of feeling that I would have knowing that I have an earthly father. I've associated with Him and known things about Him. I've gotten things from Him, prayed and had answers to prayers that I am convinced were not just chance. And so then the whole thing, as far as I am concerned, is reality.

You remember the question that was asked me when I first came here from Princeton. (I've used this often.) It was '46, I guess, one of the first years I was here. One of the regents at the University of Utah said, "Dr. Eyring, you're a scientist. I can understand how as a scientist you could be religious, but I can't understand how you could believe in a revealed religion." Well, the only thing I had to say was that I couldn't believe in any other kind. If I really believe there is a God and it suits His purpose to communicate this, I couldn't believe in anything else but a revealed religion. It would be nonsense for me to suppose that if it served His purpose—it may not serve His purpose, but if it served His purpose—that He could do it. Obviously, we can have messages and tell satellites to do all kinds of things, to take pictures and send them back, and go and change their course and do all sorts of things.

Well, to use the argument on me that there couldn't be a life after death because a resurrection isn't possible, because I wouldn't know how to do it myself—I'm not impressed by that argument. I started out with the supposition that the Being I'm dealing with is smarter than you. So when you tell me that you don't know how to, it would trouble you, and, as smart as you are, you wouldn't know how to manage a resurrection, I'd say, "Well, I agree with you. I don't think you could, and thank heaven we don't have to depend on you."

So for me, I've made a picture of the world. It may be right. It may be wrong. But for me it is very real, and I've had experiences for me which are real, and so for me the only thing that I can do is say, "Try what the Savior said; try it and see if it works, and you'll find that it does work and that it's tremendously important." Of course it's everything. I mean, you can't put anything in comparison with it. It's really true. I mean, if there is a God who cares and whether we like it or not we're going to stand in judgment (in my case you might speculate that it might be quite soon—thank you, but I don't think it will be that soon), but anyway I've always thought of this picture; I've thought this thing that kind of makes me do a little better. I've thought, if the Lord is really just and a little bit harsh, He might just put on that screen up there while all of you are watching in the hereafter and say, "Old Man Eyring—do you remember the night that he preached to you down at the BYU and sounded so noble and fine? Here is what he is really like, here's the movie of the fellow from the time he was a little boy up through the whole years. And he had the gall to go down there and preach to you and talk like a Saint, and he's a scoundrel."

Now, that would make me do better. I mean, just to think that makes me try to do a little better. But I don't think He'd do that; I don't think He'd be that harsh. But you know the test of what you ought to do? You ought to live in such a way that you would be perfectly happy to have everything that you do known. And if you don't do that, maybe you'd better change a little bit. I'd say if you're doing some things that you hope people don't know, God knows them, and if He wants to He'll turn that movie on for you. I mean, He'll at least turn it on in your own mind. He may not be so unkind as to show it to all the neighbors, but He will let you see it and He'll remind you, and if you're doing some things right tonight or tomorrow or any other time that you don't care to have anybody else know—or you wouldn't even want to know about them yourself or have to think about them very clearly—I think we better quit. I mean, that's the best test for me to try to do better. I don't want to even look at myself; I mean, I'm not very bad, I'm not even bad enough to be interesting. But dull as I am I wouldn't want to do that; so don't look for anything, because I'm kind of harsh on my graduate students and expect a little more of them and take more of the credit sometimes than I ought to; you know, just not as noble as I ought to be. My wife[12] drives me up here tonight and did it beautifully, and we get over in the parking lot and she talks a little bit about how we ought to have gotten closer, and I get a little bit out of patience and say, "Well, we can't always be perfect," and she remembers. But all of us have got things we've got to do better.

So we ought to make a picture of the world like mine or make a better one, make one that squares with reality more, and in it I think will come this idea: that you are going to have to live with yourself, and that your neighbors may have to know about you a certain amount, and that there is going to be a judgment, and that the world is really beautiful, and really it's a wonderful place to live and lots more wonderful if you live in such a way that you can live with yourself.

So this, then, is sort of the picture that I would give you and end on the note that I can't see any difference between the kinds of arguments that you make to support religion and the arguments that you make to support science. I understand, of course, that there are contradictions of all kinds in science, and there are contradictions between science and religion, and there are contradictions between various parts of religion in every human mind (but not in God's mind; in a billion years you'll have your problems solved, if you can wait).

And there aren't any problems, really, but I always feel a little bit unhappy when somebody tells me that they'll give me a beautiful picture that reconciles everything. Baloney. I mean, I can't reconcile chemistry, and they're going to take the whole world and reconcile it and religion and science and everything in it? I can't do that. I like contradictions. I like a little bit of a mess, and I am glad when one of the brethren says something that I think is a little bit foolish, because I think if the Lord can stand him, maybe He can stand me. So that's it, and I think that maybe there's a certain stumbling block that some of us have: we expect other people to be a kind of perfection that we don't even attempt to approach ourselves. We expect the brethren or the bishop or the stake president or the General Authorities to be not human, even. We expect the Lord to just open and shut their mouths, but He doesn't do that—they are human beings; but they're wonderful, and they do better than they would if it weren't for the Lord helping them. I think I would say this, that I don't think there's a finer group in the world than the bishops of the Latter-day Saint Church. Some of them aren't what they ought to be, but just by-and-large you won't find a more devoted group of men than that.

So that's my answer to this remark—somebody says that a student is down here at BYU and he's a member of the Church, but he's a mess. And I say, "Yes, I agree. But you ought to see what the fellow would be like if it weren't for the Church." And that's what the gospel does. It takes all of us with our faults and makes us better. It's a wonderful thing, and there isn't anything like the gospel. If we can live close to it and approach, at least, the life of the Savior in the kind of way that we put other people's interests before our own and in general try to be helpful, we can have a heaven on earth, and life will be a wonderful thing. And it's really true, in my opinion.[13]

NOTES

Spelling and punctuation in quotations from unpublished sources have been standardized for increased readability. In addition, in some cases extraneous material has been excised from quotations without use of ellipses, again for purposes of readability.

EVENTS IN THE LIFE OF HENRY EYRING

1. Adapted from Peck, "Register of the Papers of Henry Eyring," 6–7.

OVERVIEW

1. Eyring, "The influence of family . . . ," handwritten document, Henry Eyring Papers, box 18, folder 6.
2. Heath, "Henry Eyring, Mormon Scientist," 27–28.
3. Letter of April 22, 1969, Henry Eyring Papers, box 22, folder 7.

CHAPTER 1: SCIENCE

1. Eyring, "Men, Mines, and Molecules," 4; and Brasted, "Interview with Professor and Mrs. Henry Eyring," 753.
2. Brasted, "Interview with Professor and Mrs. Henry Eyring," 753.

3. Eyring, "Men, Mines, and Molecules," 4; and Kimball, "A Dialogue with Henry Eyring," 101.

4. Brasted, "Interview with Professor and Mrs. Henry Eyring," 753.

5. Heath, "Henry Eyring, Mormon Scientist," 39.

6. As cited in ibid., 41.

7. This quote, as well as the subsequent discussion of Henry's time in Berlin, draws from an untitled biographical transcript. See Eyring, "It's interesting to try to recall. . . ."

8. Eyring, "Men, Mines, and Molecules," 6.

9. Excerpted, with ellipsis, from Polanyi, "Michael Polanyi, the Scientist," 12.

10. Eyring, "It's interesting to try to recall . . . ," autobiographical transcript, Henry Eyring Papers, box 18, folder 6.

11. Ibid.

12. Ibid.

13. Brasted, "Interview with Professor and Mrs. Henry Eyring," 754.

14. Nye, "Working Tools for Theoretical Chemistry," 25.

15. Kauzmann, "Henry Eyring, February 20, 1901–December 26, 1981."

16. Miller, "Biography," 5, Henry Eyring Papers.

17. Eyring, *Faith of a Scientist,* 22.

18. Heath, "Henry Eyring, Mormon Scientist," 64.

19. Ibid., 65.

20. Ibid., 84.

21. Eyring, *Faith of a Scientist,* 24.

22. Heath, "Henry Eyring, Mormon Scientist," 90.

23. Kimball, "A Dialogue with Henry Eyring," 108.

24. Heath, "Henry Eyring, Mormon Scientist," 77–78.

25. Ibid., 78.

CHAPTER 2: FAITH

1. Albert Einstein to Max Born, December 12, 1926, quoted in Clark, *Einstein: The Life and Times,* 414.

2. Clark, "The Charted Course of the Church in Education," 7.

3. John 17:3.

4. Clark, "The Charted Course of the Church in Education," 10.

5. See Jeffrey, "Seers, Savants and Evolution," 41–75.

6. "Noted American Scientist Presides over Church Unit," *Deseret News Church Section,* February 24, 1945.

7. Except as noted, all of the following quotes are taken from "Science and Faith," reprinted in Eyring, *Faith of a Scientist,* 31–37.

8. John 7:17.

9. See Doctrine and Covenants 93:36; 131:6; 130:18.

10. Eyring, "Henry Eyring Speaks to Youth," 132–33.

11. Matthew 7:7.

12. Doctrine and Covenants 50:24

13. Eyring, "Henry Eyring Speaks to Youth," 132–33.

14. Ibid.

15. Eyring, "Science and Religion," 1.

16. Matthew 5:48.

17. Doctrine and Covenants 88:78–79.

18. See Doctrine and Covenants 93:36; 130:18; 131:6.

19. *Journal of Discourses,* 14:116.

20. Eyring, *Reflections of a Scientist,* 40.

21. Letter of July 20, 1951, Henry Eyring Papers, box 22, folder 5.

22. Letter of November 12, 1952, Henry Eyring Papers, box 22, folder 5.

23. Letter of February 21, 1955, Henry Eyring Papers, box 22, folder 5.

24. Letter of March 28, 1952, 1, Henry Eyring Papers, box 22, folder 5.

25. This is the classic 6,000-year Earth age inferred from the Bible. It is attributed to the Archbishop of Usher, born in 1581.

26. Letter of March 28, 1952, Henry Eyring Papers, box 22, folder 5.

27. Letter of September 26, 1967; forwarded via letter dated October 19, 1967, Henry Eyring Papers, box 22, folder 6.

28. Letter of October 19, 1967, Henry Eyring Papers, box 22, folder 6.

29. See photocopy reproduction in Heath, "Henry Eyring, Mormon Scientist," 270.

30. Ibid.

31. Letter of June 12, 1950, Henry Eyring Papers, box 22, folder 3.

32. See photocopy reproduction in Heath, "Henry Eyring, Mormon Scientist," 272–76.

33. Ibid., 277.

34. Eyring, "A Tribute to President Joseph Fielding Smith," 16.

35. Kimball, "A Dialogue with Henry Eyring," 102.

36. Letter of December 28, 1954, Henry Eyring Papers, box 22, folder 8.

37. Letter of May 23, 1957, Henry Eyring Papers, box 22, folder 7.

38. Letter of February 21, 1970, Henry Eyring Papers, box 22, folder 10.

39. Letter of March 2, 1970, Henry Eyring Papers, box 22, folder 10.

40. Letter of April 18, 1969, 1, Henry Eyring Papers, box 22, folder 7.

41. Ibid., 2.

42. Letter of July 22, 1969, Henry Eyring Papers, box 22, folder 7.

43. Letter of October 28, 1969, Henry Eyring Papers, box 22, folder 7.

44. Lorin F. Wheelwright to General Superintendency, Deseret Sunday School Union, December 15, 1964, Henry Eyring Papers, box 21, folder 15.

45. Letter of October 8, 1971, Henry Eyring Papers, box 21, folder 15.

Chapter 3: Friendship

1. Mr. Darrow refers to Henry's responsibilities as Dean of the Graduate School at the University of Utah.

2. Letter of January 10, 1982, Henry Eyring Papers, box 22, folder 11.

3. David O. McKay would become President of the Church; the school over which he presided at the time the writer speaks of was the Weber Academy in Ogden, Utah; it is now Weber State University.

4. Logan is home to Utah State University.

5. This is an argument that Henry often made.

6. Letter of October 1, 1978, Henry Eyring Papers, box 22, folder 11.

7. Eyring, "Unforgettable General Board Experiences," unpublished manuscript, February 6, 1973; found in Heath, "Henry Eyring, Mormon Scientist," 161–62.

8. I.e., crazy.

9. I.e., abuse.

10. A type of carbon-chain molecule.

11. Eyring, "Science and Religion," 7–8.

12. Student evaluation.

13. Ibid.

14. Ibid.

15. Letter of April 13, 1976, Henry Eyring Papers, box 22, folder 11.

16. Henderson, *Journal of Physical Chemistry,* 2640.

17. Eyring, "Henry Eyring and the Birth of a Graduate Program," 5.

18. Heath, "Henry Eyring, Mormon Scientist," 101.

19. Eyring, Address to members of the University of Utah Athletics Department, about 1968, Henry Eyring Papers, box 34, folder 42.

20. Heath, "Henry Eyring, Mormon Scientist," 102.

21. Henderson, *Journal of Physical Chemistry,* 2639.

22. Heath, "Henry Eyring, Mormon Scientist," 148.

23. Letter of August 22, 1973, Henry Eyring Papers, box 22, folder 10.

24. Letter of March 26, 1979, Henry Eyring Papers, box 22, folder 11.

Chapter 4: Love

1. Eyring, Interview by Leonard R. Grover, 2.

2. Ibid., 8.

3. Miner, *As a Great Tree,* 73.

4. An ecclesiastical unit comprising several thousand members.

5. Eyring, "The influence of family . . . ," handwritten document, Henry Eyring Papers, box 18, folder 6.

6. Miner, *As a Great Tree,* 26–27.

7. In this game, the players each put a piece of clothing, jewelry, or some personal belonging into a pile on the floor. These are the "forfeits." One person is chosen to be the judge, and another holds up the forfeits over the judge's head. The judge sits in front of the pile and cannot see what is being held overhead. As the sock or necklace or belt is held over the judge's head, the other player says: "Heavy, heavy hangs over thy head. What shall the owner do to redeem the forfeit?" Then the judge (without looking up) commands the owner to do some act or stunt in order to get back the property. (Description taken from childrenparty.com.)

8. Miner, *As a Great Tree,* 30.

9. Ibid., 31.

10. Ed admitted that there was also beer at this party. Ibid., 32.

11. Ibid., 30–31.

12. Ibid., 36.

13. Food poisoning.

14. To "administer" is to bless the sick to be healed.

15. Miner, *As a Great Tree,* 36–37.

16. Miner, *Life Story of Edward Christian Eyring,* 27.

17. Ibid., 30.

18. Ibid.

19. Eyring, "Autobiography of Henry Eyring written August 8, 1976," 3–4, Henry Eyring Papers, box 18, folder 6.

20. A weekly, evening Church meeting that Ed's ecclesiastical position required him to attend.

21. Eyring, Interview by Leonard R. Grover, 4–5.

22. Ibid., 8–9.

23. Ibid., 6.

24. Ibid., 26.

25. Ibid., 6.

26. Ibid., 13.

27. Ibid., 3.

28. Romney, *Life of Miles Park Romney,* 162.

29. Eyring, Interview by Leonard R. Grover, 15.

30. Letter of May 27, 1929, Henry Eyring Papers, box 2, folder 4.

31. Eyring, "Circumstances That Shape a Career," unpublished autobiography, Henry Eyring Papers, box 18, folder 6.

NOTES

CHAPTER 5: AMBITION

1. A hinged window above the door.
2. Eyring, "Men, Mines, and Molecules," 3.
3. Romney, *Life of Miles Park Romney,* 146–47.
4. Ibid., 160.
5. Ibid., 143.
6. Miner, *As a Great Tree,* 22–23.
7. Miles P., following the direction of Church leaders, went ahead to Mexico with his first wife and their children.
8. Wilford Woodruff was then the President of the Church, who was also in hiding.
9. A town in Chihuahua, Mexico.
10. Miner, *As a Great Tree,* 23, 25.
11. Ibid., 81.
12. Ibid., 74.
13. Ibid., 80.
14. Ibid., 81.
15. Ibid., 75.
16. Stoops, "A Half-Century of Learning," table 2.
17. Heath, "Henry Eyring, Mormon Scientist," 27.
18. Henderson, *Journal of Physical Chemistry,* 2639.
19. "Another milestone for Eyring."
20. Ibid.
21. Kimball, "A Dialogue with Henry Eyring," 100.

CHAPTER 6: BELIEF

1. Planck, *Scientific Autobiography of Max Planck,* 159.
2. Eyring, University of Wyoming baccalaureate address, 6–7, Henry Eyring Papers, box 34, folder 9.
3. Eyring, *Faith of a Scientist,* 173.
4. A type of bacteria.
5. Eyring, *Faith of a Scientist,* 173.
6. Letter of January 27, 1971, Henry Eyring Papers, box 22, folder 10.
7. Letter of February 28, 1958, Henry Eyring Papers, box 22, folder 5.
8. Eyring (Henry's grandfather), "I was born on the 9th day of March 1835. . . ."
9. Ibid.
10. Ibid.
11. Ibid.

12. Ibid.

13. Ibid.

14. Elder Henry B. Eyring is a member of the Church's First Presidency and the second son of Henry Eyring, the subject of our story. His summary of his great-grandmother Mary Bommeli's conversion was presented in a semi-annual general conference of the Church, broadcast worldwide. A transcript can be found in the Church's monthly magazine: Henry B. Eyring, "The Power of Teaching Doctrine," *Ensign*, May 1999, 73.

15. I.e., without money.

16. "Alma" is one of the major sections, or "books," within the Book of Mormon.

17. In her letter Mary agreed to leave Berlin.

18. Eyring (Henry's grandfather), "I was born on the 9th day of March 1835. . . ."

19. Heath, "Henry Eyring, Mormon Scientist," 27–28.

20. The School of the Prophets was established by Joseph Smith prior to the Mormon's westward migration and continued for a time in Utah; Grandfather Henry Eyring was a member.

21. Eyring, *Faith of a Scientist,* 50–51.

22. Ibid., 133.

23. Ibid., 60.

24. Ibid., 61–62.

CHAPTER 7: FEAR

1. Eyring, Interview by Leonard R. Grover, 9.

2. See Heath, "Henry Eyring, Mormon Scientist," 12–13.

3. Ibid., 13.

4. Romney, *Life of Miles Park Romney,* 214–17.

5. Ibid.

6. This is Henry's uncle, the son of Miles P. Romney.

7. Eyring, Interview by Leonard R. Grover, 10.

8. Recollection of Henry B. Eyring.

9. Coincidentally, this Ammon Tenney is the one whose father was killed trying to break up the fight that Henry's mother, Caroline, described in "Ambition."

10. Romney, *Life of Miles Park Romney,* 217.

11. Ibid., 218.

12. Eyring, Interview by Leonard R. Grover, 10.

13. Kimball, *Autobiography of Camilla Eyring Kimball,* 10–11.

14. Eyring, "Autobiography of Henry Eyring written August 8, 1976," Henry Eyring Papers, box 18, folder 6.

15. Eyring, Interview by Leonard R. Grover, 11.

16. Eyring, "Men, Mines, and Molecules," 2.

17. Miner, *As a Great Tree,* 42.

18. Eyring, "History of Henry Eyring and His Descendants," 20.

19. Eyring, "Circumstances That Shape a Career," unpublished autobiography, Henry Eyring Papers, box 18, folder 6.

CHAPTER 8: MASTER OF CONTRADICTIONS

1. Kimball, "Great Treasures of Knowledge, Even Hidden Treasures," 392–94.

2. Biographer Steven Heath deserves credit for first writing about Henry's facility with paradox, which he identifies as "Janusian Thinking." See Heath, "Henry Eyring on Scientific Creativity," 191–92.

3. Fitzgerald, "The Crack-Up," 69.

4. This discovery of the dual nature of matter initially disrupted all the scientific thinking that had preceded it. However, it also opened up new scientific possibilities, including the discovery of Henry's Absolute Rate Theory. Thus, for him, the otherwise troubling duality of matter, while impossible to explain, was a great scientific gift.

5. Henry had a historical analogy for the duality of God's nature: "If we read the story of Robert E. Lee, the great military tactician, we find that even at Gettysburg his army was maneuvered as though Lee himself were storming Cemetery Ridge alongside Pickett, as well as being everywhere else on the battlefield. Lee's success as a general depended to a very great extent on the gathering of information about the strength, position and intentions of his adversary before and after the battle started. The result is that any story of Lee as a general would tell about his influence permeating the whole sphere of his activities and very little about Lee the man. In this sense Lee is two people, the man like anyone else, and the far-flung intelligence system which governed the motion of himself and his army much as the wave is spread out in space and governs the motion of a photon or a material particle.

"In an analogous manner, we may think of God as the all-wise arbiter of the Universe, with His infinite wisdom having an influence which permeates the most remote recesses of space, and yet being Himself an exalted being with personality and deep concern for struggling humanity. One of the many things the Restored Gospel has done is to emphasize, as the scriptures have always done, the deep personal concern of God for His children." (Eyring, *Faith of a Scientist,* 84–85.)

NOTES

CHAPTER 9: CONFIDENCE AND HUMILITY

1. Temple Square refers to the block in Salt Lake City that includes the Salt Lake Temple. It is not commonly used as a metaphor for heaven, even among Church members. Henry's use of it as such would have gotten a good laugh.
2. Eyring, "Science and Religion," 6–7.
3. Eyring, *Reflections of a Scientist,* xviii.
4. Eyring, *Faith of a Scientist,* 183.
5. Ibid., 72.
6. Ibid., 53–54.
7. Letter of March 4, 1981, Henry Eyring Papers, box 22, folder 11.
8. Eyring, *Faith of a Scientist,* 184.
9. Ibid., 54–55.
10. Miller, Interview of Glenn Seaborg and Kenneth F. Pitzer.
11. Ibid.
12. *Salt Lake Tribune,* January 30, 1973.
13. Eyring, "Men and Molecules," 5.
14. Kimball, "A Dialogue with Henry Eyring," 106.
15. Heath, "Henry Eyring, Mormon Scientist," 143.
16. Brasted, "Interview with Professor and Mrs. Henry Eyring," 755–56.
17. Eyring, "It's interesting to try to recall . . . ," 2, autobiographical transcript, Henry Eyring Papers, box 18, folder 6.
18. Henry means that, because we are now seeing light that began traveling from the edge of the universe 2 billion years ago, we know what was happening there at that time. He suggests in the next sentence that, if we waited 100 million years, the light we would see then would tell us what happened at the edge of the universe 1.9 billion years ago.

CHAPTER 10: DISCIPLINE AND CREATIVITY

1. Henderson, *Journal of Physical Chemistry,* 2640.
2. Brasted, "Interview with Professor and Mrs. Henry Eyring," 756.
3. Henderson, *Journal of Physical Chemistry,* 2639.
4. Heath, "Henry Eyring on Scientific Creativity," 192.
5. Brasted, "Interview with Professor and Mrs. Henry Eyring," 753.
6. Henry's direct supervisor at Berkeley.
7. Eyring, "Men, Mines, and Molecules," 2.
8. Heath, "Henry Eyring on Scientific Creativity," 189.
9. Eyring, *Faith of a Scientist,* 125.
10. Henderson, *Journal of Physical Chemistry,* 2639.

11. Doctrine and Covenants 88:79.

12. Doctrine and Covenants 88:80.

13. Kimball, "A Dialogue with Henry Eyring," 105.

14. Heath, "Henry Eyring on Scientific Creativity," 189.

15. I.e., nearness at hand.

16. Eyring, "Men, Mines, and Molecules," 10.

17. Kimball, "A Dialogue with Henry Eyring," 106.

18. Lund, "Elder Henry B. Eyring," 10.

19. Brasted, "Interview with Professor and Mrs. Henry Eyring," 755.

20. Eyring, "Write upon My Heart," 85.

21. Kimball, "A Dialogue with Henry Eyring," 108.

CHAPTER 11: FREEDOM AND OBEDIENCE

1. A senior Church Apostle.

2. The Church was redesigning its official magazines at the time; one of those magazines, *The Instructor*, was published by the Sunday School organization, on whose board Henry sat.

3. Kimball, "A Dialogue with Henry Eyring," 101–2.

4. This council and its consequences are alluded to in Job 38:7; Isaiah 14:13; Luke 10:18; and Revelation 12:7. The council in heaven is described in greater detail in modern-day scripture, especially The Pearl of Great Price (see Moses 4:3 and Abraham 3:22). Henry summarizes the story of the council later in this chapter.

5. The celestial kingdom is the highest degree of heavenly glory.

6. Eyring, *Faith of a Scientist*, 144.

7. Ibid., 104.

8. Ibid., 108 (citing Doctrine and Covenants 121:37).

9. Ibid., 110.

10. "This Changing World," American Association for the Advancement of Science Bulletin, September 1965.

11. Eyring, *Faith of a Scientist*, 37.

12. Albert Ray Olpin was president of the University of Utah from 1946 to 1964.

13. Eyring, in printed program for December 8, 1980, dedication of the Henry Eyring Building at the University of Utah.

14. Heath, "Henry Eyring: The Utah Years," 151.

15. Eyring, *Faith of a Scientist*, 113–14.

16. See Doctrine and Covenants 130:21.

17. Eyring, *Faith of a Scientist*, 56.

18. Eyring, "The Search for Scientific and Religious Truth," 2, Henry Eyring Papers, box 20, folder 16.

19. Eyring, *Faith of a Scientist,* 122.

20. Address to members of the University of Utah Athletics department, 13–14, about 1968, Henry Eyring Papers, box 34, folder 42.

21. Eyring, Interview by Leonard R. Grover, 15

22. Eyring, "The Search for Scientific and Religious Truth," 2.

23. Eyring, Interview by Leonard R. Grover, 9.

24. Eyring, *Faith of a Scientist,* 103–4.

25. This statement was made before the first lunar landing.

26. J. Golden Kimball was an early Church general authority to whom was attributed numerous humorous sayings, many of which involved cursing or other foul language.

27. Eyring, *Faith of a Scientist,* 52.

28. Kimball, "A Dialogue with Henry Eyring," 107.

29. Eyring, *Faith of a Scientist,* 53.

30. Ibid., 61.

31. Ibid., 114.

32. Ibid., 106.

CHAPTER 12: REASONING, MORE THAN REASONS

1. Franklin S. Harris Jr. to Henry Eyring, January 3, 1970, Henry Eyring Papers, box 22, folder 7.

2. pi (pronounced "pie") is the mathematical constant best known for its role in determining the circumference and area of a circle (the circumference of a circle, for instance, is pi multiplied by two times the radius of the circle). Pi's approximate value is 3.14, but there are an infinite number of numerals behind the 4. Thus, pi cannot be known to its precise value, only approximated.

3. Eyring, *Faith of a Scientist,* 70.

4. Ibid., 157.

5. Ibid., 139.

6. Eyring, "Science and Religion," 6.

7. Eyring, *Faith of a Scientist,* 121.

8. John 7:15–17.

9. Eyring, *Faith of a Scientist,* 103.

10. Eyring, "Science and Religion," 6.

11. Eyring, *Faith of a Scientist,* 98.

12. Ibid, 126.

13. "Heat Death" is the theoretical temperature of a universe in which all

the heat of the stars is equally distributed through space; that is in fact what is happening now, very slowly.

14. Eyring, *Faith of a Scientist,* 74.

15. Ibid., 80.

16. Kimball, "A Dialogue with Henry Eyring," 103–4.

17. Eyring, *Faith of a Scientist,* 103.

18. Ibid., 98–99.

19. Ibid., 98.

20. Ibid., 101.

21. Ibid., 97.

22. Eyring, "Science and Religion," 3–4.

23. Eyring, "What Are the Things That Really Matter?"

24. Letter of April 8, 1954, Henry Eyring Papers, box 22, folder 5.

25. Eyring, "Science and Religion," 1, 5, 10–11.

26. Eyring, *Faith of a Scientist,* 61.

27. Ibid., 57.

28. Ibid., 65.

29. Ibid., 39.

30. Letter of June 28, 1971, Henry Eyring Papers, box 21, folder 15.

31. Eyring, "What Are the Things That Really Matter?"

32. Eyring, *Faith of a Scientist,* 63.

33. Ibid., 34.

34. Ibid., 166.

35. Letter of January 5, 1969, Henry Eyring Papers, box 22, folder 10.

36. Eyring, *Faith of a Scientist,* 88.

CHAPTER 13: FUNDAMENTALS, NOT CONVENTIONS

1. Eyring, in Henderson, *Journal of Physical Chemistry,* 2637.

2. Eyring, *Faith of a Scientist,* 26.

3. Letter from Arthur A. Frost, March 13, 1967, Henry Eyring Papers, box 16, folder 14.

4. Joseph Smith—History 1:25, in Pearl of Great Price, 51.

5. Eyring, *Faith of a Scientist,* 127–28.

6. Kimball, "A Dialogue with Henry Eyring," 103.

7. American Association for the Advancement of Science Bulletin, September 1965.

8. Brasted, "Interview with Professor and Mrs. Henry Eyring," 755.

9. Letter of February 9, 1968, Henry Eyring Papers, box 22, folder 7.

10. Eyring, "A Child and a Disciple," 29.

11. Letter of August 1, 1975, Henry Eyring Papers, box 22, folder 18.

12. The *Ensign* is the Church's official magazine, in which semiannual general conference talks are reprinted. President N. Eldon Tanner was the second counselor in the Church's First Presidency at that time.

13. Letter dated only June 6, Henry Eyring Papers, box 22, folder 17.

14. This is one of Winifred's four daughters, all of whom enjoyed close association with Henry.

15. Anonymous, "Dear Missionary . . . ," undated, handwritten note, Henry Eyring Papers, box 22, folder 18.

16. Eyring, *Faith of a Scientist,* 132–33.

17. Mormon Saints in Missouri were driven out in the late 1830s, shortly after Doniphan's defense of Joseph. In 1863, the citizens of Jackson and three other Missouri counties were driven out in a similar manner by the Union army; most of the county was burned to the ground.

18. Eyring, *Faith of a Scientist,* 133.

19. Ibid., 60.

CHAPTER 14: PEOPLE, NOT PUBLIC OPINION

1. Kimball, "A Dialogue with Henry Eyring," 106.

2. Letter of February 16, 1972, Henry Eyring Papers, box 22, folder 10.

3. Letter of March 1, 1972, Henry Eyring Papers, box 22, folder 10.

4. Eyring, Interview by Leonard R. Grover, 11.

5. I.e., non-Mormons.

6. Eyring, Interview by Leonard R. Grover, 14.

7. Ibid.

8. Ibid., 15.

9. An established scientist who criticized the work of the much younger Newton.

10. Brasted, "Interview with Professor and Mrs. Henry Eyring," 754.

11. Eyring, "Men, Mines, and Molecules," 3.

12. Eyring, "Science and Religion," 10.

13. Heath, "Henry Eyring, Mormon Scientist," 7.

14. Brasted, "Interview with Professor and Mrs. Henry Eyring," 752.

15. Mark 9:35–37.

16. Matthew 18:6.

17. Eyring, *Faith of a Scientist,* 129–30.

18. Ibid., 186.

19. Kauzmann, "Henry Eyring, February 20, 1901–December 26, 1981," 5.

20. Letter of February 22, 1965, Henry Eyring Papers, box 21, folder 15.

21. Letter of April 21, 1955, Henry Eyring Papers, box 22, folder 3.
22. Eyring, "A Tribute to Joseph Fielding Smith."

Chapter 15: The Kind Father Who Created It All

1. Walker, "Man of Science, Man of Faith," 5.
2. Ibid.
3. Ibid.
4. Eyring, Journal, Henry Eyring Papers, box 18, book 1.
5. Eyring, *To Draw Closer to God*, 101–2.
6. Ibid., 102.
7. Henderson, *Journal of Physical Chemistry*, 2640.
8. Ibid.
9. Eyring, "Communication," 92–93.
10. Eyring, *Faith of a Scientist*, 115–17.
11. Ibid., 140–41.
12. Winifred.
13. Eyring, "You don't have to make all the mistakes there are . . . ," speech given at Brigham Young University, no date, Henry Eyring Papers, box 20, folder 23.

BIBLIOGRAPHY

"Another Milestone for Eyring," newspaper clipping from unknown source, in possession of the Eyring family.

Clark, Ronald W. *Einstein: The Life and Times.* New York: Avon Books, 1972.

Brasted, Robert C. "Interview with Professor and Mrs. Henry Eyring." *Journal of Chemical Education* 53 (December 1976): 752–56.

Clark, J. Reuben, Jr. "The Charted Course of the Church in Education." Address to seminary and institute of religion leaders at the Brigham Young University summer school in Aspen Grove, Utah, August 8, 1938. Reprinted by Intellectual Reserve, 1994.

Doctrine and Covenants. Salt Lake City: The Church of Jesus Christ of Latter-day Saints, 1981.

Eyring, Edward Christian. "History of Henry Eyring and His Descendants." Unpublished autobiography. In possession of the author.

Eyring, Edward M. "Henry Eyring and the Birth of a Graduate Program." Unpublished. In possession of the author.

Eyring, Henry (1835–1902). "I was born on the 9th day of March 1835. . . ." Unpublished, unpaginated journal. In possession of the author.

Eyring, Henry. "Communication." *Improvement Era,* February 1954, 92–93.

319

———. *The Faith of a Scientist.* Salt Lake City: Bookcraft, 1967.

———. "Henry Eyring Speaks to Youth." *Improvement Era,* November 1970, 132–33.

———. In *Salt Lake Tribune,* January 30, 1973.

———. Interview by Leonard R. Grover. June 19, 1980. Charles Redd Center for Western Studies. Brigham Young University, LDS Oral History Project.

———. "Men, Mines, and Molecules." *Annual Review of Physical Chemistry* 28 (October 1977): 1–14.

———. Printed program for December 8, 1980, dedication of the Henry Eyring Building at the University of Utah.

———. *Reflections of a Scientist.* Salt Lake City: Deseret Book, 1983.

———. "Science and Religion." BYU Leadership Week Devotional, June 14, 1962.

———. "A Tribute to President Joseph Fielding Smith." *Dialogue: A Journal of Mormon Thought* 7 (spring 1972): 15–16.

Eyring, Henry B. "A Child and a Disciple." *Ensign,* May 2003, 29–32.

———. "The Power of Teaching Doctrine." *Ensign,* May 1999, 73–75.

———. *To Draw Closer to God.* Salt Lake City: Deseret Book, 1997.

———. "Write Upon My Heart." *Ensign,* November 2000, 85–87.

Fitzgerald, F. Scott. "The Crack-Up." In *The Crack-Up.* Edited by Edmund Wilson. New York: New Dimensions, 1956.

Heath, Steven Harvey. "Henry Eyring, Mormon Scientist." Master's thesis, University of Utah, June 1980.

———. "Henry Eyring on Scientific Creativity." *Encyclia: The Journal of the Utah Academy of Sciences, Arts, and Letters* 63 (1986): 191–92.

———. "Henry Eyring: The Utah Years." *Encyclia: The Journal of the Utah Academy of Sciences, Arts, and Letters* 61 (1984): 151.

Henderson, Douglas. *Journal of Physical Chemistry* 87 (1983): 2637–40.

Henry Eyring Papers. Manuscript Division. Special Collections. J. Willard Marriott Library. University of Utah. Salt Lake City, Utah.

Holy Bible. Salt Lake City: The Church of Jesus Christ of Latter-day Saints, 1989.

Jeffrey, Duane E. "Seers, Savants and Evolution: The Uncomfortable Interface." *Dialogue: A Journal of Mormon Thought* 8 (autumn–winter 1973): 41–75.

Kauzmann, Walter. "Henry Eyring, February 20, 1901–December 26, 1981." Biographical Memoirs. National Academy of Sciences.

Kimball, Camilla Eyring. *Autobiography of Camilla Eyring Kimball.* Salt Lake City: private publication, 1975.

Kimball, Edward L. "A Dialogue with Henry Eyring." *Dialogue: A Journal of Mormon Thought* 8 (autumn–winter 1973): 99–108.

Kimball, Spencer W. "Great Treasures of Knowledge, Even Hidden Treasures." *Liahona: The Elders Journal,* January 31, 1933, 392–94.

Lund, Gerald N. "Elder Henry B. Eyring: Molded by 'Defining Influences,'" *Ensign,* September 1995, 10–15.

Miller, Robert. "Biography." Register of the Papers of Henry Eyring (1901–1981). Special Collections Department. University of Utah Libraries, Salt Lake City, Utah (1988).

———. Interview of Glenn Seaborg and Kenneth F. Pitzer.

Miner, Caroline Eyring. *As a Great Tree: The Life Story of Caroline Cottam Romney Eyring.* Salt Lake City: private publication, 1962.

———. *The Life Story of Edward Christian Eyring.* Salt Lake City: private publication, 1966.

"Noted American Scientist Presides over Church Unit." *Deseret News Church Section,* February 24, 1945, 5.

Nye, Mary Jo. "Working Tools for Theoretical Chemistry: Polanyi, Eyring, and Debates over the Semiempirical Methods." *Chemical Heritage* 23 (spring 2005): 25.

"Party games for children." In http://childrenparty.com/partygames/classicgames.html#Forfeits.

Pearl of Great Price. Salt Lake City: The Church of Jesus Christ of Latter-day Saints, 1981.

Peck, Allesen. Register of Henry Eyring Papers. Manuscript Collection. Special Collections. J. Willard Marriott Library. Salt Lake City, 1988.

Planck, Max. *Scientific Autobiography, and Other Papers.* Translated by Frank Gaynor. New York: Philosophical Library, 1949.

Polanyi, John C. "Michael Polanyi, the Scientist." *Chemical Heritage* 23 (spring 2005): 10–13.

Romney, Thomas C. *Life of Miles Park Romney.* Salt Lake City: private publication, 1948.

Stoops, Nicole S. "A Half-Century of Learning: Historical Census Statistics on Educational Attainment in the United States, 1940 to

2000." http://www.census.gov/population/socdemo/education/phct41/table2.xls

"This Changing World." American Association for the Advancement of Science Bulletin 10, no. 3 (September 1965). AASS Misc. Publ. No. 65–18.

Walker, Joseph. "Man of Science, Man of Faith: U. of U. Building Named for LDS Chemist Henry Eyring." *Church News,* December 13, 1980, 5.

Young, Brigham. In *Journal of Discourses.* 26 vols. Liverpool: Albert Carrington, 1872, 14:114–18.

INDEX

Illustrations are indicated with italicized page numbers.

Absolute Rate Theory (ART): conception of, xvii–xviii; rejected by *Journal of Chemical Physics*, 26–29, 272–73; published by *Journal of Chemical Physics*, 29–30; broadens Henry's fields of study, 253

Agency: Henry's views on, 208–16; obedience and, 223–24; eternal progression and, 238

Allred, Priscilla, 275–76

American Association for the Advancement of Science, 25, 35, 256

American Chemical Society, 23, 27, 34–35

Aquinas, Thomas, 245

Awards, 34–36

Bandits, 140–43

Baptism, of Henry's grandfather, 128

Barlow, Belva, 84

Bathwater, 245–47

Beanie, 109–10

Bennion, Adam S., 60–63

Bennion, Howard, 69

Bennion, Mildred, xi, xii

Bentley, Joseph C., 219

Berkeley: Henry's education at, 15–16; Henry's work at, 22–23

Berlin, Germany: Henry's research fellowship in, 17–19; Mary Bommeli Eyring preaches gospel in, 130–32; Henry remains optimistic in, 178–79

Berlin Wall, xix

Birth, of Mary Eyring, 99–100

Bonaparte, Napoleon, 244

Book of Mormon, 239–40, 259–63

Born, Max, 43

Brezelius Medal, 35

Brigham Young University, professors required to obtain Ph.D., 59–60

British Isles, Miles Park Romney called to, 111–12

Brown, William, 128

Bryan, William Jennings, 42

Bureau of Mines, 13–14

Callister's Department Store, 148

Cancer: Henry researches, 192; Mildred Eyring passes away from, 201–2; Henry suffers from, 285–89

Canoe, 197–98

INDEX